GW00458601

Getting Away

Amelia Short

Copyright © 2021 Amelia Short

All rights reserved.

ISBN:
ISBN-13:

Chapter One

The story I am about to tell is the truth, the whole truth and nothing like the truth, so God help me!

It was a hot Friday afternoon in the middle of summer 2002, and I was waiting to be called in to my annual appraisal. My manager, Mr Stiles, was running late, so I was having a quick cheeky game of solitaire on my desk computer while I waited. He would ask me the same questions as every year, "How are things going?", "How could you improve things?", "Wouldn't you just love to be an arsehole Job Centre Manager like me one day?", blah blah blah. Naturally, I would say all the right answers, so I could get my pittance of a pay-rise and get out of here for the weekend.

'Nancy!' I heard my name being yelled across the room and quickly minimised my screen before heading in to the Manager's office and taking the seat in front of the desk. Mr Stiles, or Nobby as he was unaffectionately known behind his back, sat on the other side in a high-backed chair, swivelling from side to side.

'So, er … Nancy Smart,' Mr Stiles began, looking down at the paper in front of him as if he couldn't remember my name. Of course, he knew my name – I'd worked here for five years. This was an appraisal, not an interview, for goodness' sake, but I knew this was a way he liked to put me on the back foot and assert his authority.

'Yes, Mr Stiles.' Of course, I was going to play the game.

'So, you've been with us, what, five years now? You came as a trainee and you've worked your way up to Customer Career Assistant. So … how're things going?'

'Fine.' I replied. Trainee to Customer Career Assistant in five years wasn't exactly an impressive resume.

'How could you improve things?' He read from the list of questions in front of him with all the enthusiasm of a three-toed sloth.

'What things?' I decided I'd shake it up a bit. That stumped him. He checked the piece of paper for clues and subsequently panicked when there were none.

'Well, things. Things in the office, things in general.'

'Oh, things in general,' I repeated, pretending to consider it. 'Well, I suppose I could do things better, you know, a bit faster.'

He made it obvious that he wasn't listening to my stupid answer by moving on to the next question. 'Nancy, where do you see yourself in five years' time?' *There it was.* He looked up at me, expecting the usual, "I would like to be doing my job to the best of my ability and move up through the ranks to Assistant Manager and ultimately Manager and have my own office just like you," answer, preparing to greet it with a smug smile.

But it had been a long, hot week and, quite frankly, I couldn't be arsed – so I told the truth. 'Erm, I'm not sure. Anywhere a million miles away from here, I suppose.'

His eyebrows shot heavenwards. 'Nancy, be serious. There are plenty of training courses and development days we can send you on to get you up the ranks. There's some home learning, but a bright girl like you could do very well. You just need to commit to a career at the Job Centre.'

Training courses, development days (which sounded unbelievably dull), home learning, commitment to the Job Centre and a life of sweaty chairs and ungrateful customers. I suddenly felt filled with dread. I should have said "yes, thank you" but instead I went for honesty:

'But I don't want to work at the Job Centre for the rest of my life.'

This had clearly never come up in an appraisal before, and

Nobby's eyebrows immediately shot to the top of his head again. He was more than a little perplexed. 'Really? Why not?'

'Well, it's just not exactly my dream job.'

'Well, what exactly is your dream job?' He highlighted the word "dream" with air quotes, his nose evidently put out of joint.

'Honestly, I'm not exactly sure.'

'Well, I suggest you start thinking long and hard about it. The Job Centre isn't here to accommodate you until you find a better job elsewhere.' The irony was lost on him as he continued. 'This is an excellent place to build a career, just look at me.' And I did look at him. I looked at his red, puffy face and receding hairline. His collar still buttoned up and his tie still tied tight, even on a scorching day at 4 o'clock on a Friday afternoon. I saw a man who would work out the rest of his years, however many that may be, behind that desk, carrying out thankless tasks and pointless appraisals.

'I definitely will think about it, thank you, Mr Stiles.' I decided to be polite in order to undo any offence I may have caused to a man who so obviously prided himself on the position he had reached.

'You may go now,' he said, calm returning to his voice.

I thanked him again as I backed out of his hot and sweaty office and back into the hot and sweaty Job Centre shop floor. Back at my desk, I turned off my computer, grabbed my bag and headed towards the door. Ok, it wasn't strictly 5 o'clock yet, but Nobby had said I could go, so I decided to take him at his word. Anything else could wait until I returned on Monday.

I walked the short route through town towards my apartment. Even at this time of day, it was still hot and my body was sweating profusely under the nylon Job Centre uniform of white blouse and knee-length skirt. The matching nylon blazer that they insisted we wear all year round hung over my arm like an electric blanket, and my feet slid around in the corporate-style black court shoes.

As I passed the main town square, I noticed the usual group of drunks, already several cans into their White Lightning cider and several sheets to the wind. As I looked over, one of them waved. It was Poncho Pete, one of my regular customers, shirt off, dancing (for want of a better word) around the grass in front of his drinking buddies who were lolling about on the grass. I acknowledged his wave and headed into Oddbins for a bottle of something cold. It wasn't that I was jealous of Poncho Pete and his pissed-up pals per se; it was their unabashed sense of freedom that I envied. Yes, it was important to earn a living and not depend on the state or rich parents (chance would be a fine thing), but to earn that living on your own terms, in your own good time – *that* was freedom.

'You're home early,' my flatmate, Steph noted, as I huffed and puffed my way into the hallway and up the stairs to our shared flat.

'Appraisal.' Was my non-explanatory reply, as I kicked my sweaty shoes off to one side and plonked myself down at the kitchen table.

'And I'm guessing it didn't go well, judging by the early departure and the bottle of white.'

'Not great,' I admitted.

'I see. Well, you're a sweaty mess, so go have a shower while I open this—' She grabbed the wine '—and you can tell me all about it.' Steph was no stranger to telling it like it is – I was a sweaty mess – so, I took her advice and had a nice cool shower to wash off the heat of the day and the grime of the working week.

Feeling a lot fresher after the shower, I wrapped myself in a light cotton waffle robe and headed out to find Steph. She had set up shop on our small balcony, which was much cooler than the street outside but still pleasantly warm.

Normally on a Friday night we'd be going out around the bars, but because Steph was off to a hen do in Blackpool the next day, and I'd accidentally agreed to give my parents a lift to Luton Airport in the morning, we'd agreed to a quiet night in and takeaway food.

'Have you been out at all today?' I asked, noticing she was in her silk kimono, the long triangular sleeves rolled up slightly as she sat painting her nails. Her long blonde hair was pulled to one side and draped over her shoulder. Steph was an aspiring actress who devoted her time to amateur dramatics and honing her craft for when she hit the big time. She was always overdramatic, so she was already halfway there.

'Yes,' she replied defensively. 'I've only just got back myself. I've been to a Chromatic Creature Discovery workshop.' She saw me raise my eyebrows. 'It was actually very enlightening. I learnt things about myself I had no idea about.'

'Really, like what?' I was intrigued.

'Like …' Steph stopped painting mid fingernail. 'Like, were you aware that I am purple and my spirit animal is a woodpecker?' I honestly was not aware of that, and I told her so. I was a tad confused.

'But woodpeckers aren't purple?' I pointed out.

'That's not the point, it's about confidence and assuredness. I'm a go-getter, I keep pecking at that wood until I get what I want.'

'Don't they make their homes in other bird's nests?' I enquired, and she thought about it for a second.

'No, that's cuckoos.'

'And what's with the purple?'

'Erm, something to do with confidence and putting yourself out there for all to see. It stems from royalty or something. It made sense at the time.' She looked up at me and saw me smirk over my glass of wine. 'It did!' she protested, as we both broke into fits of giggles.

'Money well spent then.'

'It was! It was actually fantastic, honestly! Anyway, enough about my purple woodpecker, what happened at your appraisal?' She turned her attention to her toenails. It was so nice sitting on the cool balcony, I'd almost forgotten about the dreadful appraisal.

'Oh, you know, the usual.' I sighed. 'Although he did ask me if I wanted a career at the Job Centre, and I told him "no".'

Steph looked up sharply. 'You did?'

'Yes, I told him I wanted to do something else, live the dream.'

'And what did Knobhead Stiles say to that?'

'He told me I'd better think long and hard about what I want to do with my career. And it's Nobby, by the way.'

'And have you thought long and hard?' She asked with a cheeky glint, emphasising the words to make the innuendo obvious.

'No, not really, but I seriously need to. I'm a woodpecker pecking at the wrong wood!'

'Haha, you ain't no woodpecker.' She said, laughing. 'You're a … hmm … you're a …'

'Yes? What am I? Careful what you say now!'

'Ok, I know what you are, you're a chameleon.'

'Hmm, that doesn't sound too bad. They're pretty cool, right?'

'Yeah, they're pretty cool, they just kind of adapt. Fall into wherever they fit without really finding their own colour. No offence.'

I was offended. 'Offence taken! Is that really how you see me?'

'I meant it in a nice way.' Steph tried to backtrack. 'Like you fit in anywhere, you fall into situations without really trying and make the best of it.' It was clearly supposed to make me feel better, but it didn't.

'You're saying I'm like a floater, a big old colour-changing floater?'

'No, I wouldn't put it like that. Well actually, yes, a little bit like that. You never go for anything, put yourself forward, strive for a goal. You just sort of fell into the trainee position and never left.'

'That's because I don't know what I want to do!' I whined. 'It's all right for you, you've always wanted to be an actress and have a goal to work towards. If I don't have a goal, how can I work towards it?'

'So, find your goal! What did you want to be when you were young?'

'Debbie Harry.'

'Well, I'm pretty sure that ship has sunk. You work at the Job Centre, you have different listings coming in every day! There must be something that takes your fancy?' It was true, I had practically first dibs on all the vacancies and none of them appealed to me.

'What's wrong with me?' I wondered aloud.

'There's nothing wrong with you, you're just a bit late to the game.

But the good thing is you're only twenty-six, so the world is your oyster. I hate to say it, but I agree with Knobhead Stiles. It's time to get your thinking cap on, time to make some decisions.'

Steph was certainly a go-getter. For instance, she would just walk up to a guy she fancied and get chatting. She had the confidence of a rock star and the hide of a buffalo. She believed in herself and if she got rejected, she just put on more lipstick and moved onto the next.

I, on the other hand, cared too much. Potential humiliation was far too great a risk to take unless I was 100% bona fide sure I would be successful. If you didn't step up, you couldn't get knocked down, and your pride was kept intact. Like with boyfriends, for instance. It's not that I hadn't had boyfriends, but they had generally been the boy next door, a friend of a friend, a guy from work, all fallen into my lap with little effort. None of them had worked out.

Later that night, after we'd eaten chicken chow mien and polished off a bottle of Chardonnay, I lay in bed deliberating about the day's events. What did I want to do? In what direction did I want my life to travel? I felt like I was waiting. Waiting for something to ping up into my brain, waiting for something to happen. But what?

The next morning, I met Steph in the hall, She was on her way out, her bag stuffed to bursting with killer heels, a feather boa and an inflatable man.

'So, have you thought any more about what we talked about last night?' she asked.

'Yes, loads, but I still haven't come up with anything. I remember I used to be pretty good at writing … maybe I could do something with that?'

'There you go, that's a start!' Steph said encouragingly. 'When I get back, I want you to have a few options and a career plan, yes?'

'Ok, I suppose.'

'No, not "I suppose", the answer is "yes, Steph".'

'Yes, Steph!' I saluted.

'Now are you sure you don't want to come to Blackpool? Kiss-me-quick-hats and a grope on the Ghost Train if you're lucky?'

'As appealing as that sounds, I've unfortunately promised to do the airport run for my folks.'

'Ah yes, I'm not sure which is worse!'

'Yours is definitely more exciting. I can't wait to hear all about your adventures and sexcapades.'

'Haha, yes, let's hope so. And in the meantime, go forth and find your own adventure at Luton Airport.'

'Yeah, right.' I rolled my eyes as I hugged her goodbye and she walked out of the flat.

After Steph had left, the flat fell suddenly quiet, and I felt a despondency descend on my shoulders. Time was running out; I really *did* have to make some decisions.

Speaking of time, I had to get going or my parents would miss their flight. Ugh, hours driving in the heat of the day through London traffic filled me with dread, but I had agreed and couldn't pull out now. I slung on an old, comfy, greying T-shirt and denim skirt, ran my fingers through my shoulder-length, brunette waves and stepped into the nearest pair of flip-flops I could find.

My mobile phone battery was almost dead, so I plugged it in to charge. It would be fun to message Steph later to find out what she and the hens were up to. I grabbed my shoulder bag, threw in the essentials – purse, sunglasses, deodorant, hairband – picked up my car keys and navy hoodie and headed out into the late morning sun.

The airport was heaving with people and smelt of sweat, Duty Free perfume and anticipation. And there I was, sticking to my plastic chair, wishing to buggery that I had dropped my folks off at the door and not seen them off in to the bustling terminal with screaming kids and frazzled parents bustling around me. The only good thing about the day so far was that dad had bought me a cold beer (albeit a small one, he's not Rockefeller). He must have felt guilty for asking me to chauffeur them on my day off. In fact, going by the price of the beer, he must have felt *very* guilty indeed.

I always wondered why children had no qualms about walking straight up to you and staring with that look of total bewilderment and distaste. When one of those brats gawped at me in the manner of an inquisitive chimp (usually with at least one grubby finger placed up a nostril), I always had the urge to turn boss-eyed and scrunch up my face with a hideous expression. I had one staring at me now. I tried smiling and then ignoring him, but he seemed to become even more intrigued so I had to resort to face pulling. It worked as a deterrent perfectly as the small boy ran and hid behind the stubbly legs of his mother, occasionally peering from behind the human shield with apparent fear and dread.

I wished the plane would bloody hurry up. My beer was a little too warm to be enjoyable anymore. I was now welded to my seat and had frightened all the under-eights within half-a-mile radius to seek refuge behind various items of scattered luggage and now I'm bored. Bored, bored, bored. Bored as a very bored thing; a very, very bored thing indeed. A bored thing on a bored seat waiting for a bored plane to board. Normally when you're sitting waiting in an airport, you have the delayed gratification of getting on a plane and flying off to somewhere fabulous, so the waiting is worthwhile. You have the promise of new adventures and making memories stretching out before you. When you're not actually getting on a plane, it's all just boring and anti-climactic. If I had been more prepared, I could have brought a book to read. The only silver lining here was that I had realised something else that I liked to do: travel. Maybe I could write about travel and faraway places.

At last, after I'd chiselled off most of my nail varnish and heard the life story of the rather large man next to me (oh, and what a life, I'll tell you about it sometime when you've got three days to spare, or you're in a coma or something) and made my plastic cup into a pretty water lily, I was eventually saved. The flight was called, I said my goodbyes and begged for the final time for my parents to take me with them. They disappeared into the babbling crowd, leaving me alone in the airport lounge, which, unbeknown to me, would change my life forever.

After my folks had gone to board their plane, rather than get in my car and head for home, I made the strange decision to head up to the viewing area. My hot car and the heavy afternoon traffic could wait for another half an hour. I had the beginnings of an idea and needed time to think away from the horns and roadworks outside.

On standing up, I instantly regretted wearing my three-year-old denim skirt. It was fraying at the edges and saggy in the rear, and now, thanks to the said skirt, I was sporting a matching pair of gorgeous red patches on the back of my thighs, as if I didn't look rough enough already. I just hoped I wouldn't bump into anyone I knew – although this far away from home, it was highly unlikely that I would and a pretty safe bet I could pass by with no notable loss of pride.

Chapter Two

 With wrinkly clothes and legs like malfunctioning traffic lights, I
followed the signs up the escalators to the observation area. Here, it
was slightly less crowded with seats covered in a non-colourful
'airline-grey' fabric. Although less full, it was no cooler as the wall of
windows intensified the afternoon sun. I felt like a tomato in a
greenhouse and understood why they turned red. I was psychedelia
personified. Thank goodness Danny Greenslade wasn't here to see
me. What? Who's Danny Greenslade? You mean I haven't mentioned
him yet? That is most unusual because he's usually foremost in my
thoughts and conversation. Danny Greenslade is my lover. Well,
perhaps "lover" is not the right word. He's the guy who I'm totally in
love with and who is totally in love with me … no, that too is a slight
exaggeration, well okay, an enormous exaggeration … but I have
spoken to him twice and I'm sure it's only a matter of time.

   The first time I spoke to him was at a friend's party. In truth, I
wasn't the biggest fan of Shelly Babcock, but there was free grog and
she had a swimming pool (yes, she was one of those people), so I
thought I would tag along on Steph's invitation. I remember when I
first glimpsed Danny. The party was well underway. The ice had
melted, most of the potted plants had been urinated in, and there'd
been a catfight over some guy who nobody honestly wanted anyway,
which had ended in tears. The inevitable loomed as one drunken guy
was thrown into the pool and the floodgates were opened. Soon

clothes were flying from drunken extroverts with a generous helping of money but a definite shortfall of sense. Although I'd had a few, my clothes were staying exactly where they were; for one, I didn't think the public was ready for my pasty thighs, and for two, I wasn't ready to gamble with whatever bodily fluids were lurking beneath the murky depths of the pool. No, I was just chillin' out on a lounger next to Steph, or, in other words, I'd sat down rather than fallen down and was making slurred conversation with my friend, putting the world to rights whilst hoping that the churning in my stomach would stay there. I'd just finished the dregs of a bowl of Hula-Hoops when in he walked.

I was struck dumb for approximately one nanosecond before screaming at Steph, 'Who the hell is that?'

Steph followed my eyes and then told me rather too calmly, 'Oh, that's Danny Greenslade,' as if she'd just said, 'Oh, that's my Auntie Sheila,', and not that this was the man I'd been waiting my entire life to meet. He was stunning – a literal Adonis. Tall, fit, blond, well – and remarkably *still* – dressed, with the darkest brown eyes and the most beautiful smile I had ever seen. I mean Brad Pitt would have been jealous of this guy; he was definitely the best-looking bloke I'd seen in real life. He sat three loungers down from me with some mates, all male I was pleased to note. Perhaps you're wondering when I made my big move, when I strolled on up and introduced myself as the angel in his heaven. Well, it wasn't quite like that and the only move I made was a quick one to the downstairs WC where I introduced my guts to the lavatory basin. It wasn't pretty. It was actually probably the worst possible time for a gorgeous hunk to appear and say,

'Hi, I'm Danny.'

'Hi, I'm puking,' was my rather disappointing reply.

'Hey are you ok?' he asked, handing me some toilet paper and brushing my hair out of my face. I was in love. A guy who cared with such lovely eyes, as dark and adorable as the Andrex puppy - whose product I was now flushing away along with any hope of making a good first impression. I composed myself and told him I was fine.

'Well, if you're sure you're ok, I really have to go.'

I couldn't let this vision of loveliness walk out of my life just like that, so I muttered rather lamely, 'So soon?'

'Well, it is kind of what I came in here for.'

Ah, the penny dropped. He needed to pee. Oh, the shame. My face turned from green to pink as I made a rather quick but inelegant exit, apologising a little too much. He gave me a last smile showing his perfect teeth (my mother would love those teeth) and disappeared to find Steph waiting for me to embark on the walk home. All the way home, I whinged at what a fool I'd made of myself and relayed how wonderful Danny had been nursing me back to health. I marvelled at the fact that he'd actually used the toilet in the conventional manner rather than urinating in the plants like everyone else. Of course, he may just have used that downstairs loo because he knew I was in there. It was certainly a possibility in the land of drunken make-believe.

So that's how I met and fell in love with Danny Greenslade. I saw him a few times after that across crowded rooms, through car windows and once in the queue at the dole counter – apparently he was claiming benefits until he made it as a musician (*so* cool!) – but nothing too memorable.

My second major encounter with this hunky chunk of perfection was in, of all places, the public library. My brother, Stuart, had come back to stay with my parents while his wife was away on a business course. My brother is eight years older than me, which always seemed quite a lot. By the time I started secondary school, he'd already left home and had shacked up with a tart from Coventry and only re-appeared when they'd had a row or he missed my mother's cooking. I'm pleased to say that he eventually moved on from the tart who, in fairness, probably wasn't a tart but when you are eleven and you visit someone who wears lipstick all day and has a bathroom strewn with black lacy underwear, you tend to brand them as a tart. He's now married to an incredibly modern woman called Lucinda ('don't call me Lucy') and they have two little girls, Atlanta and

Verity. Where they dug those names up from, I'm not entirely sure, although I know that I personally wouldn't like to be known as "At" or "Very" but beggars can't be choosers. Although if it was up to Lucinda their names would never be cut short.

Anyway, this particular day when I was visiting my parents, my brother had turned up to dump the kids on Mum while he settled down in front of the match with Dad. Verity is only six months and so is still a novelty with my parents who turn all gurgly and talk to her in funny voices. Atlanta is four going on forty-two and wants to know everything, which can get truly annoying after a while. While Stuart tucked into a plate of starchy carbs, I got lumbered into taking Atlanta down to the library. Sometimes she can be a cool kid; like a mini adult in disguise. She's the kind of kid who uses the word "poo" instead of "woopsy" or "poopoop". It's only a mild difference, but it's noticeable – more than likely Lucinda's influence. Had it been Stuart's, she would probably talk about "dumps" and "turds". I suppose it's only a matter of time.

The library wasn't far, so we walked – well, sort of stopped and started, picked up an old cigarette packet, climbed up and down every set of steps and walked along every wall we could find on our way before eventually reaching our destination. Actually, I think I had more fun than Atlanta. I sat and read Miffy and Thomas the Tank Engine while she headed straight for the play area where I heard her telling a boy of three that she could play with the rubber toolkit, even though she was a girl. I just managed to whisk her away from a hand which was about to grab hold of her curls, apologised to the parents and told her to choose a book or two. We eventually settled on one about animals and their babies and a second called I Can Do That, which depicted little kids using remote controls and computer games. What was the world coming to? Whatever happened to how to tidy a Wendy house and dollies that wet themselves? Engrossed in Atlanta's books, I queued to get them stamped out, while Atlanta picked her nose and stared at a student girl who was sat studying. I was jolted from my reading when she came running to hide behind my legs, elbowing the guy waiting patiently behind me. Yes, you guessed it: the point to this extremely long and winding story had finally arrived. The patient guy was the one and only Danny Greenslade, looking so exceptionally appetising I could have eaten him up, or at least settled for a bit of a nibble.

'Sorry,' I squeaked, digging deep into my classic repertoire of chat-up lines.

Danny smiled. 'Oh, you're all right. Puking, isn't it?' he joked. *Holy shit, he remembered me!* It was good he recognised me, but that he remembered me for having vomit all over my chops was not ideal.

'Why have you gone all red, Auntie Nancy?'
Thanks for that, Atlanta. I glared at her.

'She yours?' Danny asked. *My goodness, this was a real actual conversation situation thing going on here!*

'No, no, no, no!' I replied a little too eagerly. 'She's my niece. We just came to get some books … obviously, us being in a library and all.'

Danny checked out the books in my hand. 'You've got some good ones there. Shall I tell you who dunnit?'

I laughed one of those silly, false, girly laughs and instantly regretted it. 'So, how are you?' I asked, secretly rather proud of myself for saying one thing to this guy which wasn't totally ludicrous.

'Oh, you know, I'm cool, nothing much happening. Bit of song writing, bit of playing, might have a gig coming up, that sort of thing.'

'Yeah, I know what you mean.' *We were kindred spirits.* This was it, the longest conversation I'd had with my dream bloke. I was trying hard to think of my next line, anything to keep the conversation going when I noticed Atlanta tugging at my sleeve.

'I think it's your turn,' Danny said. I plonked our books on the counter and handed over my card to the librarian. While we waited for her to stamp the books, Danny continued, 'Perhaps you should—' and, sadly, I never found out what I should have done, as the librarian interrupted him and a bored four-year-old dragged me outside.

I managed a 'Nice talking to you,', To which he replied, 'Yeah, see you around.' *You betcha!* So, what had he been trying to say? Perhaps I should … what? Perhaps I should go out to dinner with him? Marry him? Pop round for passionate sex? Get out more often? Get a haircut? Lose three stone? Keep out of his way from now on?

Oh, the list is endless; I know I still keep coming up with new endings. Some are non-repeatable and, needless to say, those are my favourites. But Danny Greenslade, or Dan if you knew him really well, which of course I do, had spoken to me; he had remembered me from that fateful party, puke or no puke, he had remembered me. That was a positive sign. Next time I saw him I would almost definitely ask him out, maybe.

If you remember a while ago, when I started this story, I was at the airport. I apologise, but my mind wanders liberally when I'm bored. Did I mention I was bored? So, now I was upstairs in the viewing lounge and with nothing in particular to rush home for, I had bought myself a cool bottle of Diet Coke. I walked over to the window to spot my parents' plane. There were so many, I didn't have a clue which one was theirs, so I waved at the next three to take off just in case my mother was looking out of the window. Everyone around me must have either thought I had hundreds of jet-setting friends, or I was a bit of a nutter with a plane-waving-off disposition.

I'm not saying I'm a plane-spotter, but I do find them fascinating to observe. Passengers returning from their destinations, tanned and regretful to be back home; those departing, excited and happy to be finally boarding. Those big metallic birds were the enablers of dreams to so many, whether holidaymakers, travellers or reuniting family and friends. I loved to discover new places. After months of reading guidebooks and holiday brochures, the joy of touching down in an unfamiliar land to explore was terribly exciting. I am a realist and understand that no-one gets paid for travelling around the world …

but perhaps writing about it was a start.

I was on the verge of wishing bon voyage to the fourth jumbo jet when I became distracted by a draught wafting my limp hair over my face. Spotting the one and only opening in the sweaty hothouse, I moved towards its absolute luxury. *Ah, bliss!* To my delight, the breeze was sneaking in through a fire door which had accidentally been left ajar. This was just too tempting for words. A quick glance around the room, à la Bodie and Doyle, and I was through the door into a secret outdoor world. Well, it wasn't another world, just a different area of the same old one I'd been living in for the past twenty-six years. But here, it was almost cool, almost humane.

I was standing at the top of a vast tower of steep stone steps. *I wouldn't want to run down those in a hurry,* I thought as I peered over the steep flight looming down to the depths of the forecourt below. Here, I had the most fantastic view of the planes, which made being here almost bearable. As I said, quite emphatically, I'm not a plane-spotting geek, but the sheer size of these things this close up was incredible. I gathered my hair up with my hand behind my head to allow the cool breeze to dry my sweaty neck.

Uh oh, I'd been spotted, ironically, by a young, pimply faced porter, of about seventeen or eighteen in bright red overalls, who looked remarkably like an acne-faced Leonardo di Caprio but in *Gilbert Grape* rather than *Titanic*. He swung through my secret door and invaded my draughty haven.

'What are you doing out here?' he asked me rather predictably and with a good attempt at sounding authoritative.

'Practising my lambada moves,' I replied, for some reason.

'Well, you're not supposed to be out here,' he said, ignoring my stupid answer.

'C'mon mate, give me a break, it's sweltering in there,' I pleaded, nodding towards the sweatbox from which I'd escaped.

'But it's not allowed,' he told me in a manner rather reminiscent of a school prefect. 'What would happen if everyone came out here, eh?'

'It would become jolly crowded,' I answered with mock sincerity.

My mother always said one day my sarcastic mouth would get me into trouble. I could tell he was rather lacking in the sense of humour department, so I tried the last resort; the old woeful female look and some whining. 'But it's so hot in there! I thought I would faint, so I just came out to get a breath of fresh air. I'll be ok in a minute,' I said, glancing down at my nearly finished Coke.

'Well ok, but just for a minute then.'

Crikey! It actually worked – that must be a first. How innocent, how naïve this guy must be. He turned to leave, but then thought better of it. 'I think I'd better stay so I can keep my eye on you.'

Hooray! I almost retorted. What did he think I was going to do, nick a bloody Boeing 747!? But I figured I shouldn't push my luck, so I just smiled a sickeningly sweet smile and turned away to watch the planes and finish my drink.

I was far from relaxed standing there and was beginning to feel a little bit stupid now with this jobsworth keeping his beady eye on my back, so it wasn't surprising that I dropped my glass bottle over the edge and onto the tarmac below when a loud yelp rang out behind me. I whipped round, expecting to see a spotty scowl demanding that I retrieve the splinters of glass below, but no, it was worse – much, much worse.

In front of me stood the pimply prefect with his back towards me and his hands quivering above his head. Beyond him, between his waving arms, I saw two shotgun barrels pointing in a direction that was frighteningly close to the line directly towards my head.

'You! Hands above your head!' I didn't need asking twice and my arms shot up so fast my elbows made a loud cracking noise. The instruction had come from a balaclava'ed face, one of two, with piercing blue eyes that stunned me into silence.

'Don't move!' it shouted. *Hey, I wasn't going anywhere.* I looked back to the viewing area window for help, but all I saw was the reflection of the sky and the planes, and I wasn't sure if anyone could see us. One of the gunmen pushed past my co-victim (I still didn't know his name). *This is it*, I thought, *this is how I'm going to die, at the age of twenty-six, in a crumpled T-shirt and three-year-old denim skirt.*

'You! Down the steps!' The blue eyes commanded. He was obviously the leader, as the other one had not yet uttered a word. I told my legs to get me down the steps in one piece and, bless them, they did as they were told, although rather shakily. It was strange the things that went through your mind at times such as this, like, have I got sweat patches under my arms? Did I leave the iron on? What if someone finds my diaries? Would Danny Greenslade care if I died?

Standing now at the bottom of the steps, I felt the barrel of a gun in my back as I waited for the other hooded man and my co-victim to reach the ground. I was grabbed by the wrist and taken round the corner of the building to a blue transit van, which I assumed was the getaway van as this seemed to be the only reason people bought blue transit vans. The rear door was opened, and they forced me inside, closely followed by Blue Eyes and his ever-present bullet carrying death machine. My co-victim and the biggest of the two men got in behind me while a third man, a black guy I hadn't seen before, jumped into the front seat of the van and was already changing into first gear by the time they slammed the doors fiercely shut.

'Go! Go! Go!' was the shout as the van sped away, it was like something from *Starsky & Hutch,* but I was far from safe with no predictable end in sight – *and* with David Soul and Paul Michael Glaser nowhere to be seen.

Well, so much for security. So far, I had seen no attempt to rescue us. No police, no guards, no megaphones, not even an alarm bell, nothing at all, just the smell of burning rubber as we sped out over the tarmac and away from the airport. Because of the lack of help, a small part of me hoped that this was all a joke; maybe these guys were Terrorist-O-Grams, or Noel Edmonds would turn up at any moment. Instead, our hands and feet were tied, our eyes were blindfolded and our mouths were covered with that black sticky tape kidnappers always seem to have handy. Now I was really scared. I was scared because I didn't know where I was or where I was going. I was scared because Steph was away for the weekend, my parents were halfway to Tenerife and I wasn't due to see anybody until Monday morning at work so no-one would miss me. I was scared because I was at the mercy of three men with very big guns, and I was scared because I really didn't know if I would live or die. Suddenly, my pathetic chameleon life seemed something worth holding on to.

It wasn't much, but it was my life and I didn't want it to end like this, with no warning. All at once, I felt like my future, if I had one at all, had changed completely from what it used to be.

My head was against the door of the van, as I lay on the floor rolling backwards and forwards at each sharp bend, and with every twist and turn the driver made. I could detect a draught through my hair, now sweatier than ever. If I wasn't going to die at the mercy of a bullet, I would surely die with a cracked head on the road outside. Over my shoulder, I could hear the other chap whimpering as he lay on the van floor beside me and our captors were conversing at the front.

'Are you sure it's him?' one man was saying.

'Yeah, I'm sure, all right!' came the reply. 'So far everything's going according to plan.'

'Yeah, apart from her,' interjected a voice I hadn't yet heard, in a tone that I didn't exactly care for.

'No, she's just an added bonus.'

'Bonus? How do you work that out?'

'Well, pretty girl, sympathy vote.'

'Have you shut that door properly? God, you're useless, we don't want to lose them yet!'

Although not utterly thrilled, I was slightly relieved when somebody clumsily straddled us, sat me upright and yanked the door closed. At least I wouldn't lose my life by falling out the back of the van, but it was the word "yet" that troubled me somewhat. So, Blue Eyes thought I was pretty, eh? The sitting position was not as comfortable as I would have liked, but it was definitely an improvement to lying on the petrol smelling, dust mite infected scrap of carpet I'd been lying on.

The journey seemed to take hours as I attempted to remember every turn in the road and every noise I could make out on the outside, desperate for any clue to my whereabouts or destination. I guess that's what comes of being an avid *Crimewatch* viewer. Eventually, after a long while, the van turned left onto an uneven track, and I was bumped up and down so harshly that I had little chance of keeping my balance. At last, any scrap of composure I had retained flew out of the window as I was flung off the seat, landing with a bruised bang on the floor, about as delicate as a sack of spuds.

'Careful!' someone yelled. *Like it was my fault*, I thought, but then as someone helped me back to my seat, I realised he had been talking to the driver.

'What are you trying to do, kill her?'

Please say no, please say no, I mentally pleaded.

'Sorry about that, love,' came the surprising but most satisfactory reply. 'Look, she's bleeding now! Shit, we'll have to sort her out when we get there.'

Great, now I'm bleeding to death and I don't even know where from.

The van eventually came to a halt, and they steadily bundled us out into the fresh air where someone untied my legs and I slowly peeled them apart.

'Watch your step now,' came the oddly reassuring, but stupid considering-my-blindfold, remark. 'We're nearly there now.'

'Mmm,' I replied as the baked soil underfoot turned to wooden planks. I warily baby-stepped straight ahead with the careful guidance of my captor.

'Now, step up,' said the voice at my side as it took me three attempts to find my footing on the rocking surface. It was a boat. As the realisation hit me, I could now hear water gently lap the sides. I was taken through, what felt like, a narrow gangway, down some small and precarious steps, finally coming to rest on a cushioned seat that felt good to my rather bruised and battered derrière and my sticky thighs. The air smelled like musty plastic, like a window needed to be opened. Other people followed.

'C'mon, mate, park your arse down there.' My co-victim had joined me. Curtains were either closed or opened and the rev of an engine started to churn. It took a couple of turns, but soon the whole boat was vibrating with a loud whining noise. We seemed to be turning slowly around, perhaps preparing to leave the shore, as we headed out into unfamiliar waters. We began rocking slowly from side to side with such a gentle lull that, for a moment, I was filled with a hope that maybe everything would be okay after all, like a baby comforted by being rocked in its mother's arms. But then the boat thrust forward, flinging me back into my padded seat, as we jetted off into the unknown.

Chapter Three

We had not been on the water for long when I heard a cabin door open and someone come in.

'Well, we're off guys.' A voice told us as if it was the exciting beginnings of a long-awaited holiday.

'Can I do it now?' another voice asked. *This is it*, I thought, *I am now as good as dead.* How could he be so callous as to sound like he was actually enjoying this? It sickened me to the pit of my stomach, which was now to all intents and purposes in my throat. My heart was pounding so hard it was almost painful.

'Yeah, hang on a second, I'll give you a hand,' came the reply as a second man came into the room.

'I'll take her.' It sounded like Blue Eyes, but did was he holding a knife? A gun? Or just a heavy blunt object? My face was burning hot and nervous sweat rolled down the inside of my blindfold. The knot behind my head was untied, and it hurt as strands of my hair were caught in its twists and folds. Although the inside of the cabin was dim, what light there was shocked my eyes as I blinked away the darkness.

'That's better, huh?' Blue Eyes asked me, with no anger and, even more pleasingly, no murder weapon. He had half removed his balaclava upwards, and I was not surprised to see that the lower half of his face, with its five o'clock shadow, was as attractive as his eyes. His lips moved upwards in a quick nervous smile as he must have seen the terror in my expression.

'This might hurt a bit, I'm afraid,' he told me as he peeled away the corner of the tape across my mouth, bit by bit. Believe me, that was an understatement if ever there was one. I made a mental note never to have my top lip waxed, not that I needed it now. It felt as though most of my face came off with it, leaving the discarded sticky tape twice as thick as it had been to start with and my skin feeling raw. He untied my hands next, and it ached as I slowly arched my arms back into place around the front of my body. I put my fingers up to my face and was reassured to find my lips were still in their rightful place, if a little sore.

In front of me was a table with green legs secured to the floor and across it, at the far end of the padded green seating, was my co-victim and a boiler-suited, much bigger man, trying his utmost to untie his knotted blindfold. Blue Eyes went to his aid but was of very little help.

'Got a knife?' he asked, at which the boy shuddered.

'Shall I have a go?' I offered, my voice shaking.

'Sure, let's see what you can do, you've probably got smaller fingers.' Eventually, I loosened the knot that was tangled in his sweaty hair and allowed the poor boy to see again. I winced as they ripped the tape from his mouth, taking the heads of several zits with it – like the boy didn't have enough problems. Then I remembered that I should be feeling sorry for myself, not anyone else, but he was a bit of a sorry sight.

As soon as they untied him, he started ranting and raving, shouting all sorts of crap like, 'You wait until my father hears about this,' and 'Do you know who I am?'

The two kidnappers stood staring at him, their heads cocked to one side as if observing an animal in the zoo.

'What? What? Can't you speak? What are you going to do with us?' The boy stopped himself just in time to prevent his head exploding and began fidgeting with his hands as if he had only just noticed everyone was staring at him.

Our two captors looked at each other. 'We got the right one,' they said in unison.

'Why, who is he?' I blurted out, annoyed that I was missing out on something everyone else knew.

'Well, I suppose you might as well know. This is Mark Cheriton,' The boy looked up, his eyes wide. 'Isn't that right, Mark? And yes, I do know who your dad is. That's why you're here.'

'So c'mon, who's his dad? I don't understand.' I whined as if talking to an old mate.

'Max Cheriton,' I was told, but I still didn't understand. 'Max Cheriton? The owner of Giant Airlines, not to mention Giant dot com and several other successful companies.'

'No way! That's amazing, I've got one of your dad's Giant mobile phones!' I squealed in surprise. Mark couldn't seem to stop himself from beaming ear to ear with pride, even though, at this particular moment, I questioned whether he should be so thankful to be the offspring of England's most successful business mogul. There was a strange silence in the small cabin as it filled with a variety of emotions.

Blue Eyes' smile disappeared as he glanced at me and said, 'Oh my god, your face!' *Cheers, you really know how to bring a girl back down to Earth with a bump.* I sat motionless as he disappeared out the room, returning minutes later with a First Aid kit and a bowl of water. He gestured for me to scooch along the bench as he sat down next to me, dipped some cotton wool into the tepid water and began dabbing the dried blood on my forehead. His warm breath was gentle on my face as he inspected my wound, so gentle and so close, and it made me a little nervous.

'So, why am I here?' I almost whispered the words so as not to break the comforting dabbing motion on my face.

'I'm not sure,' he whispered back, 'I'm afraid you were just in the wrong place at the wrong time.' For a moment, he looked apologetically into my eyes, which would have been a tender moment had he not still been wearing half a balaclava. Then he jolted upwards. 'Well, that's all clean now. You'll be fine'. He put the antiseptic cream and plasters back into the box and returned it and the bowl of water to whence they came.

'What's your name?' Mark asked me in a calmer voice than before, like a primary school teacher on a child's first day.

'Nancy,' I told him. 'Nancy Smart, who happened to be at the airport one day to see her parents off on holiday and ended up on a boat in the middle of nowhere.' The other two men present were both looking at me with a mixture of interest and pity. In their research of Mark Cheriton, heir to the Cheriton fortune and means to a very lucrative end, they had obviously not banked on meeting Nancy Smart, the girl from nowhere and of no importance.

'Well, Nancy Smart …' old Blue Eyes said, 'pleased to meet you.' He held out his hand to shake mine, and being a well-brought-up girl, I responded accordingly,

'I wish I could say the same,' I replied with an edgy politeness. 'And who might you be?'

'Oh, yes, I'm sorry! How rude of me. I'm Bill and this is Ben,' he said gesturing to the larger of the two men. 'We will be your hosts for the next few days. If you behave yourselves and all goes according to plan, you'll be back home by the end of the week and you will never hear from us again. Now, who's for beans on toast?'

We all looked at him in silence, including Ben, who eventually said, 'I love beans on toast!'

'Great!' said Bill as he clapped his hands together. 'Beans on toast all round.' He walked through the little stable door to what I presumed would be a small galley kitchen. Ben followed him like a devoted puppy, leaving me and Mark on our own.

'Can you believe this?' I whispered.

'I know, it's mad. My father will go crazy.'

'Well, mine won't be very pleased either. What shall we do?'

'I suppose we could jump overboard and swim for shore?' he suggested.

'Yeah right, have you any idea where we are?' Mark shrugged his shoulders as I opened one of the little curtains and peered out. There was nothing but water. No land, no other boats, and we were getting further and further out to sea by the second. To make it worse, it was getting dark. The sun was almost below the horizon, and the water looked less than inviting and distinctly cold.

'We'd never make it, Mark. Ooh, have you got your mobile phone with you?'

'No, we're not allowed them at work. It's in my locker. You?'

'Would I need to ask you if I had?' I snapped for no reason. 'Sorry,' I quickly apologised. 'I know none of this is your fault. I'm just hot and tired and shit scared, that's all. Sorry.'

'It's all right, I understand. We're in the same boat, remember?' He looked at me as he said this, and we both burst into nervous laughter. Bill came in quickly, closely followed by Ben, each with eyebrows raised in surprise and confusion. I don't think this particular scene was in their plan.

'What's so funny?' Bill asked, looking rather unnerved.

'Nothing.' Mark and I said in unison, suddenly aware of the inappropriateness of our behaviour.

'You stay here,' Bill ordered Ben, 'and keep an eye on them.' He pointed to us with a butter knife before disappearing back through the door to dish up the beans. Ben stood to attention and did what he was told until Bill returned with the dinner.

Having never shared beans on toast with two kidnappers and an heir to a fortune on a boat in the middle of the ocean before, I was unsure what the mood should be and quite how to behave. I wished I was one of those people who couldn't eat in a crisis, who said things like 'No I can't face the sight of food,' or 'I really couldn't eat a thing,' but I loved food, to which my bottom and thighs were testimony, and I tucked in with the rest.

We ate most of the meal in silence, with each of us looking up every now and again to meet someone else's eyes before quickly looking back down to their food. It was Mark who spoke first.

'Have you contacted my father yet?'

Bill and Ben looked at each other before Ben spoke. 'Well ... not exactly ... shut up and stop asking questions!' he barked as if suddenly remembering that they were in charge. Then he disappeared out towards the front of the boat and was replaced by the driver of the car from earlier who was wearing big sunglasses and smoking a hand-rolled cigarette.

'And you're "Weed", I presume ...' I ventured, wondering if all of these guys had not-very-intimidating Flowerpot Men aliases. The man appeared puzzled as he looked down at his roll-up.

'Well, it ain't no-one else's now, is it?'

My resolution to stay alert and in control at all times had failed miserably, as I could no longer keep my eyelids from closing and my head lolling about like a balloon on a stick. I finally gave in, figuring that it might be better to sleep now and recharge my batteries for my dramatic escape later on.

I had no idea how long I'd slept, but I woke up as the sun was rising on a new day. Mark was lying asleep on the seat next to me and was breathing so heavily it was almost a snore. The boat's cabin was in semi-darkness with shafts of orange glowing light sneaking through the gaps in the ill-fitting curtains, and the whole place smelt stuffy and in desperate need of air. I pulled open the curtain next to me but could see nothing but sea stretching all the way to the reds and golds of the horizon.

'Mark,' I whispered. 'Wake up.' He didn't, so I poked him. 'Oi, Mark, wake up!' I shook him gently until he stirred.

'What ... what's going on?' he stammered, clearly trying to remember where he was.

'C'mon, we've got to do something,' I urged.

'Like what?'

'I don't know, but something. We can't just lie here all day.' To be honest, I thought he might have a plan, but it was pretty evident he was as clueless as me.

'Well, I've got to get some air anyway. Are you coming?' Although

I had seen no evidence to think he could protect me, I reasoned that it would help to have safety in numbers – somebody to witness my murder if nothing else. He began to get up, and I tried my hardest to undishevel myself. I folded my body into the tiny toilet cubicle and threw water on my face and the unruly mop of frizz that had previously been my hair, which I tied back in a knot. When I emerged, Mark was waiting for me with a quizzical expression on his face.

'What's the matter? What's happened?' I asked.

'Can you smell bacon?'

I looked at him, surprised by his response, but I sniffed – and, yes, I could indeed smell bacon.

I followed Mark up the little cabin steps and out onto the deck where we found a small barbecue covered in sizzling bacon rashers. Behind it stood the black man we had seen the previous evening. He was whistling while he turned each slice one by one with a pair of tongs. He was now sporting a red and white spotted handkerchief over his face in the manner of the Lone Ranger or a bandit. Strangely, the hanky reminded me of the type that fairy story characters used to pack up their belongings, like Dick Whittington or The Three Little Pigs.

'Ah, look who's up,' he announced joyfully in a thick Jamaican accent. 'Anyone fancy some bacon?' He looked questioningly at me and Mark.

I wanted to tell him to shove it up his stupid kidnapping arse, but as it is widely known that it is impossible for any meat eater to resist the tempting aroma of a bacon sandwich, I instead replied, 'yes please,' rather meekly.

Mark accepted a sandwich also, and we sat down together at the back of the boat, wolfing them down while commenting on how nice a bacon sandwich tasted in the open air. It reminded me of when I was little and the family would travel to the seaside for our annual holiday. We would set off exceptionally early in the morning to avoid the traffic, Mum having packed some bacon sandwiches for breakfast.

Halfway there we would park up somewhere to eat the cold bacon sandwiches, me and my brother still in our pyjamas. Those sandwiches signified the start of our holiday, and I felt a pang of nostalgia for those days and the safety only parents can give. I realised how far away I was from that now as I sat on a boat with several strange gun-wielding men, going I knew not where.

From where we sat, we still could not see land. The only people we saw were ourselves and our three kidnappers, who by now were all sporting bandit-like bandanas and sunglasses – well apart from the biggest man they called Ben, who seemed to be sporting a checked tea-towel. Clearly it was too warm to be wearing balaclavas today.

The hours came and went. And then the days. They provided meals at appropriate times. Sometimes they included fresh fish one of the men had caught, but mostly it was some shit out of a tin or a packet. As far as I knew, the boat never stopped and I couldn't tell how they refuelled or restocked the food. Perhaps they did it at night when Mark and I were asleep. As much as I tried to stay awake, the sea air and the lethargy of the days made it impossible, and I'm ashamed to say that we both slept like babies, both at night and even periodically throughout the day.

Several days into the trip there was a breakthrough. *Land ahoy!* My heart skipped a beat, and I became alive with excitement. Land meant people – people I could alert to our situation. We finally had a glimmer of hope for escape from our tormentors and their bacon sandwiches. As luck would have it, we seemed to be heading straight for the strip of white sand I had spotted. As we drew nearer, I scanned the skyline for hotels and houses, anything to show that it was inhabited, but I saw nothing except some smoke curling up into the dusky sky from somewhere close to the beach.

'Nearly there,' said Blue-Eyes Bill as he came to the back of the boat.

'Nearly where?' I asked casually to see he would fall for that old trick.

'That, my friend is—' He was about to answer as I had hoped but managed to stop himself '—is your new temporary home,' he finished. *Damn, that was close.* 'I will have to put these back on you,' he said, holding up a couple of cloths I recognised as the blindfolds they had used when they picked us up. As the three of them still had guns and there seemed absolutely no point in refusing, we let them tie the cloths around our eyes and then tie our hands together behind our backs.

I heard the engine slowing down as the little boat chug-chugged towards the wooden jetty. The men shouted instructions to each other as they brought the boat to a halt and tied it securely with ropes. Mark and I sat still until they guided us to our feet and helped us over the side of the boat and onto the wooden planks of the jetty. This was by no means an easy feat as not only had I no vision, my tied hands gave me no balance and, having just found my sea legs over the past few days aboard ship, I wobbled precariously as I searched high and low for my land legs. It seemed they were nowhere to be found, and I staggered along on jelly legs like a decrepit old lady being helped along by a nice young man on community service.

When we reached the end of the jetty my feet, unsurprisingly, stepped onto sand and started up an incline.

'Who's that girl?' I was startled to hear the voice of a woman and tried to work out where it had come from, stopping in my tracks. *Hooray, a woman!* I thought. *Surely she will have some sympathy and help me out of this, woman to woman.*

'Oh yeah, bit of a mistake,' came the response. *Hmm, story of my life,* I thought as they pulled me forward.

'I'll tell you about that in a minute,' Blue-Eyes Bill shouted over my head.

Despite my blindfold, I could tell I was walking through a doorway into what smelt like some kind of shed. My blindfold was at last removed, as was the rope that bound my hands. They closed the door, locked it, then left.

Chapter Four

I found myself standing in the middle of what appeared to be a small wooden shack-like structure with Mark by my side. He appeared just as confused as me.

The room was approximately four metres square and was nothing more than a shed made of wooden planks with no features other than a small window nailed up unevenly with wooden slats and the door through which we had entered. The wooden floor was covered in a light layer of sand. The only furniture was a small camp bed evidently made for a pygmy or an Oompa Loompa, and in the corner what appeared to be some kind of chemical toilet.

'Hmm, cosy,' I announced sarcastically as we both surveyed our surroundings.

'Mmm, just like a home from home,' added Mark.

I peered out through the slats of the tiny window and onto brilliantly white sand stretching out to the gentle waves of a clear blue sea. It was late in the afternoon; the sun was low, and the glassy surface of the water shone in the light. It looked so inviting, especially considering I was very hot, very tired and very much in need of a good wash.

'Wow!' was all I managed. In different circumstances, extremely different circumstances, this would have been anyone's dream getaway place.

'What's out there?' Mark asked as he was took off his shoes and emptied them of sand.

'Come and see.' I moved over slightly so Mark had room to join me by the window.

'Oh my God!' he exclaimed. 'That is stunning.'

'It really is. I wonder where the hell we are?'

'I've no idea, but by looking at that view, we must be on some tropical island – maybe the Caribbean or something?'

'Hmm.' I agreed. We had been travelling for several days solid, in God knows what direction. From this angle I could just about make out the tiny jetty with the boat moored to it, bobbing up and down harmlessly in the shallow waters.

Mark tried the door. 'Worth a try,' he said when it rattled but remained firmly shut.

'Shit!' I announced as I slumped down on one end of the camp bed and nearly went flying. Mark sat on the other end to steady it. 'What are we going to do now?' I asked wearily.

'I'm not sure there is much we can do, is there?' Mark replied. 'We might as well get some sleep. It's starting to get late, anyway.'

'What if they come and kill us while we're sleeping?' I asked in a voice that said I was far too exhausted to care.

'Well then, we'd probably be better off asleep – at least we won't be aware of what's going on. Anyway, they won't kill us.'

'What makes you so sure of that?'

'Well, they wouldn't have hauled us for miles on some boat if they wanted us dead, would they? They'd just have thrown us overboard.'

'I s'pose,' I concluded, nodding off sleepily and slumping against the planked wall of the shed. 'I guess we should replenish our energy anyway, as we might need it later.'

'Yeah? What for?'

'For escaping, fighting, that sort of thing.'

'Yeah, course,' Mark half-heartedly agreed, and we both closed our eyes and gave in to sleep.

I don't know how long we were sparked out for, but someone

banging about outside woke me up and I had no idea where the hell I was. Mark jumped up, and I plummeted to the floor off the end of the camp bed, arms and legs flailing into the side of the hut and my head banging against the rough wood.

'Argh!' I screamed and uttered a few choice words of disdain, continuing to thrash about in terror and confusion, kicking aside the hands that had reached out to help me.

'Ok, ok.' I saw the silhouette of Blue-Eyes Bill as he backed away, his arms raised in surrender. 'Are you ok?' he asked with a look of concern.

'Yeah, just great,' I spat at him. 'Bloody marvellous!' *Ah, sarcasm, my old friend.*

'Are you hurt? Are you bleeding?' Although this didn't exactly sound like the voice of a cold-blooded killer, I kept my defences up just in case.

'I said I'm fine!' I answered, annoyed, as I put my fingers up to my throbbing head to check out the damage. Just a graze, I assumed.

'Well, if you're sure,' he added gingerly, 'I just brought you some food and stuff.' I ignored him in disgust so he turned to Mark who was also staring at my crumpled heap of a body on the floor.

'Well look, that's drinking water but that one's just for washing in, ok? Don't drink it.'

Mark was nodding.

'And this is an oil lamp but it'll probably only last a couple of hours so, erm, well that's about it. Oh, and there's some food in there, and I guess you've already found the toilet which ... yes, I'm sorry about that but hopefully it won't be for long, eh?'

'Yes, thanks, righteo,' replied Mark as if talking to a hotel porter pointing out the room's facilities.

'Righteo?' I mumbled as Mark closed the door behind Blue Eyes and started checking out the food.

'What?' he looked at me in surprise.

'Bit polite, aren't we, to the man that chained us up and nearly killed me?' I could be a little overdramatic sometimes.

'First of all, we're not chained up to anything, and you blatantly fell off the bed – no-one touched you at all. Now come and have some food before I eat it all.'

I felt wretched. I was dirty and tired and now had another great throbbing gash on the side of my head. I wanted my mum, and I wanted a hug. There was no point having a go at Mark seeing as he was the only "friend" I had right now, so I shuffled across the sandy floor on my bottom towards him and the smell of food.

'I'm sorry,' I said softly. 'But you could have punched him out of the way and run out and got help or something.'

Mark sighed and smiled at the same time to show that he was a bit weary of me but that it was ok. He took a bite of the meat stew-like dish in front of him before answering. 'Well, to be honest, I can hardly punch anyone on a normal day, let alone when I'm this knackered. Plus, he had his gun. Plus, I wanted to make sure you were ok. You hit your head with quite a bang.'

'Ah, thanks.' That was nice of him, although it did make me relive the embarrassment of my fall all over again. I decided it would be better for me to shut up now and started tucking into the homemade bread and tasty stew.

'Mmm, this is good,' Mark said, dipping his bread into the gravy.

'Mmm, it certainly is. Those kidnapping bastards really can cook.'

We finished it all, not a crumb of bread or a drop of gravy was left, and I collected the empty plates together; an old habit from my waitressing days.

'Let's just hope it wasn't poisoned, eh?' Mark said, watching me.

'What?' I said, stopping in my tracks and looking down at the empty plates.

'Joke,' he said. 'That was just a joke!'

'Ha, ha, you won't be laughing if that's true.'

'Neither will you,' he retorted, laughing at his own joke, which made me snigger too.

'You are *not* funny,' I told him as we continued laughing and I went to dump the dishes in the corner of the room.

'I can see you and me are going to fall out before too long.' He laughed again as he pretended to kick me. I saw it coming and quickly dodged out of its way before wobbling into the doorway and falling through the unlocked door onto the cold sand below. *What was wrong with me tonight?* I was giving Norman Wisdom a run for his money – all I needed was a garden rake, and I'd have done the set. I looked back up towards the light and saw Mark standing in the full length of the doorway.

'Oh my God!' he whispered loudly.

'I know, how clumsy am I?' I asked incredulously.

'No, I mean oh my God, the door's not locked! We're free!'

'Oh yeah, you're right!' I shouted back up at him.

'Shh!' he whispered, putting his finger up to his lips. I signalled for him to go back in and I followed, closing the door behind me.

'What shall we do, just make a run for it or wait for a bit and bide our time?' I asked.

'I don't know, what do you think?' he answered unhelpfully.

Not known for my decision-making skills, as Steph would testify, I was rather hoping that Mark would come up with a plan and save the day. I was a loyal follower, but not a brilliant leader. I was that drab chameleon, who just moulded in with everyone else's plan. Admittedly, I was totally an armchair critic when someone else made an unpopular decision but concocting a solution myself, without weighing up the pros and cons and dithering about it for at least two weeks, was exceptionally rare. And in this situation time wasn't on my side, so what to do?

'Ok, let's think.' There was only one logical way to decide. 'What would the Famous Five do?' I pondered.

Mark looked a little taken aback and then said thoughtfully, 'Is that the same as the Secret Seven?'

'No.'

'Why not?'

'Because there were seven of them and only five of the Famous Five,' I said, annoyed at his stupid question and wishing Steph was here to take control of the situation.

'So, who wrote the Secret Seven?' he continued.

'Enid Blyton.'

'So, she wrote them both?'

'Yes, she wrote them both. Now what would either the Famous Five or the Secret Seven do in this situation?' I tried to bring him back to the matter in hand.

'Oh sorry, yes, erm … I don't know.'

'Hmm.' I was getting frustrated that the full responsibility of our escape seemed to land on my insecure shoulders. 'Well, didn't that guy say that the lamp would go out in two hours?' I questioned.

'Yes, that's right,' Mark said with sudden enthusiasm. 'So we should go now while we've got some idea where we're going.'

'Yes!' The adrenaline was pumping now, 'Yes, and we'll take this blanket to hide the lamp until we're far enough away so they don't see us. If you carry that, I'll carry this bottle of water. C'mon let's go.'

'Hey, you're good at this,' Mark whispered as he covered the lamp and slowly opened the shed door. He stepped out, looking left and right. 'Ok, we're clear, come on.'

The boat and the light from what seemed to be the kidnapper's camp was far off to the right, so we crept out towards the left before breaking into a run, or our best attempt at a run on a beach in pitch blackness. Once we were far enough away that the light from the camp was no longer visible, we removed the blanket and let our eyes become accustomed to the glow from the lamp we were carrying. The light didn't reach far. To our left was a dark mass of trees, and to our right was a long stretch of sand and then an expanse of blackness and the sound of rolling waves.

We kept walking along the beach as far as possible. We agreed it would be safer than walking through a wood, especially as I was just wearing my flip-flops. At least this way, we would inevitably come across some hotel, holiday home or some other type of civilisation, even if it was just some cannibalistic tribesmen looking for company. We walked along in silence for some distance, both pondering our own thoughts. Mine were of stumbling across Brad Pitt's holiday home and him tending to my wounds in the jacuzzi while the police rescuers were taking their time to fly in and chopper me back to reality. Mark's thoughts had clearly been quite different.

'So, were the Famous Five the same as the Secret Seven after they'd lost a couple or something?'

'What? No! They're all different people – well, actually, eleven different people and one different dog.'

'Oh yes, that's right, there was a dog.'

'Yeah, called Timmy.'

'So, what were the others called?'

'Oh, I can't remember,' I said, trying to recollect. 'Dick.'

'What?' he asked.

'Dick was one of them, Julian and Dick.'

'Oh, right. And wasn't there a tomboy one? Jeanette or something?'

'I don't know. I don't remember a Jeanette. There was a Susan in the Secret Seven, though.'

'I'm sure there was a Jeanette. I can picture her in a school uniform.'

'You're not by any chance thinking of Jeanette Krankie, are you?' I laughed.

'Oh yes, I might be.' He laughed too. 'They were a bit of a freak show, weren't they?'

'Hmm, they were a bit strange,' I agreed. What a strange and diverse world we were in, where we meandered from Brad Pitt to Enid Blyton to *The Krankies* in the space of a ten-minute conversation.

The last look at my watch before the lamp fizzled out told me it was nearly ten-thirty, and we had been walking for an hour and a half with no signs of life whatsoever. We decided to keep going for as long as our legs would hold out to put as much distance between us and the kidnapper gang as possible. We walked on and on, too tired to speak. Our conversation had died and the only sound was the flip-flopping of my footwear, the crunch of the sand beneath and the gentle crashing of the waves on the shore.

It was a long way off, and at first I thought I was imagining it, so I stopped in my tracks and put my hand out to halt Mark.

'Do you hear that?' I whispered.

'What?' he whispered back, straining to hear.

'Maybe I imagined it. It sounded like … like some kind of music.'

Whatever it was, it had stopped, but we continued to walk in the same direction, this time with a quicker pace and a glint of hope. *There it was again.*

'I heard it that time.' Mark looked at me as we stopped to listen.

'It sounds like … something familiar … hang on a minute … that's only bloody Boney M and "Rivers of Babylon"!'

'I think you're right,' Mark agreed. 'Come on.' And we started off in a jog towards the music.

'It must be some kind of English bar or hotel or something.'

'Yeah, I bet it is!'

We sang along gleefully as we got nearer and nearer, and the music became louder and louder. We were nearly there! We saw lights and hazy half-illuminated figures were just visible through a small clump of trees. We jogged towards them, excited and relieved, happy with the certainty of our impending rescue and of returning to our friends and loved ones. *Hooray, we were free!*

We were reunited all right, but not in the way we had expected. We ran straight into the camp a la Batman and Robin, completely out of puff, trying to shout, 'Hi', 'Help!' and 'We've been kidnapped,' as we both doubled over to catch our breaths. To my surprise, I looked up to see a man with the most stunning face I had ever seen. *Thank you, God!* I mouthed, looking up into the heavens. He was as fit as a butcher's dog with a tan to die for, rugged good looks, chiselled features and the most amazing blue eyes …

Chapter Five

'Oh my God!' I gasped through my half-regained breath. As I looked around the assembled group, I saw that to the left of me was the Jamaican man from the boat. Next to him was the big man, Ben, who seemed to be a bit slow and was looking from one man to the other, confused. Last but not least, there was a woman – perhaps the one I'd heard when I first arrived. She too was black, wearing a brightly patterned sarong dress and had a perfect complexion. She was also holding a microphone, and I realised that she might have been behind the music which had guided us here.

'Shit!' It was Mark who said what everyone else was thinking. No-one knew what to do next.

Blue Eyes reached for his gun and nervously waved it around in our direction, clearly with no idea how to react. 'What the ...? How did ...? Oh shit, I must have left the door unlocked!' he said to the others sheepishly.

'Oh no, man,' said the Jamaican guy. 'How on earth did you let that happen?'

'I'm not sure. I'm sorry.'

'Who are they, Joe?' The bigger guy, Ben asked.

'You know, thingy and whatsit – Nancy and Mark.'

'Oh yeah,' he replied, the realisation dawning.

It felt like we were two unwanted guests at a party. I wondered whether we should just start to back out slowly.

'We should put them back in the hut while we decide what to do next,' Blue Eyes, or Joe as we now knew him, suggested.

'Maybe they'd like a bit of drink or somethin' first,' said the woman kindly, looking at us in our pitiful refugee state.

'This ain't supposed to be a party, woman,' the Jamaican guy told her. 'Although—' He trailed off as he glanced around the camp at the various people, several bottles of alcohol and what appeared to be a karaoke machine '—it is lookin' a bit like one.' He laughed a deep laugh that was somehow comforting and made me smile at him.

'No!' yelled Joe. 'We should … well, I think it would be best if we put 'em back. Don't you?'

These were the worst, most indecisive bunch of crims I'd ever met, and, believe me, working at the Job Centre I'd met a few.

'Look, I'll tell you what …' I announced, surprising everyone, especially myself. 'We are obviously crap at escaping, and frankly I'm too knackered to even try again tonight, plus it seems like we're on some inescapable island. If you just give us a couple more blankets, we'll go back into that shed thing and go to sleep. A bottle of that stuff you're drinking wouldn't go amiss either. You lot can then decide what you're going to do, and as long as you don't decide to kill us, that's fine by me.

They were all looking at me in astonishment, including Mark. 'But we've seen their faces now,' he said to me. *Oh yeah*, I thought, but the others said nothing.

'Ok, look. We have seen your faces …' I began again, looking particularly at Joe's. I would not be forgetting that one in a hurry. 'But we promise that if you let us out of this alive, we won't say anything about what you look like.'

Mark chipped in. 'Yes, we'll say you wore balaclavas the whole time. Just please don't kill us,' he tagged on the end for good measure.

'Ok, that seems fair,' agreed Joe as he shrugged his shoulders at the rest of the group who, in turn, nodded and murmured their approval. I sighed heavily, not quite comprehending this whole ludicrous situation. They gave us some more blankets and a couple of bottles of beer before escorting us back to the shed with a refill for the oil lamp.

'Well, good night then,' said Joe as he closed the door behind himself, securely clicking the padlock shut this time.

'Good night,' Mark and I echoed in unison as we tucked ourselves up in bed (me on the camp bed, him on a bundle of blankets on the floor). We cracked open the bottles, and the contents warmed our throats and sent us both cosily off to sleep.

The insides of my eyelids glowed red, and I opened one eye slowly as a shaft of bright sunlight came streaming through the slats in the window. This light and the uncertainty of my situation gave me a nauseating twang deep in my stomach. However, the brightness was nothing compared to the intensity of the sunlight which poured into the shed when the door was yanked open.

'Sorry about that,' a woman's voice said as I blinked frantically, desperately trying to save my sight. The outline of the Jamaican woman I had seen holding a microphone yesterday appeared in the doorway. Though most of her was in silhouette, I could still make out her long plaited braids swinging about her shoulders. Her voice sounded a little shaky as she asked us if we would like to come and have a wash and some breakfast. She sounded like she was almost more scared of us than we were of her. The shed was hot and sticky, and the promise of a cold shower was the nicest possible thing I could imagine right then. That was until I stood up and stepped towards the door. There, in front of me, was the sea – the beautiful sea I had seen on arrival but had been too stressed to appreciate. Its beauty surpassed any beach I had ever been to, easily matching ones I'd seen in holiday brochures and the ones Judith Chalmers visited in the Maldives.

'Oh, my …' was all I could say as I gazed out at the glistening water and golden white sand stretching out forever before me.

'Mmm, isn't it just?' said the woman standing next to me, and we smiled at each other like two lifelong friends stepping off a tourist bus on our package holiday.

'Can I ...?' I asked, nodding towards the inviting water ahead. I noticed her hesitate. 'It's ok, I'm not exactly going to make a swim for it, am I?' I assured her.

She weighed it up in her mind before saying, 'Yeah, sure, why not? Here, have this towel.' She handed me a blue towel which had very little nap on it. I took it and turned to Mark, who I could see was considering whether to join me or go for breakfast first. As is typical for most young boys, he chose his stomach and headed off towards the camp with the woman. They looked to be discussing the weather, which seemed bizarre and yet pleasantly reassuring. As they walked, the woman idly swung a gun round her fingers as if forgetting it was there.

I turned and headed in the opposite direction. I walked a little way up the beach until the camp was out of sight, along with the hut and the jetty, and made my way down to the water's edge. The water was so clear I could see the sand stretching out along the seafloor, its rippled texture mirroring the tidal ripples of the sea's glassy surface. I paddled for a little while, letting the water gently lap at my knees, but it looked so inviting, and I felt so grubby, that before long I felt the need to dive right in.

After a quick glance up and down the deserted shoreline, I removed my top and skirt, flinging them backwards onto the dry sand, before ducking down into the cool water and stretching forward into a swim. I swam a little further out until I was able to bob gently with my feet still touching the bottom. It was truly wonderful. I felt cleaner than I had in days, and as the soothing water caressed my bruised and battered body, my skin came back to life and I understood the true meaning of the word "revitalised". I swam and I bobbed and I floated under the water, through the water and on top of the water – and it felt good.

Looking out to sea, I saw nothing but ocean stretching out for miles. I looked back at the shore and saw nothing but sand and trees.

I was, to all intents and purposes, alone.

Although my future was uncertain, from my current vantage point it was no longer looking so bad. If the worst came to the worst and I was going to die, what a place to go in! The notion still scared me, of course, but the beautiful surroundings most definitely sweetened the pill.

I must have been in there for about fifteen minutes when I began to get real pangs of hunger, so I dragged myself out of the water in the manner of Ursula Andress, had Ursula been wearing her old bra and pants, and attempted to dry myself with the towel, before putting my wrinkled, and now even more sandy, clothes back on.

I ambled back towards the camp, trying my best to dry my soaking hair on the wet towel as I went, imagining I was an adventurous bounty hunter. I smelled something cooking and could see Mark and the Jamaican woman sitting in foldaway deckchairs at a circular, rustic-looking wooden table. They were laughing and making easy conversation with each other. Mark was resting back on one arm and patting his belly subconsciously with the other, as if he had just enjoyed a hearty meal – which, judging by the empty plate pushed to one side, he had. The woman stood up as she saw me approaching and began dishing up an array of English breakfast components: sausages, bacon, black pudding, fried egg, mushrooms, tomatoes and fried bread. It looked good and, as I soon found out, it tasted even better.

'How d'you like the water?' she asked as I was tucking into the highly stacked plateful.

'Mmm,' I answered.

'Yes, there is nothing like a swim to wake you up in the morning.'

'Mmm,' I answered again.

The three of us had a brief chat about how beautiful the place was, and it was a while before I noticed Mark's attire. He was no longer wearing the standard-issue bright red Giant dungarees he had arrived in and had changed into shorts and a T-shirt. He looked much better out of uniform, much less out of place.

'How come you've got different clothes on?' I asked with my mouth full.

'Rio had some spare clothes for me,' he answered matter-of-factly, as if I should have known.

'Rio?' I questioned.

'Ah yes, sorry – this is Rio,' Mark introduced us.

I turned to the woman, and she smiled back. 'Should you be telling us your name?' I asked.

'No, probably not, but I guessed it was bound to slip out some time. Figured I may as well introduce myself.'

'Oh, ok.' *Fair point*, I thought. 'So, have I got any other clothes?' I asked hopefully.

'Well, no, I'm afraid not. You see, we were expecting Mark but not expecting you. You were a bit of a mistake, … sorry.'

She actually appeared like she was sorry, so I told her it was ok and that I would make do with the clothes I had on. She informed me that Joe had gone to get some supplies and that she had asked him to pick up something for me, but in the meantime, I was welcome to borrow one of her sarongs so I could at least wash the clothes I was in. I thanked her, and after I'd had an outdoor shower with proper shampoo to wash the salt water out of my hair, she gave me a red and orange sarong combo to wear. It was light and floaty and made me feel like an exotic Arabian princess.

Rio was nice, I liked her. She helped me wash my clothes and underwear in a bowl of water, then wring them out before stringing them up on a makeshift washing line between two trees. To the untrained eye, no-one would know we were kidnapper and victim. While we "worked" we had a giggle and chatted away like washerwomen (which, in fact, we were). She told me she was married to Coultan, the big Jamaican guy, who was at that moment attending to the homemade rum distillery he had set up in the woods where it was cooler. She explained it was a tricky time as another batch was almost ready and had to be constantly monitored. Apparently, it had to be left until just the right minute – left too long, and it would be undrinkable.

'He's not far though. He'd come if I shouted,' she added quickly as if she felt she should. What was I going to do anyway? I didn't even have any underwear on.

To say there wasn't much for us to do was putting it mildly. There were no books, no newspapers or magazines, no TV, stereo or even a radio. For most of the morning, I sat with Mark in the sun, chatting like we were on holiday. Rio pottered around the camp, tidying things away and peeling vegetables. Coultan appeared periodically and then disappeared back into the undergrowth to check on his rum.

'They seem to be pretty stupid kidnappers,' Mark said to me as we sat out of earshot.

'I know, we've already seen all of their faces and know three out of four of their names.'

'Four out of four. I heard them refer to the other one as Frankie,' Mark informed me.

'Ah, so that's Rio, Coultan, Joe and Frankie. Hmm, good work, Columbo.'

Mark laughed. 'I like your thing,' he said, pointing to my outfit.

'Thanks. Yeah, it was nice of Rio to lend it to me, wasn't it?' I said, playing with the floaty fabric.

'Yes, Rio is nice,' Mark said, his eyes glazing over as he turned to see if she was around.

'Do you fancy her?' I asked, poking him in the ribs playfully like a little brother.

'No,' he answered quickly, then, 'no no no,' more slowly. 'I just think she's nice,' and then he added almost to himself, 'anyway, she's married to Coultan.'

I smiled at him knowingly.

'Stop it!' he said, laughing. 'Ok, ok,' he conceded. 'She's very attractive, but as I said, she's married. Still, it will make it a lot easier being here with her around.'

'Yeah, because it certainly is tough. Stuck here in this shitty tropical paradise.'

'Indeed. I suppose if you're going to be kidnapped, this is the way to do it. Beautiful place, gorgeous weather.'

'Nice food,' I added.

'Yes, great food,' he agreed. 'You know what? I think my spots are even clearing up,' he added, touching his face with his fingers.

'Great! It's like a hostage detox programme.'

We lay in the sun for a while, enjoying the warmth on our faces. At lunchtime, Rio brought over a selection of doorstep sandwiches filled with cheese and a variety of meats. If it were not for the limited bed situation and no proper sanitation, this would have been better than a five-star hotel. The food service, in particular, could not be faulted.

As Mark and I tucked in, I asked him, 'So, you reckon this is so they can scam your dad for money?'

'Yep, definitely. He is *loaded*,' he answered.

'You don't seem too bothered,' I noted.

He shrugged his shoulders. 'I know. To be honest, I feel a bit guilty about not being bothered.'

'Do you not get on?' I enquired.

He paused before answering. 'Yes and no.' *Well, that cleared things up.* 'He's not a terrible father, he's just a very busy one. I don't see him very much and when I do, it always seems so … so formal, you know? I'm never able to relax around him.'

'What about your mum?'

'I get on better with her, but I guess from as long as I can remember I always spent more time with my nanny or at boarding school. I just never really had the opportunity to bond with either of them.'

'Did you learn that in therapy?' I asked, half joking.

'No, *Trisha*,' he mocked.

'Haha,' I laughed along with him before turning more serious again. 'So, do you think your parents screwed you up?' I continued to dig.

'No. Honestly, I'm ok with it. I suppose it made me build

relationships with other people outside my family, you know friends, teachers, that sort of thing. I guess we're all different, that's just life. I don't believe I'm any the worse for it.'

'Hmm,' I agreed.

'Anyway, my father's idea of trying to bond with me was to have me go to work for him. I remember thinking that would be cool, assuming I would be one of his executives with a windowed office halfway up Canary Wharf, but no, what does he do? Sticks me in a uniform and gives me a mop!'

'Is that because he knew you'd be a crap exec, or to teach you some kind of life lesson?'

'Yes, that life lesson thing, I think. Working your way up, learning to be humble, all that kind of stuff.'

'Yeah, but look at you now.'

'Yes, this certainly beats mopping floors any day of the week,' he agreed. 'So, what about you? What would you be doing if you weren't here right now?'

'Erm ...' I tried to recollect the life I'd had before I took on the unexpected role of kidnappee. 'I don't know ... what the hell day is this?'

Mark scrunched up his nose. 'Hey, Rio. What day is it today?' he shouted over his shoulder.

'Wednesday, sweetheart,' Rio shouted back.

'Wednesday,' he told me as if I hadn't heard.

'Ah, Wednesday lunchtime. Jobs paper day. I would usually be sitting in the canteen pouring over the local paper looking for any new vacancy arrivals, like everyone else in there looking for my perfect dream job.' I smiled at the image of them all sitting there, while I was here thinking about them.

'Which is?' Mark asked.

'Well, that's the problem, I don't know. I guess that's why I've never found it.' I looked at Mark as I voiced my revelation. This is exactly what I had spoken to Steph about only a few days ago and had been contemplating at the airport, just before ... well, just before I met Mark and everything changed.

At that moment, I was sure that, whatever happened, I would not go back to that black-and-white world I had spent too long in already. I'm very much an "everything happens for a reason" type of girl and up until now, I could see no reason for my current predicament other than that it had forced me out of the inertia of my humdrum existence. *Something had to change.*

Whilst the midday sun beamed down, Mark and I sat under a tree to prevent us from burning. The cool breeze nestling in the branches soon lullaby'd us off to sleep, and we dozed lazily, with the fresh sea air and leafy aroma in our nostrils. We were awoken sometime later by the distant whirr of a boat's engine, and I momentarily panicked that we might be rescued.

'Who is it?' I asked Mark as we peered out to sea and watched the little boat shape approaching closer and closer.

'I think it's just that Joe chap coming back,' he said, and my stomach turned involuntarily, both in anticipation that something was going to happen and in the knowledge that I would get to see Joe again.

He moored the boat to the little jetty while Frankie peered over the side, steering the boat gently to line it up. Joe was shirtless and his biceps flexed as he pulled on the boat's mooring ropes to steady it. *Very nice. This unquestionably beats a day in the office with scab-picker Jeff.* We both watched as Frankie and Joe unloaded the supplies they had brought and saw Rio walk down to meet them. Her plaits were swinging and her bangles were jangling as she walked serenely over the sand. She kissed them both on their cheeks and helped them carry their bags back along the jetty and towards where we were laying.

I wondered if there was anything in those bags for me. Rio had said she had asked Joe to pick up some clothes. I could imagine him now, checking out the lingerie. *Hmm, what would he get me?* He would've been torn between the classic white lacy bra and pants set and the saucy red-and-black basque slut set. For clothes, he'd surely buy me some slinky little black number, perhaps a bikini or a selection of pretty vest tops. I scanned the bags. Nope, no bags from La Senza or any recognisable brand names for that matter. *Never mind, they probably won't have a La Senza in the carribean, I thought. Maybe a Marks & Spencers.*

As they got nearer, Mark got up to relieve Rio of a large box full of fruit and vegetables that she was carrying. I got up too and walked a little way behind him. I saw Joe look over to me, his face was smiling from the conversation he was having with Frankie and Rio. He stopped in his tracks and appeared suddenly surprised to see me. He looked me up and down in my floaty ensemble and, despite the heat, a shiver ran all over my body. I was suddenly very aware that I was wearing no undies, and I liked the thrill of exciting danger that gave me.

'I, er, have something for you,' Joe said as he stepped just close enough so I could reach the bag he was holding out to me at arms' length.

'Thanks,' I said politely as I reached out to take the bag. Frankie grinned and waved at me, shouting an enthusiastic 'hello' before they continued towards the camp with their goods.

I could barely wait to open my bag but didn't want to seem too excited. As any self-respecting twenty-six-year-old woman should, I loved presents and loved getting new clothes. I loved it even more when they were given to me by tasty blokes, whether they were kidnappers or not.

I calmly walked back to my tree and peeked inside. The contents soon brought me back down to earth. Inside was a plain white vest top, size "free", some wrap-around skirt type item, which was almost a sarong but much stranger with hideous pictures of elephants and monkeys all over it. Luckily, there was a khaki green knee-length skirt which at least seemed wearable – but, worst of all, I discovered right at the bottom of the bag a pack of six pairs of pants, each with a day of the week written on them in English. I don't know what worried me most about the pants. Whether it was that the size on the packet also said "free" (How can you have free size pants? What the hell size were they?) or that there were only six pairs, the sixth of which was inscribed with "weekend". I put the so-called "goods" back into the bag, sorely disappointed in Joe and his ability to shop for girls.

After sulking under my tree for a while, I walked back into the camp. Mark was helping Rio with her preparation for the evening meal. Frankie was blowing up some kind of inflatable football with a map of the world on it, while Joe and Coultan were nowhere to be seen. I offered to help but was told that Mark and Rio had it all under control. Frankie asked me if I wanted to kick his ball around with him for a while. 'Maybe later,' I told him. Me running around braless was probably not the best idea. He was friendly though, and didn't seem to take offence at me rejecting his offer. It wasn't long before Joe and Coultan came out of the bushes from the direction of the distillery, giggling like schoolgirls.

'It's just about good and ready.' Coultan laughed his deep laugh, waving a bottle of murky brown liquid in one hand and squeezing one of Rio's bottom cheeks with the other. Rio laughingly slapped his hand away and told them both to wash up as dinner was almost ready.

'What are they like?' She laughed as the two men giggled and jostled their way towards the water pump. They looked so comical we couldn't help laughing along with them. For dinner, we tucked into pork chops with fresh vegetables, which was good enough to put any posh restaurant to shame. It was plentiful and delicious and would have been eaten in appreciative silence, had Joe and Coultan not kept breaking into inane laughter each time they looked at each other.

Like any well-mannered guests at a dinner party, Mark and I offered to wash the dishes. While we did this, Coultan and Joe disappeared back into the woods, presumably to bottle some more of their laughter potion, and Rio sat with her feet up drinking a cool glass of lemonade. She unscrewed the top of the first bottle.

'You two fancy a glass?' she asked as we dried our hands and came to join her.

'Sure,' we agreed and grabbed a couple of glasses.

'You're sure now? This is crazy stuff. You've seen what it's done to those two grown men, I don't go near the stuff myself anymore.' She said, smiling. But that wasn't enough to put us off. I took a sip. *Good Lord above!* I almost lost the lining to my oesophagus with that first sip and the rest of my mouth was on fire. This was nothing like the stuff we had drunk before. Cor, well, if they didn't shoot me, this stuff would kill me off for sure!

Rio laughed as Mark and I coughed and spluttered, wafting our hands in front of our open mouths to cool them.

'Believe me, it gets better,' Rio assured us. We drank a little more, I swear it must have been at least 90% proof, if not more. It was pretty potent stuff.

'They're probably burying it,' Rio told us. 'It keeps it cooler underground, you know?' She paused. 'Only thing is, last time they drank too much before they buried it, the next day they had forgotten where it was!' She almost cackled with laughter at the memory in her head, and Mark and I also burst out with laughter at the image.

'Did they find it?' I asked through hiccoughs that had been brought on by laughing. Rio and Mark both laughed at me before she answered. 'Eventually, but it took a good couple o' days. They were not happy days.'

This was quite a contrary image to the three men who were now ambling out between the trees, bottles in each hand, stumbling and tripping over grass and twigs as they went. Joe slipped and fell towards Coultan, who instinctively pushed him backwards. Joe lost his footing and reached out to grab something to steady himself. The nearest thing to hand was the washing line with my drying clothes still pegged to it, and as his hand closed around my bra, he took it with him as he fell flat on the sand below. We all roared with laughter at the spectacle of slapstick comedy. Joe was laughing so much he couldn't even begin to get up, and Coultan tried to offer him his hand but was having trouble staying upright himself. Frankie eventually managed to drag him up by his armpits until Joe was kneeling in the sand. He seemed to realise that there was no way he would make it to his feet, so he crawled on his hands and knees the remaining couple of yards to join the rest of us. He hoisted himself up to sit on one of the large logs placed around the fire and brushed the sand off his knees and chest. After a minute, he looked down at what was in his hand before realising with a start that he was still clutching my bra. He stopped in his tracks before flinging the said item in my direction. Everyone continued to bawl with laughter, including me, who, far from being embarrassed, was loving the fact that Joe's hands had been on my bra, even if I wasn't wearing it.

As the sun set and the night drew in, the laughter died down and heads lolled in the smoke and the warmth of the campfire. With full bellies, the mood in the camp seemed, rather ironically, to be one of contentment.

Chapter Six

The next morning, I woke up back in the shed with no idea of how I got there. Mark was next to me, snoring like a tractor, and my head felt like it was being mined for diamonds. I checked the time; it was eight-thirty. I prised myself out of the small camp bed, my bones aching from sleeping the whole night in one position. I tried the door and it opened, but the bright sunlight forced my eyes closed, so I shut it again while I fumbled in my bag for my sunglasses. Once out in the fresh air, the smell of the smoky fire reached me and I heard sounds of life coming from the camp. I walked unsteadily towards them, my head banging with each step I made.

Rio looked up from what she was doing and saw me approach. 'Hey there!' she shouted rather too loudly for my liking. 'And how're you today?'

'Not good,' I managed, slumping down at the table and holding my head in my hands.

Rio laughed at me. 'You know the best thing to stop hangovers?' she asked gaily.

'What?' I mumbled into the table.

'Not drinking.'

I peered up at her from under my hair. 'Not funny.'

'You know what the second best thing is?'

'Let me guess, chopping your own head off?'

'No, one of my special breakfast baps and a dip in the ocean.' She placed a homemade bap stuffed full of sausage, bacon and a fried egg in front of me. Otherwise known as Hangover Heaven.

'Ahh, that's so nice.' I sat up, almost crying tears of joy.

Rio smiled. 'I'll get you a nice cup of tea.' She truly was an angel sent from above. And she was right. After I'd wolfed down the enormous bap, I felt much better. We sat together for a while, chatting over our cups of tea.

'So, where is everyone else?' I asked.

'Coultan has gone to the mainland for more bottles, Joe and Frankie know better than to wake up this early after a night on the rum.' She nodded to the side of the camp, past the water pump and the little hut that she and Coultan slept in. Amongst the cool trees, I could just make out two stuffed hammocks, hanging like chrysalises, concealing their drunkard butterflies, dead to the world.

'I thought Joe usually slept on the boat?' I whispered so as not to wake them.

'Yeah, he sometimes does, but last night he didn't think his legs would make it that far.'

'I don't blame him.' I remembered the state we'd all been in the previous night. 'But how the hell did he get in a hammock?' I wondered, bemused.

'Well, it took a few attempts, I can tell you. Once he'd taken you back, he was out for the count, so Frankie, Coultan and I had to lift him in. Now that is not an easy task, no sir.'

She laughed, and I pictured the scene; the three of them, a drunk man and a hammock. It must have been a fair sight.

'So that's how I got back? I had wondered about that.' *So, Joe had taken me? Hmm, just like Sleeping Beauty.*

'Yes, just after you told us you were going to drink us under the table you fell backwards off your log and weren't able to get back up again, so Joe picked you up and carried you back to the hut. Don't you remember?'

'Yes, yes ... well, no actually, I don't. The shame.' I buried my head in my hands again. *Less Sleeping Beauty more drunken zombie.*

'Don't worry about it,' she reassured me, laughing. 'You were fine, don't sweat it. We had a good night, the best we've had in a long while.' She patted my hand, and I managed a smile back at her, feeling a little better.

'Hey, how do you fancy a swim, huh? C'mon, it'll do you good.' She stood up and headed towards her hut, looking for something. 'Here try these, they're clean.' She threw a pair of colourful Bermuda shorts at me and I tried them on under my skirt.

'They're a bit big.' I said, surprised that I was small enough to fit into any of Rio's clothes, let alone drown in them.

'Yes, they will be, they're Coultan's. They've got a string to tie at the waist and you can roll up the legs. They'll be ok for swimming. I'd lend you a cossie but I only have the one clean and I haven't got anything else for swimming in,' she said while still rummaging.

'These'll be fine—' I said, rolling up the legs to above my knees '— as long as you think Coultan won't mind?'

'Oh, he'll be fine, he's got hundreds of pairs.' She turned to look at me in the baggy, hitched-up shorts and pulled a face.

'They're fine, honestly. I'm only going for a swim, not down the catwalk.'

'Ok, c'mon then.' She took off her clothes to reveal a stunning white all-in-one bathing suit which showed off her flawless curves to perfection.

As we strolled down to the sea, it was like Beauty and the Beast; Rio like a goddess next to me in an old vest and ill-fitting shorts with my pasty white legs. But once in the water, we were like two mermaids, swimming and diving about under the rippling surface. The water was clear enough to see the bottom even when we were so far out our feet could no longer touch it. Small white inquisitive fish swam about us before darting off again at right angles, and it felt like the presence of nature was all around me.

The exercise and the chilliness of the water woke me up, and I was more than happy to realise that my hangover was practically gone. Rio gestured to me that she was getting out. 'The boys will be up soon and they'll be wanting their hangover cures,' she shouted to me as she stood up and started to wade back to the shore.

'Ok! I think I'll just stay down here for a bit!' I shouted back, and she waved her acknowledgement as she headed up the beach towards the camp. I swam for a little while longer, in and out of the tumbling waves, as free as the white fish below me. *How strange it was, I mused, that I had to be held captive to be this free.*

After I tired of swimming, I sat in the shallow waters, bobbing gently in the waves, the sun on my face and the salty water gently cleansing my body from top to toe. How peaceful it was here. Was there ever a more beautiful sound than waves lapping ashore? *Ahh, bliss.*

'Ouch!' I was suddenly awoken from my reverie by what appeared to be a beach ball ricocheting off my head and splashing in the water next to me. I turned round to see Frankie pegging it down the beach after the ball.

'Sorry!' he shouted, laughing. 'Do you want to play now?' he asked as he reached the spot where I was sitting.

'Sure, why not?' I agreed, scrambling to my feet and grabbing the ball. 'What are we playing?'

'Catch,' he told me, and for a while, we threw the ball back and forth.

'I think we're too good at this,' I said after we'd thrown and caught about twenty in a row. Frankie grinned, clearly pleased with himself.

'Ok,' I said. 'This time every time you throw it you have to shout out a different colour for each letter of the alphabet, and if you can't think of one, or you repeat one, then you're out!'

'That's a great idea!' He beamed. 'You start!'

'Aqua!' I shouted as I tossed the ball in his direction.

'Blue!' he shouted, hurling it back.

After about ten minutes, we'd both practically run out of colours and the pauses between throws were getting longer and longer. I had mentally been through every item in my wardrobe and recited as much of the multi-coloured coat song from *Joseph and the Amazing*

*Technicolor Dreamcoat a*s I could remember.

'C'mon!' Frankie shouted. 'You've got to think of one or you're out!' he yelled, jumping up and down on the spot.

'Hang on, I'm thinking!'

'You're taking too long! I'll give you five seconds. One …'

'Hey, that's not fair!'

'Two …'

'I can't think.'

'Three …'

'Erm …'

'Four …'

'Ok, I give up, you win,' I conceded.

'Five! Haha, I win! And you know what that means?'

'What?'

'You lose!' he shouted, charging towards me before rugby tackling me around the waist and throwing me into the sea. As I came up for air, coughing and spluttering, I saw Joe standing halfway down the beach, his arms folded, watching us and shaking his head as he laughed at the spectacle in front of him. I had just managed to compose myself and brush the wet hair from my face when Frankie shouted 'Again!' and dived on top of me, pushing me backwards into the water.

'Hey, be careful!' Joe shouted as he ran down to the water like a protective father. 'Don't be that rough!' I heard him tell Frankie as, once again, my head made it above the surface. 'But can I play?' he asked, smiling at me. 'It looks like fun.'

'As long as you're not gonna dive on top of me as well!' I shouted and then instantly regretted it. *What the hell did I say that for? If only!*

'No, I won't, I promise.' Damn, I thought. 'Fancy a kick about?'

To be honest, I was a bit knackered after swimming, all that throwing and being nearly drowned twice, but I didn't want to miss the opportunity to get to know Joe better and show him my fun, frolicky side.

Mark came to join in too but, unfortunately, we were soon

thrashed by Frankie and Joe who succeeded in getting the blow-up football between their set of stick goalposts more times than we did, although in my book there were plenty of dodgy tackles and a few manoeuvres that I knew weren't strictly FA. The game ended when Rio called us up for lunch, and we ambled up the beach like field workers with a hunger in our bellies.

Lunch was a mountain of fresh salad   – slices of huge juicy beefsteak tomatoes, cucumbers, peppers, olives – with cold meats and cheeses and home-baked crusty rolls.

'How do you keep everything so fresh out here?' I asked Rio as I munched my way through.

'It's all kept in the fridge,' she told me, nodding backwards over her shoulder, and I noticed a small white fridge just inside her and Coultan's hut.

'How come that works?' I asked, amazed.

'It keeps things cold,' Frankie informed me, which indeed had answered the question I had asked but wasn't quite what I'd meant.

'It's run off a small generator,' Joe interjected. 'We keep it in the trees to keep it cool and dry.'

'That's cool, having electricity,' Mark joined in. 'I was wondering how you got hot water for the shower.' To be honest, it hadn't even crossed my mind, but I nodded along in a so-was-I kind of way so as not to appear stupid.

'Yes, that was down to me,' Rio announced. 'I flatly refused to come out here unless there would be hot water. They said they would cope with it being cold, but I told them no way was I going to wash myself every day in freezing water.'

I for one was glad she'd put her foot down; a woman after my own heart. Now all I needed was a hairdryer and some straighteners.

'Did you bring anything else?' I asked hopefully.

'No, we agreed that, besides the fridge, we were only allowed to bring one electrical item each. That generator is on its last legs so we don't want to overpower it.'

'So, what did everyone else bring?' I asked, wondering if there was anything else I could use that I didn't yet know about.

'I just brought an electric razor,' Joe told me. 'But I usually keep it on the boat. There's an electric socket on there too but it's not great.' *Hmm, that wasn't at all useful to me.* 'Coultan, what about you?'

'I brought along a radio as I like the music to listen to. Only thing is, there isn't a signal so it's pretty useless. I knew I shoulda got me one o' them music players.' He smiled wistfully. 'At least we got Frankie's karaoke machine.'

That's right, I'd forgotten all about that! The first night we had arrived and tried to escape, it had been Rio we'd heard, singing Boney M into a microphone. In all the haziness and confusion of the situation and the rum, it had completely slipped from my mind.

'That's what you bought as your luxury item, a karaoke machine?' Mark asked Frankie, who was beaming with pride.

'Yep, I love singing karaoke,' he told us.

'Well, I suppose it's something to keep you amused out here,' I offered.

'Only thing is,' Joe said, 'it's not exactly top of the range. It's a bit old and only has songs by artists that begin with "B".'

'No way, that's so funny!' Mark and I laughed.

'Yeah, and nothing after 1997. It's more what you'd call a specialist karaoke machine.' Joe laughed with us.

'At least you've got the Beach Boys and Bowie,' I said.

'Well, actually we don't have Bowie because that would be under D, but we do have Barry Manilow and The Bay City Rollers.'

'Well, that's alright then. Thank God for Barry Manilow,' I concluded, and they all nodded in agreement.

After lunch, Rio took us to find the "long drop", otherwise known as a hole in the ground, for number ones and twos. So far, Mark and I had been using the chemical potty in the shed but they had decided, as it was quite obvious there was nowhere for us to escape to, that we should now use the "drop" along with the others. It was not pretty, and to get over the experience Mark and I went to have a lie down in our favourite spot under the trees at the edge of the beach. We were now like natives of the island and were quite at home on the cool, sandy carpet, the gentle sound of the waves rocking us gently off to sleep.

Several peaceful hours later, the smell of roasting meat wafted up my nostrils, triggering my brain to wake me up in time for tea. As I sat up, I realised Mark was no longer beside me and I looked around to see where he was. It wasn't long before I saw him chatting to Rio, knife in hand, cutting up some kind of vegetable. I left him to it and decided to go for a paddle to wake myself up. I stood up and dusted the sand from my wrinkled clothes before giving an almighty stretch to awaken my sleeping muscles. As I stretched, I spotted something moving to my left, a little farther down the beach.

From where I stood, I peered through the trees to try and make out what it was. It was Joe, an axe in his hand, chopping logs into chunks while Frankie collected them into a heap. I took a few steps forward to where I had a better view and kept watch from behind my tree. From here I was able see Joe clearly; he had removed his T-shirt and had stuffed it into the waistband of his shorts. His brown sinuous skin glistened with sweat from the late afternoon sun, and his muscles tightened as he swung the axe over his head and down to split the wood below. His face was pink with the effort, and every now and again he would wipe the dripping sweat from it with his T-shirt. The scene was all very manly and caveman-esque.

As I watched, I began to feel a little guilty, as if I was a naughty voyeur viewing a scene that I had no earthly right to take such pleasure from. Mortified at the thought that someone might catch me spying, I dragged myself away and walked down to the water as previously planned. As I made my way down, I couldn't resist turning back for one more look. As I stood knee-deep in the shallow waves, I washed my face and arms in the cool water and casually glanced back up to where the wood was being chopped.

'Hi, Nancy!' Frankie yelled, and Joe turned round to see where I was.

'Oh, hi!' I yelled back as if I hadn't noticed they were there.

From where I was standing, I couldn't make out what Frankie said to Joe, but it resulted in them downing tools and racing each other down to the water, playfully pushing each other out of the way as they ran, before flinging themselves into the shallows and drenching me as they did. It was Frankie's head that appeared first shouting, 'I won, I won!'

Joe closely followed him shouting, 'No you did not, I was miles in front of you!'

They both looked towards me to decide. 'Err, I think we'll call that one a draw,' I said diplomatically.

'Yeah, right,' said Joe. 'She knows I won. She just doesn't want to hurt your feelings.' He poked Frankie in the ribs.

'No,' Frankie retorted, as he began striding out of the water. 'Anyway, I'll beat you back to camp!' he yelled as he started pegging it up the beach.

'Yeah, like that's fair!' Joe shouted after him, scrambling to find his feet on the seafloor. He looked at me, shaking his head and rolling his eyes, before running after him. I followed too, but at a much slower pace. It was way too hot to be running around like a lunatic.

After a tea of fresh meat and fish, potatoes and salad, Mark and I did the washing up while Joe put more freshly chopped logs on the fire and Coultan cracked open a fresh bottle of rum. It was still warm but becoming dusk, so Rio was making her way around the camp lighting lanterns and lamps until it looked like a tropical fairy garden. I heard Frankie pestering Joe to get out the karaoke machine.

'No, Frankie. Not tonight,' Joe was telling him, and then I heard, 'because I said so!' in the manner of a frustrated parent at the end of their tether.

After we had completed all the after-dinner chores, we gathered around the fire; some sitting on the thick logs, and some on blankets on the ground using the logs as backrests. Mark, Frankie and I drank cold beers while the others started on the homemade rum, and we made idle conversation about the day and the weather.

Eventually, Mark asked casually, 'So, how's the old ransom thing going?' which shocked everyone into silence. Joe 'erm'd' and looked at Coultan, Coultan 'err'd' and looked at Rio, Rio looked down at the floor in front of her and took a sip of water.

'Well, have you at least contacted my dad?' Mark continued. 'Has he said he'll pay up?'

After a few more seconds of silence, Joe finally said sternly, 'Look, that's none of your business.'

'Of course, it's our business! It's totally our business!' Mark answered back.

'Yeah,' I added. 'It determines how long we have to stay here.' As I spoke, a strange thing happened in my brain as a small piece of anxiety dislodged and was replaced by a tinge of regret that I would have to leave the island and the half-life I was now living. No-one said any more about it. Instead, to break the awkward silence, Joe suddenly blurted out, 'Ok Frankie, why don't we get out the karaoke?'

Chapter Seven

'But you said no before,' Frankie said.

'I've changed my mind,' he told him.

'Yay!' Frankie shouted and ran to get the karaoke equipment and plug it into the generator. He also grabbed an old builder's pallet, which was evidently the make-shift stage.

'Ok, I'll go first!' He beamed as he selected a disc from the pile.

'Let me guess, the Blues Brothers?' Coultan sighed.

Frankie merely grinned and put on his sunglasses. After a rather fluid rendition of 'Everybody Needs Somebody to Love', Frankie took a bow and we all clapped.

'Now Nancy!' he shouted, holding the microphone out towards me.

'Oh no, I'd rather not. I'm not a very good singer.'

'Hey, none of us are.' Rio laughed. 'Watch Coultan.'

'Thanks for that, my dearest,' Coultan said as he took the microphone and started singing 'Baby, We Better Try to Get It Together' by the unmistakable Barry White. It was true that he didn't hit all the notes, but with his gyrations and smouldering looks to the audience, it was most definitely an entertaining performance.

'Ready yet?' Joe asked me when the song ended.

'No, I don't think so,' I replied.

'What that girl needs is rum!' shouted Coultan as he passed the microphone on to Rio and while Joe filled up a glass and handed it to me. Rio sang a strangely soulful version of Belinda Carlisle's 'Heaven is a Place on Earth', which made me shiver and gave me goosebumps. Joe's 'Uptown Girl' by Billy Joel gave me shivers for totally different reasons. He was completely out of key, but as I clapped along with the others, I could stare at him unashamedly, and I watched as his attractive face crinkled with laughter when he got the words wrong or couldn't hit the top notes. He was positively lovely.

Mark was next with a half decent rendition of Bryan Adams' 'Summer of '69', which had us all up dancing around the fire as the alcohol reached our dancing feet. After Mark finished, I was all too aware that I was the only one who hadn't been up there – and it was clear everyone else knew this too, as all eyes were on me. I took a sip of rum.

'C'mon we'll do it together.' Joe said, taking the microphone in one hand and holding the other one out for me. It was obvious that I had to bite the bullet, so I downed the rest of the glass and reached out for Joe's hand.

'Ok, I know,' Joe said as he selected a disc and pressed play. When the first few familiar bars of Bonnie Tyler's 'Total Eclipse of the Heart' came on, I smiled – and when Joe started singing, I melted. I'm not sure whether it was singing with Joe or the effects of two enormous glasses of rum, but I began to warm up, and before long I was belting out the song too.

The others joined in the singing, swaying their arms in time to the music. As we finished, we were met with a standing ovation and Joe gave me a squeeze, I felt tingly all over again.

Now there was no stopping me, and after I'd murdered 'Manic Monday' by the Bangles, they had to practically prise the microphone out of my hand so someone else could have a go.

What a night! The next morning, if truth be told, some memories were kind of blurry, but I remembered singing and dancing and laughing. Yes, I remembered laughing a lot, really laughing, the kind of laughing that makes your stomach hurt and your face ache. I hadn't laughed that much for a long time.

I'd learnt my hangover lesson and didn't emerge from my camp bed until after ten, by which time Mark had bravely already left the hut. The outside air hit me like a slap in the face, but the view was so beautiful I couldn't be mad at it for too long and soon forgave it. I ambled into the camp to get some breakfast, and Rio made me scrambled eggs on two doorstep slices of hot, buttered toast which seemed to do the trick.

'How come you're always so fresh in the morning?' I marvelled at her glowing skin and constant perkiness.

'I'll tell you a secret—' she said, sitting down next to me and smiling '—the good skin is down to the ocean and the night cream, and I avoid that dreadful rum at all costs.' I smiled back at her and we had a bit of a giggle.

'What's so funny?' It was Joe coming out of the trees, trying to untangle a length of white rope as he made his way over.

'Never you mind, women's secrets,' Rio told him and she winked at me.

'Oh yeah?' he raised his eyebrows and looked at me. I played along, giving him a coy "wouldn't you like to know?" smirk.

'Ok, don't tell me. I thought you were laughing about last night. How are the bruises, by the way?'

I assumed he was talking to Rio so turned towards her for a reply. 'Why, what happened?' I asked her.

'I think he's talking to you, sweetie.' She laughed at my puzzled face. 'Don't you remember? You were singing "When Will I Be Famous?" when you went flying off the edge of the stage.'

I put my hands to my head. Shit, there was definitely some vague memory clawing its way back in.

'And when you fell over the log you banged your leg pretty badly, but you assured us you were fine,' Joe added.

Shit! My hands were now covering my face and I shook my head from side to side. 'Oh God, I'm such a loser!' I whined.

The other two laughed. 'You're not a loser,' Joe comforted. 'I think you're hilarious.' I peeped out at him through my fingers and saw him smile at me before announcing his departure and heading off back into the trees with his rope.

Rio gave me a friendly pat on the back and got up to busy herself around the camp. After a shower, I felt a lot perkier so when Frankie and Mark asked me to join in a game of catch, I agreed. This time we had to shout out the names of different pop groups beginning with every letter of the alphabet – after my Velvet Underground and Frankie's Wombles, Mark failed on the dreaded letter "X" and was spectacularly given the now customary dunking by me and Frankie. Coultan had been out on the boat getting supplies, and as he drew nearer, we waved at him before rushing over and helping to moor the boat and carry the bags up to the camp.

As I helped unpack, I found the suntan lotion I had asked for and gave him a peck on the cheek. After lunch, I headed down the beach with a towel and the lotion to start working seriously on my tan. With only a rolled-up vest top and hitched-up skirt to play with, my attire wasn't going to win any style awards in St Tropez, but I had to work with what I'd got.

After about a quarter of an hour of soaking up the glorious sunshine, a dark shadow fell over my face and I opened my eyes to see Joe towering over me.

'Mind if I join you?' he asked.

'Sure,' I answered casually as he laid his towel down next to mine and began rolling up the legs of his shorts like the archetypal Englishman abroad. We lay there for a while, just your average kidnapper and kidnappee enjoying the peace and quiet of a summer's day in paradise.

'So, you've had enough of playing football, have you?' I eventually asked him to start up a conversation. It was nice to get him alone for once. At last, I could finally get to know him better.

'Yeah, I'm too good. I had to give them a chance,' he said, referring to Mark and Frankie who were still playing a game further up the beach.

'Yeah, right,' I said playfully.

'It's true, I could have been the next David Beckham.'

'What, if you hadn't turned to a life of crime?' It was supposed to be a joke, but I regretted saying it almost as soon as it had left my mouth. It was true, but it was a mood killer.

'What do you mean?' I heard from his voice that he had turned to look at me, and I opened my eyes to see him lying next to me, his chest close enough to rub suntan lotion into.

'Erm, well, the whole kidnapping, blackmailing, ransom thing,' I answered, wondering if I'd missed something or got my wires crossed.

'Oh yeah, that.' He sounded uncertain.

'You know you've got to do something soon. You either have to ask for the ransom or let us go. We can't stay here indefinitely.'

'Yeah, I know. We're gonna get that money. We need to get that money.'

'Yeah? What do you need it for?' I asked in a rather accusatory tone.

'Stuff.'

'Oh well, I didn't realise you needed it for stuff. In that case, go ahead and rob Mr Cheriton, get some for me while you're at it, I could do with some stuff too.'

'You don't understand.'

'No, I don't, I don't understand at all.'

'So, you should just accept what life gives you? Some are born rich and the rest are born to live their lives in the gutter so tough shit?'

'No, that's not what I'm saying at all! I'm saying that if you want something more, a better life or whatever, you've got to work for it, not just take someone else's!'

'So, tell me, you work don't you? Where is it again?'

'The Job Centre, why?'

'Right the Job Centre. Do you work hard?'

'Yeah, I guess.'

'And what do you work, 9 to 5, five days a week?'

'Something like that, what's your point?'

'Do you get paid as much as you deserve?'

'No, but who does?'

'So, you're worth more, right? The money you earn is enough to buy you the odd CD, some new clothes every now and again, and maybe a couple of nights out a month, but it will never make you rich. There will always be things you want that are just out of reach, things that you see other people with; a new car, an extra holiday or even a house. Things you spend your entire life dreaming of, saving for or paying off.'

'Of course, but that's the same for everyone. You have to accept it.'

'Exactly! But it's not the same for everyone, is it? Some people have all that. Some people never have to worry if they can afford the electricity bill this month or pay for the kids' school trips. They worry about getting a scratch on their Lamborghini or whether the pool cleaning man can switch from Tuesday to Thursday.'

'Ok, I see your point, of course, some people are better off than others, but it doesn't mean you can go round stealing from them. I'm sure he's worked bloody hard to get to where he is.'

'It's not like I'm leaving him destitute. I'm not shagging his wife or anything. He's got way more than any human being needs. Once you have a bit of money, you get all sorts of perks; expenses, business lunches. Money goes to money. I'm—' he paused for a moment to find the words '—redistributing the wealth.'

'Redistributing the wealth! Don't you have to be wearing Lincoln green and have your arrows in a quiver before you can say things like that?' I sniggered at my Robin Hood joke and he looked hurt.

'Forget it,' he said and stood up to leave. 'You obviously don't understand, you just think this is one big joke.' He turned and strode away across the sand to the shoreline.

'Hey!' I yelled. 'Hey!' I yelled again, scrambling to my feet and stomping after him. 'Hey, you know what?' I shouted at his back, as he continued to ignore me and walk away. 'I'm the one who you bundled into the back of a van, I'm the one who you drove God knows where for God knows why. I'm the one who has no idea if I will end up getting killed or if I'll ever see any of my friends or family again, so no Mr Dramatic, I don't think this is a joke, I don't think any of it is a joke. All I want is an explanation or even a few hints as to why the bloody hell I'm here, and if this is just so you can cruise around in a fast car or go to Klosters ski-ing every Christmas, I …' After such a good speech, I suddenly realised I couldn't find the words to end it.

Joe turned round to face me expectantly. 'You what?' he said, rather more gently than I had anticipated. *Good question.*

'I don't know,' I answered stupidly but honestly, as a wave lapped my toes and I looked down sharply as if it had bitten me, blinking away the tears that had been brimming in my lower lids. Joe was looking out at the ocean and he crouched down in the shallows, letting the cool water run through his fingertips. He picked up a floating twig and subconsciously let it go and float past him to the beach. He said nothing, so sighing loudly, I turned to head back up onto the sand.

'I'm sorry,' he whispered without looking up. 'I'm sorry, I was just too involved with my own problems.'

'I am your problem,' I replied, just as solemnly, and made my way up the beach with heavy feet that suddenly became very weary. I sensed him turn to watch me go, but I didn't turn back. Instead, I let the tears roll down my face. The tears that had been wanting to escape ever since that dreadful day at the airport. Along that bumpy track in the van when the blood and sweat had poured out of me, the tears hadn't come, but now they did. As I walked and walked, past the hut, past Mark and Coultan building a campfire, oblivious to me, and past Frankie, who was now bobbing lazily on the marooned boat. I walked until the shed became small and the only audible sound was the gentle waves of the sun-soaked waters and the breath of the breeze ruffling the leaves of the trees.

I sat down in the shade of a palm, dragged my heat-frizzed hair away from my face and tucked it behind my ears. I tried to wipe the tears away from my hot and sticky face; nevertheless, they came. Tear duct sluice gates gaped open, and I cried and cried until my eyes were almost swollen shut and I found it difficult to breathe. I sat on my shady spot for what seemed like hours, long after the initial bout of tears had ceased, and tried to make sense of my position. Here I was, on a beautiful beach, looking out at the ocean which would not have been out of place in a brochure for Eden – yet I had been through so much to get here.

But why was I filled with such emotion now? Why was it today that the tears had come? Why not when the duct tape had been stuck to my face and a gun held to my head? Perhaps it had all been brewing inside me for days and my body eventually had to let it out, or maybe it was my hormones rampaging through my blood … or was it something else? Why was the sight of my captor, of a man, of Joe looking hurt that had prised open the gates? All I could see in front of me now was his blue eyes, hurt and lost. Panic had filled my stomach when he had risen to leave, and a desire not to let him go. I wanted him to share my thoughts almost as much as I wanted to share his. There was still a great precipice between us that could not be bridged with palm trees and vine leaves. The tears were for the realisation that I may never reach the other side, and it was only at that moment that I recognised how very much I wanted to.

I awakened to find that the shadow of the tree above me had moved round to leave my feet exposed and baking in the early evening sun. I awkwardly stood up, inspected the ridges on my arms and back where they had been resting against the bark and shook the sand out of my skirt and pants. Still dazed from my nap and weary from all that crying, I ambled down to the water's edge, placing one red glowing foot timidly into the water, followed hesitantly by the other, to cool them down. Once they had become accustomed to the change in temperature, I sat myself down fully clothed in the shallow water and soaked my face and hair. The coolness felt so inexplicably good on my fiery extremities that I lay myself down flat, letting the waves wash over me from burning head to burning toe.

It was lying there in the gentle ebb and flow that I made my vow. I admitted that I had some kind of romantic attachment to Joe, however this was simply a reaction to the predicament I was in. I was travelling an emotional journey unlike any I had ever travelled on before, and I had lost sight of the map for a while. I couldn't and didn't have feelings for Joe. It was a crazy fantasy that would soon disappear when I realised how stupid I'd been, like a crush on a school teacher. I laughed a little to myself at my analogy. *That's it, like a crush on a teacher.* I didn't really want him. It was an illusion, created in my mind to make the time go faster and that's just what girls did; made the best of a bad situation with a romantic fantasy. And then it hit me, I knew what this was all about. *It's Stockholm Syndrome!* When those who are held hostage develop feelings and sympathies for those imprisoning them – like Patty Hearst, back in the 70s. Thank God, it was a syndrome which meant it wasn't real. What a relief. What an idiot I'd been! All this fuss over nothing. I didn't really fancy Joe at all!

So why was I nervous with anxiety at the prospect of returning to the camp? Why had I stayed away for the best part of a day in case my reactions gave me away? *I can do this. I can go back there and do what I'm told until the time comes for me to go back to England. I will tell myself I can't possibly have feelings for him, like a silly school girl crush. I'm twenty-six years old goddammit, and I can do this!* I vowed adamantly to myself, as I floated back and forth like a piece of driftwood in the water.

This newly made pledge was subsequently literally blown out of the water along with my body as someone yanked me up with two firm hands under my armpits and pulled me back onto the sand. I yelped in shock and wriggled in an ungainly manner to release myself from the grip I found myself in.

'What the hell are you doing?' I shouted as I turned round to see Joe's worried face looking back at me.

'I'm sorry, I ... well, I saw you walk down to the water, and you were in there so long and, err, I came to check you were ok and saw you lying there with your eyes closed and I thought you were … you know … dead or something.'

Oh holy moly, he looked lovely, kneeling next to me with his big blue eyes and his tanned chest. What a bastard. It certainly made my new vow very difficult to keep.

I had to come up with something to say quickly, something that was mean and did not include any words like, "I bloody love you!" Instead, I opted for, 'I'm surprised you bothered, it would have saved you the hassle of killing me!'

It was totally overdramatic, but I figured it was better than the alternative. I'm not sure what reaction I was expecting, but it wasn't the smile and the shake of the head that I received.

'C'mon,' he said, patting my shoulder as he stood up, 'burgers are almost done.' With that, he started back towards the camp, and I watched the muscles in his back jostling with each swing of his arms. I stood in the sea to wash the newly acquired sand off my body, affirming that I must try harder or my plan to resist was doomed to failure. And then I realised … he said he saw me walk into the water, which means he also saw me shaking sand out of my pants. *Marvellous*.

Chapter Eight

Dinner was a subdued affair with no-one having much to say. It made a change to the lively chit-chat of previous meals. I was mulling over my conversation with Joe, it could have been a lovely afternoon of laughs and idle conversations, but I had to go and bring up the whole kidnap situation and spoil it. *Stupid, stupid.* Or maybe it had needed to be said; although it was an unusual situation, we were in fact captives and it would be irresponsible to become too close.

Sitting by the fire made me sleepy, and I hadn't the energy to make polite conversation. I announced that I would have an early night, stood up to leave and turned towards the shed.

'You still sleepin' in that shed?' Rio asked, as if surprised.

'Well, yeah,' I answered, looking around the group in case they were aware of something I wasn't. I mean really, where else would I be sleeping?

'You don't like your hammock then?' She looked at me, her eyebrows raised, then looked at Joe.

'What?' I asked, following her eyes towards Joe.

'Oh yeah,' he said shyly, looking down at his feet. 'I made you a hammock. I thought you might like one ... for a change, you know.' He lifted his face to meet my eyes. *What to say?*

'Really?'

'Yeah! Show her, Joe!' Frankie piped up excitedly, and Joe almost reluctantly stood up from the log he had been sitting on and nodded toward the trees at the edge of the beach.

'C'mon,' he said.

I obediently followed him. There, in my favourite spot, between the trees with a clear view of the sunset on the horizon to the west, I saw a low-slung, white canvas hammock, with slats of wood at each end to keep the width, tied up with the white rope I had seen Joe untangling earlier that day.

'I don't know what to say,' I managed. 'Thank you.'

'You're welcome. I hoped you might like … well it seemed to be the right time … anyway, it's nice to sleep outside sometimes,' he said with his hands shoved deep down inside his pockets, looking at me for a reaction.

'It's lovely, really, I love it, and I love this spot,' I said, looking up at the starry sky above.

'Well, that's what I thought,' he said nonchalantly. 'I was going to show you earlier, before … well before you kicked off at me.'

My cheeks pinked up in the twilight. 'Yeah, listen, about that … I'm sorry. I didn't mean to go off on one.'

'No, I'm the one who should be sorry. I can be a right twat sometimes.' We looked at each other and smiled.

'Friends?' he asked.

'Friends,' I agreed, although in the real world we had no earthly right to be so.

'C'mon, let's go and get you some blankets.'

We wandered across the sand to the shed and loaded ourselves up with blankets and pillows, bringing them back over to where the hammock was strung up.

'Well, go on then,' he said, gesturing towards it. I knew it would not be easy, but I managed to get on it with some semblance of decorum and, more amazingly, stayed on it without flying off the other side, or spinning round and round like they do in cartoons. I didn't dare move too much for fear of the above, so Joe stuffed the pillow behind my head and even covered me up with the blankets. For a moment, I thought he was going to give me a goodnight kiss, but instead, he just smiled and said, 'Well?'

'Actually, it's comfy. I'm as snug as a bug in a rug.'

He looked at me strangely before advising, 'Just don't move all night and you'll be fine.'

I was pretty sure that would be easier said than done. 'Thanks,' I said, 'and thanks for this, I'm honestly touched.'

'You're welcome,' he said, nodding at me before disappearing back through the trees to the camp. I could hear the low voices of the others and see the glow of the fire through the trees and didn't feel alone. To my right, I could make out the black sea as it made its eternal reach for the shore, the twinkling stars above me glittering on its smooth surface, looking more beautiful than any diamond jewellery or tiara. This world had been here for millions of years and would still be here for millions more, and I felt privileged to be a part of it, even for just the brief time I was here.

In the morning I woke up and watched the colour of the sky change from purples and pinks to reds and yellows as the sun began its steady ascent. Thanks to the absence of alcohol the previous night, my head was clear for once and, unusually, I couldn't wait to get out of bed, or hammock in my case. I clambered out without too much difficulty, and although I was a little stiff from sleeping in one position, I jogged down to the sea. The day was still breaking, but the air was already warm and I ran into the water before diving headfirst below its cool surface. It was freezing, but it certainly beat any power shower for waking you up in the morning. I felt alive, really alive – in fact, I felt so alive it was as if I was the only person in the world who was awake, and I swam alone while everyone else slept on.

The camp was silent when I crept in to grab a towel. Even Rio wasn't up yet. I quietly made myself a cheese sandwich and sat at the table, with a towel and blanket wrapped cosily about my shoulders. I looked around the camp they had made for themselves. The little hut for Rio and Coultan made of logs and some form of bamboo, from whence I could hear Coultan snoring through the open window. The remains of last night's fire, surrounded by the tree trunk seats scattered with various blankets and pillows. Beyond that, on the edge of the woody area, Joe and Frankie's hammocks hung full and still. To the left of them were the open-air shower and washing-up station, housing pots and pans, plates and other general kitchenware. Further round the corner, I could just about make out the shed where I assumed Mark was still asleep.

A couple of hours later, the camp was once again full of life; breakfast had been eaten and morning swims had been taken. I had just finished a tough game of catch with Frankie, Mark and Joe where the alphabet topic of the day was different types of food, and I was now oiling up ready for the sunbathing that I had missed out on yesterday. My feet, however, were still very red, so I covered them up with a towel. Lying on my belly, I had a view up the shore and it wasn't long before I could see Joe heading in my direction, towel in hand. As I watched him approach from beneath my sunglasses, I decided that I definitely wouldn't be so confrontational today, I would just relax and chill.

'Mind if I join you?' he asked, smiling as both of us clearly recognised that it was reminiscent of yesterday.

'Sure,' I replied, relaxed and chilled.

'So, how was your first night in the hammock?' he asked as he sat down next to me.

'Fantastic, actually,' I told him enthusiastically. 'Sleeping under the stars, waking up in the open air with that view. It was awesome.'

'Yeah, there's nothing quite like waking up and having the sea right there. You can literally roll out of bed and dive straight in, you don't even have to get changed.'

'Yes! That's exactly what I did this morning!'

'Now where else would you get to do that, eh?'

I had to agree that I was surely in a unique position, but after a while I couldn't hold it in any longer.

'So go on then,' I ordered him.

He looked a little scared. 'Go on then, what?'

'Tell me the reason. Why are we here?'

'What, you mean the meaning of life?' He looked puzzled, and it made me laugh.

'No, silly,' I said, trying to be playfully cute. 'Why do you need the money? What's the big secret?'

'There's no secret.'

'There is if you don't tell me what it is.'

'It's a long story.' He shook his head and looked down at the sand between his knees.

'Well, I ain't exactly going anywhere.'

He looked up and smiled at me, exhaling an almost laugh. 'Ok, as you asked, I'll tell you.' He stretched out his legs to get himself comfortable and propped himself up on one elbow, facing me. I did the same in his mirror image and he began. He told me the sad truth of his childhood, that he'd never known his parents and been brought up in a series of care homes. When he was about ten years old, he met Frankie who came to the same home as him and they became friends. Joe was sent periodically to foster homes with a view to having him adopted, but Frankie wasn't, it was thought that no-one would want to adopt a little boy who had learning difficulties.

'That's barbaric!' I was outraged. 'What is this, Victorian England? It's like something out of a Charles Dickens novel!'

'Tell me about it.' Joe shook his head. 'I was only ten and even I knew it was wrong, but that's the way it was back then.'

'So, what did you do?' I asked him to continue.

'Well, naturally loads of couples wanted to adopt me.'

'Why?' I asked to be cheeky.

'Because of my charm and my good looks.'

'Yeah, right.' I sniggered sarcastically, and he playfully punched my arm.

'Hey, I was cute back then.'

I bet you were. 'Ok, I believe you. So did you get adopted?'

'Nope! I decided I didn't want to go anywhere unless they

adopted Frankie as well, so I'd mess around and be naughty so they wouldn't take me.'

'Really?' I imagined him for a moment messing around and being naughty, but that story was perhaps for another day …

'Yeah, I'd stay out late after school, rip my school uniform, throw stuff through windows, that kind of thing. They would always send me back after a while, but there was this one couple who saw me as a challenge. God, they were tough nuts to crack.'

'What did you do?' I was intrigued.

'Well, I started with the usual slamming doors, skipping school, cutting up photographs, then moved on to putting my fags out on the carpet, robbing top-shelf mags from the corner shop and sticking the pictures up around the house – I even stuck one on the cat! I was a right little shit.'

I tried not to laugh.

'It's not funny,' he told me, trying not to laugh himself.

'I know it's not. You were a little gobshite.'

'Indeed I was, but the sad thing was that it was all unnecessary. If they had just let me stay at the home with Frankie, I wouldn't have done any of it.'

'So, Frankie stayed at the same home all that time?' I'd stopped laughing now.

Joe sighed, 'Yeah, we'd write to each other and stuff while I was away, but it always made me sad to picture him there alone. Sometimes new boys would come in and take the piss out of him and bully him. I just wanted to stand up for him. He's a top bloke when you get to know him. We used to have some brilliant times when we were together. Once we ran away, hitched all the way from North London to Cleethorpes.'

'Cleethorpes, that's miles away!'

'It is, to us it was the other end of the earth. I remember we bought a bag of chips and ate it on the pier. God, that was the best bag of chips ever.' He smiled to himself at the memory.

'So, how come you went back?'

'We broke into an empty caravan, one of those static ones in a park. We were doing alright until I tried to clamber back out the window and got the fur on my parka caught on the window latch. Some bloke from the next-door caravan caught us and called the police who took us home.'

'Did you ever run away again?'

'No. It was soon after that, when we were about thirteen or fourteen, that this lady came, Mabel, her name was. She'd been fostering troubled kids for years, housed about forty of them in her time, and it turns out she'd heard about my troublesome ways and reckoned she'd have a bash. I remember telling her not to waste her time and I'd only end up coming back here to my mate Frankie. She asked me about Frankie and why I liked him so much, so I told her what a laugh he was, but that no-one wanted him because of his learning problems. She was cool, and after speaking with one of the assistants, she asked me and Frankie if we'd both like to stay with her for a while. Well, we couldn't believe it. I swear I've never seen Frankie that happy before or since, just someone choosing him, he was made up. A week later, we were packed and ready to go.'

'And? She didn't turn up?' I was mortified.

'No, she did, and we moved in with her. She was fantastic. She didn't have much money, but we did loads of fun things, like going to the swings, swimming, going sledging in the winter, and of course, because me and Frankie were together, we didn't play up. After about a year, she adopted us officially and we had a party with cakes and balloons; it was well cool.' While telling the story, it was clear that in his head Joe had reverted back to being that little boy, unwanted and unloved for years, discovering the genuine love of a family for the first time, enjoying the simple pleasures of life. In his face, I could see that happy little boy once more and I welled up. Luckily, I was wearing my sunglasses so he couldn't see, and I coughed to clear away the lump in my throat.

'That's cool. It must have been great for you and Frankie.'

'Yeah, it was. They were great years.'

'So, what happened? Where does the money come in?'

Joe took a deep breath and continued. 'A few years ago, me and Frankie got a flat together. I'd done an apprenticeship in carpentry and was working for a small firm, and Frankie was doing the odd bit of work in restaurant kitchens. It wasn't much, but we earned enough to pay the rent and it was cool. Then one day we found out that Mabel had had a stroke and was in the hospital. It was awful, Nancy. We panicked and ran over to the hospital but she seemed ok to me, still recognised us and everything, just a bit bruised from where she'd fallen. We were told that she wasn't able to live on her own anymore in case it happened again, so me and Frankie said we'd move back in and look after her. We were told that that wasn't good enough, and she needed a proper carer which we couldn't afford. It was all taken out of our hands, and they took her out of her own home and stuck her in some old people's home.' He was shaking his head. 'I couldn't believe it, she was fine, we knew she was fine, she knew she was fine, but they still went ahead and did it. It was heartbreaking to see her. She doesn't belong there.'

'So that's why you need the money, to get her some proper care?' The penny was dropping at last, but it was dropping in the wrong place.

'Well, not really. She doesn't need any special care. She hasn't had any more falls or strokes since then, she's still totally compos mentis in the marbles department. It's just that place that's sending her doolally. No, we want to bring her here.'

'Here?' I looked around. Beautiful as it was, I didn't think hammocks and mud huts were quite suitable for an old lady.

'Well, not while it's like this. The money is to get the place sorted. We're going to build a lodge, just a couple of luxury rooms, for guests that fancy a retreat, like all them posh types who want to live on the edge for a week. We've got it all planned out – a few rooms, a bar serving home-cooked food, that's pretty much all we need. When it's up and running, we'll fly Mabel over. It will do her so much good to be out here in this fresh air.'

'With her boys,' I added.

'Yeah, with her boys.' He smiled at the thought.

'So, where do Coultan and Rio come in?' I asked.

'Well, it's Coultan's island, you see. We wouldn't be here at all without him.'

'He owns this island? Is he rich?' This all seemed very exciting.

'No, he's a gambler. He won it in a poker game in prison – that's where we met him,' he said a little too matter-of-factly as if to shock me, which he did.

'Prison?!' I felt like I'd missed out on a whole chunk of the story. 'What was he doing in prison? What were you doing in prison?'

'Ah yes, prison. Not one of my favourite places, like a big care home for adults. But with no care and nothing like home, obviously. I don't like to blame Frankie for it, but it was all his fault. After they had put Mabel into the home, we tried desperately to come up with ways to get money to get her out but came up with nothing. He then got involved with a bloke who promised him loads of money to do a job for him. He didn't tell him any details, just that he had to drive a car. I twigged something was fishy when he asked me which was the brake and which was the accelerator, and I tried to talk him out of it. But he was adamant he was going to do it with or without my help, so I said I'd do it with him. I thought it was the only way that we'd get away with it, but I was wrong and we got a year's stretch in Wormwood Scrubs.'

'Oh my God!'

'Yeah, but we were out after six months.'

'Yeah, even so. You hear so many stories about prisons. I've seen *The Shawshank Redemption*.'

'Well, it was bad, but not that bad. It could have been, but we ended up sharing a cell with Coultan who had been in and out of prisons for years. No-one messed with him, and as we became friends, no-one messed with us either. In that place you have hours in your cell with nothing to do but talk and dream, and that's where we came up with our plan. Coultan told us about this island he'd won in a poker game and we told him about Mabel. At first, I thought he was lying about this place, that he was just Mr Big trying to impress the new little guys, but it turns out it was true … and here we are.'

In the afternoon, the others joined us down by the water's edge where we played games and took it in turns to be thrown into the sea for the ultimate cool down. As we lay on the sand, Joe, Coultan, Rio and Frankie showed us the plans for the retreat they were planning to build while Mark and I listened intently. Their voices became more animated as they described the luxury bedrooms, the kitchen, even the plumbing they planned and the solar panel energy system they would install. Rio's eyes lit up when she described the Egyptian cotton sheets, hand-woven rugs and batik paintings she would make for the walls, and Coultan spoke excitedly about the little bar he would build with its homemade rum distillery where his guests could unwind and watch the sun go down.

'Sounds impressive,' I said.

'Sounds like a lot of hard work,' said Mark.

'Yeah, it will be, we're prepared for that,' Joe said, jokingly flexing his bicep. 'We just need the materials … and the money, of course.'

'So how much is something like that going to cost?' Mark asked.

'A million pounds,' Frankie told us, and the others nodded.

'Ok, so you've worked it all out, and it comes to exactly one million pounds, does it? All the wood, the sanitation equipment, solar panels?'

Mark sniggered at my question and added, 'one million dollars,' in the style of Austin Powers' arch-enemy, Dr Evil.

'Well, near enough, give or take.' Joe laughed.

'You're joking, that's all you've asked my dad for? A million pounds? He spends more than that in a year on wine!'

'You reckon we should ask for more?' Coultan interjected.

'You can't ask Mark that!' I laughed, which started the others laughing. It genuinely was a surreal situation to be in.

As the afternoon turned into evening, a cool wind started to blow in from the sea and I helped Joe try to light the fire by shading it from the wind. Eventually, he got it going but it soon blew out, and before long the wind was whipping clothes, blankets and anything that was not pinned down across the beach. I was frantically trying to unpeg the clothes off the line before they blew away, while everyone else was chasing things left, right and centre. Rio and Mark were grabbing lamps and taking them into her and Coultan's hut, closely followed by Coultan loaded down with bottles of beer and rum. As I ran down to mine and Mark's shed for extra blankets, the sky was darkening with rapid pace and I heard Joe hollering for Frankie to leave his beach ball globe and get into the hut, which he obediently did.

'C'mon Nancy!' he shouted at me. 'We've got to get in!'

I waved acknowledgement before disappearing into our shed to grab my bag along with more blankets and pillows. I held them tightly as the door flung open and practically blew me out. I battled against the wind, being blown this way and that along with the palm trees and the tide, taking two steps forward and one step back as I attempted to reach the others. Joe came lumbering down the beach, grabbed a pillow from me with one hand and with other he grabbed my wrist and pulled me across the sand. With my hair blowing all over my face, I couldn't see where I was going, so let myself be dragged along amidst the ensuing gales and the sandstorm it was creating.

After what seemed like an eternity, we made it into the hut. I wobbled as I tried to get my bearings, before plonking myself down on the mattress next to Mark, who already looked at home under the blankets next to Rio, who was next to Coultan and then Frankie. Joe forced the door shut before sitting down on the end next to me, pulling the blankets over us. Handily the fridge was next to him, and it wasn't long before he reached across and handed out bottles of lager to myself and Mark. The room was tiny, undoubtedly not made to house six people, and with no glass at the small window, gusts of wind periodically swept through our little shelter covering us in sand

and the odd wayward piece of foliage. The wooden walls creaked as they rocked from side to side and I had visions of us taking off like the house in *The Wizard of Oz.* Way down the beach, we could hear the white waves of the unruly sea crashing down, its usual tame smooth surface riled up into a wild beast angrily battering the shore.

Chapter Nine

We all simultaneously gasped or screamed as the first flash of lightning lit up the sky, forking down into the black horizon. It was closely followed by a deep rumble of thunder, which vibrated through the hut and made us all hitch a little closer together and a little further under the blankets. As we watched the following frequent bouts of lightning from the window, there began a gentle patter of rain on the roof. It became increasingly louder and louder as the huge raindrops forcefully pelted down. Coultan had a protective arm around Rio, who had an arm around Mark. I had my arm linked through his other arm, and Joe had his arm around me, which he'd put there when I'd yelped at the first flash of lightning. Although I was terrified at being at the mercy of nature's ill-temper, it was all so very cosy sitting in the hut snuggled under the blankets, watching the weather do its worst outside, only a matter of feet away.

As we continued to observe the spectacular display of lightning and listen to the powerful rain beating a steady rhythm on the roof, we started to relax a little and even laughed and joked. It started with Mark suggesting we should sing about our favourite things which expanded into us discussing our real favourite things: the smells of freshly cut grass, of just-lit matches and skin that's been soaking in the sun; the sound of the sea, of children laughing or hearing a song on the radio that you love and had forgotten all about; getting into a bed with fresh clean sheets, coming in from the rain or having someone's arm around you. As we talked, I realised that we weren't that different after all.

The next morning, we all stirred at the same time which was not surprising as we had been squidged together so tightly we had all fallen to sleep on one another's shoulders, our arms and legs tangled as if we were doing the cygnet dance from *Swan Lake*. The storm of the previous night had completely subsided, but as Frankie opened the door, we were faced with the effects it had left behind in its wake. The shower unit had blown down, bits of wood and branches were strewn across the beach and everything that hadn't blown away was now covered in a thick layer of sand. We all set to work clearing the camp of debris. Coultan and Joe began rebuilding some of the structures, while Rio cleaned out the fire and retrieved what was left of the pots and pans to start on breakfast. Frankie, Mark and I volunteered to walk around the island and collect anything that the sea hadn't washed away. On our travels, we discovered that although my hammock had broken at one end, the other was still intact and, thankfully, it was fixable. We also found some pieces of clothing, a towel, some planks of wood and, remarkably, Frankie was thrilled to find his globe beach ball stuck up a tree between two branches.

After lunch, Joe and Frankie checked over the boat which had been slightly battered but was still in one piece, and thankfully still tied to the small jetty which had also survived the storm. As Mark and I settled down for an afternoon of sunbathing, the boat chugged into life and we waved as they sailed past on their way to fetch fresh supplies.

'You like him, don't you?' Mark asked me out of the blue. Perhaps I hadn't concealed my feelings quite as well as I'd hoped.

'Yeah, I like them all,' I replied in my best casual manner.

'Yeah, but you *really* like Joe,' he said, looking at me knowingly and somewhat sympathetically.

'You're right ... I do,' I reluctantly admitted.

'Thought so,' was all he said.

Relieved that I finally had someone to share my thoughts with, I asked, 'But how can I? I mean, this guy kidnapped me and held me hostage.'

'Indeed, a good-looking guy took you away from your little humdrum existence and brought you here,' he said, nodding down the sparkling white sand to the translucent sea beyond. 'What a bastard!'

I looked over at him and sniggered, aware of the craziness of our situation.

'If it's any consolation, I feel the same way you do,' he said.

'What? You're in love with Joe too?!' Now that was something I hadn't bargained on.

'No!' he said, laughing, 'I mean I like them all too!' He paused. 'So, you're in love with Joe, eh?'

'No,' I was quick to deny. 'I just find him, you know, quite nice.'

'Nice? You think he's nice? I get the impression you think he's more than nice.' He seemed to think about it and then added more seriously, 'You are in love with him, aren't you?'

I took a deep breath and stared out to sea while I considered what my answer should be. There was no way I was actually in love with Joe, was there? I'd only known him a short time. Mark had obviously noticed something, but to admit it out loud would change everything.

'Well, if it helps,' Mark started before I spoke further '... he thinks you're nice too.'

'Really?' I asked with rather too much excitement.

'Yeah, durr brain, it's obvious. Everyone knows.'

'Has he said something? What did he say? Tell me, tell me!' I was like a kid in the school playground.

'Well, it's not anything he said, you can just tell.'

'How?' I fished.

'Trust me, I'm a man,' he said matter-of-factly, as if this phrase would convince me. 'I know how men's minds work.' I could tell this was the only confirmation I would get from him, so I put my fishing rod away and stopped angling for more. Why is it that blokes are so useless at this kind of thing? Steph would have given me at least three examples of obvious attraction by now, probably including dialogue, facial expressions, the clothes that everyone was wearing plus some surrounding scenery.

'Well, I guess it doesn't matter anyway. It's not like anything can come of it, given our situation. We have to forget we ever had this conversation.' As if to mark the end of our discussion, I rolled over onto my belly to let the sun toast my back and legs.

'Funny, though ...' Mark continued to my back, regardless.

'What's funny?' I asked, not looking at him.

'I was just thinking how much I love it here. Yes, I'm supposed to be trying to escape and hating my captors, but they're all so great. I mean, I can't remember a time when I've laughed so much as with Coultan and Frankie, and Rio's great, and Joe too, of course. We're all so different, but it's almost like ... I don't know, like a we're family somehow.'

I considered what he was saying as I ran my fingers through the sand in front of my face. 'I know what you mean,' I said, still not looking up. 'Sometimes I forget what's going on here and start imagining I'm here on holiday with my friends.'

'That's it. Same as me,' Mark agreed.

I sat up to face him and we smiled at each other, thankful to acknowledge our mutual feelings. I felt relieved and a little excited that I could finally talk about what was going on in my head.

'And so, tell me, do you feel guilty for feeling like that because our families and friends are probably going through hell imagining the worst, and we're here having the time of our lives?'

Mark was nodding as I spoke. 'Yes, yes, unbelievably guilty. But it's not my fault I'm in this situation. I didn't ask for any of it, so I have no reason to – and I suppose I can't help who I like.'

'Exactly.'

We both sat pondering for a while.

'You know what I think?' Mark asked after a short silence.

'What?'

'If we asked them, they would probably just let us go now. I mean, I can't imagine any of them turning a gun on us, and it's obvious we can't stay here forever.'

'I bet you're right, but, with no disrespect to your dad, I kinda want them to get the money. I want it to work out well for them. Does that make me sound crazy?' I asked for Mark's opinion, hoping it would be similar to my own, and it was.

'Well, yesterday I sat with Joe and Coultan and helped them make adjustments to their plans for the holiday village. So, if you're crazy, that must mean I'm crazy too.'

'I can imagine it – the holiday apartments and complex thing. It would be a fantastic place to come and get away from it all. Coultan making cocktails at the bar, Rio serving the guests with her fine cuisine, Frankie at the mike on his karaoke machine …'

Mark smiled and nodded as we pictured the scene. But then his face turned serious again. 'And where would Joe be?' he asked softly.

I pictured Joe. 'He would be sitting at the water's edge, listening to the music and watching the sun go down with a glass of wine and a smile on his face.' I was wistful as I imagined him there.

'And would he be alone?' I turned back to check Mark's face to see if he was mocking me, but all I saw was concern.

'Well, when I'm back in England imagining him, he definitely will be,' I replied with a little laugh. Mark laughed too and gave my shoulder a playful punch.

'Come on, I think a swim is in order. You are in desperate need of a cool down,' he said, climbing to his feet and holding out his hand to pull me up.

'Oh, you are so funny, Mark Cheriton,' I joked, ignoring his hand and running past him to the sea. The cool water was lush on our sweating skin as we dived straight into the waves.

'We'll not ask if we can leave right now then, eh?' I shouted to Mark as he swam out ahead of me.

'No, I agree we should stay a few more days. After all, it would be rude for us to go now!' We both laughed as we drenched ourselves in the water.

A little while later, I walked towards the shore, but, reluctant to completely leave the sea, I sat in the shallow water to allow the gentle tide to wash over me as my bottom bounced gently up and down on the clean sand below. Mark came to join me and the conversation resumed.

'You do know, that they're all going to end up in prison?' I began.

'Not necessarily.'

I tilted my head with an "oh-come-off-it" expression. 'This plan of theirs can't possibly work. To be honest, they have no idea what they're doing. There's so much that can go wrong.'

'Mmm.' Mark stared out to sea. 'You never know, they may have some grand plan up their sleeves.'

'I suppose, but I doubt it. The fact that they got us here at all was one big fluke. They don't seem to have a clue about how they'll get the money.'

'Maybe you're right,' Mark agreed. 'Perhaps we *should* leave, at least then they wouldn't get caught.'

'Even if we did, they would only try some other harebrained scheme that would go tits-up.'

'That's true. Did you hear why Joe and Frankie ended up in prison in the first place?'

'A robbery, wasn't it?'

'Yeah, a robbery they would have got away with, had they remembered to put petrol in the getaway car!' Mark laughed.

'No! They've got the will and determination, I'll give them that, but they are severely lacking in the common sense department.'

'So, what are you saying? They're all doomed to failure?'

'What I'm saying is that they're the worst bunch of criminals ever, and the only way they stand a chance is …'

'What? Spit it out, Nancy.'

I looked across at my toes sticking out of the water in front of me, and quietly said, '… if we help them.'

Mark didn't speak but stared at me in wonder, which made me feel a little foolish. I had surely gone mad in the sun.

'Ok, I get it, it's a stupid idea. Just forget I said anything.'

'No, no. Do you really think if we helped, we could get them the money and keep them here on the island?' he asked more with interest than sarcasm.

'Well, it would give them more of a chance.'

'Nancy, do you know what you're saying? That would make us co-conspirators. We would get locked up.'

'Only if it went wrong. It's not like we'd benefit from any of the money, and we can't stay here on the island indefinitely. We've agreed we don't want anyone to get caught, haven't we? So, we're gonna have to make up some story to the police anyway, because if we tell the truth it would lead them straight here.'

'Yes, but bending the truth and blatantly assisting in a crime are two completely different things.'

'Oh God, I'm sorry, Mark. I shouldn't have said anything. It's like I'm using you to steal from your own dad. I'm sorry. Let's leave it to them to sort out their own mess.'

'I'm not worried about that so much, after all he had me sweeping up cigarette butts at the airport, I'm just not sure if's it's such a good idea, that's all.'

'Ok, I understand. You're right. C'mon, let's go and see what's for dinner.' I splish-splashed my way out of the water and began shaking the sand off the towel I had been lying on before folding it. But I realised that Mark was beside me again looking thoughtful.

'I'm not dismissing the idea, you understand. But I do need some time to consider it,' he said.

'Ok, that's fair enough, that goes for me too. It's not like me to burst out with things before weighing them up first.'

'Get away,' Mark said sarcastically, before hitting me with his towel and running off up the beach to beat me to the shower. *Well, he's got the measure of me.* But how well did I know myself? Me, aiding and abetting in the execution of a crime? Who did I think I was, Ronnie Biggs?

That night, with my hammock still not repaired, Mark and I went back to sleeping in the shed … only I couldn't sleep. My body was worn out, but my brain was buzzing with thoughts of prisons and my family, and most of all with thoughts of Joe. I lay on my back with my arm behind my head, looking up at the stars through the cabin window, but they gave me no answers, merely philosophical questions about star-crossed lovers and the reality of destiny. Joe was out there, under those stars, a little way down the beach. I quietly climbed off the camp bed and walked over to the window. From there, I made out the boat at the end of the jetty as it bobbed gently on the quiet waters. The light from the lantern twinkled in the night's sky but I couldn't see any signs of life; I couldn't see Joe, but I knew he was there, just out of my reach …

'Can you see him?' Mark whispered loudly, making me jump out of my skin.

'What?' I whispered back, just as loudly. 'I thought you were asleep.'

'No, can't sleep, there's too much running through my mind.'

'Same goes for me,' I said with a heavy sigh.

'Yeah, but I bet we're thinking about different things.' I saw him nod towards the window in the half-light.

There was no point in denying it so I turned back to the window. 'But what's the point?' I sighed again, not expecting an answer.

'You should go to him.'

'What?'

'You might not have long left here. I say you make the most of it.' Eighteen-year-old Mark giving me advice on my love-life didn't seem quite right, maybe even a little indecent, but he continued. 'If you do nothing, you'll regret it. When you get home and you remember these days, you'll kick yourself for being so sensible … or stupid, as it seems to me.'

'You're right! I have to do it. Thanks, Mark.'

'Well, what are you waiting for?'

'What, *now*? I should talk to him now?'

'Well, it's as good a time as any. Strike while the iron's hot, that's what I say.'

'But ...' I looked back out the window.

'But nothing. Get out of here so I can get some sleep.'

'Ok,' I said, walking determinedly towards the door and releasing the latch. 'Wish me luck?'

I heard Mark wishing me the requested good luck as I stepped outside, closing the door tightly behind me. *I'm gonna need it.*

With bare feet and wearing nothing but the crumpled T-shirt I had been sleeping in and Thursday's pants, I made my way down towards the shore. The sand had lost its warmth and gave the crunchy sound underfoot, which it only seemed to do at night. Still with no idea what I was going to say when I got there, I silently walked the length of the jetty, eventually reaching the swaying boat. I saw Joe now; he was on the deck, tidying away anything liable to move during the night.

'Hey,' I said, barely loud enough for him to hear me.

'Nancy, what are you doing here?' he asked, surprised. *Good question.*

'Can I come on board?' I replied, not giving him a direct answer.

'Yes,' came the reply, as he moved over to take my hand and help me clamber over the side of the boat. 'C'mon, let's get inside where it's warmer.' I followed him down the steps. 'Er, sit down,' he told me, shifting a pile of clothes from the seat. As I did so, he grabbed two bottles of beer from the fridge. I realised I must have shocked the hell out of him turning up out of the blue because he seemed a little awkward as he nervously sat down, a little away from me.

'So, what can I do for you?' he asked in the manner of a bank manager. In my head the possibilities were endless, but making such suggestions was not the way to start this conversation. Instead, I chose to sit there like a bumbling idiot.

'Um, I couldn't sleep and fancied a chat.' *At half-past midnight, yeah right*, I added to myself.

'Ok, er ... what do you ... er ... want to talk about?'

'Um, I'm not really sure,' I replied, feeling more than a little stupid. Deciding to cut my losses and leave, I got up. 'I saw your light and … well, actually, I'd better go, it's late and you want to go to bed, er, I mean sleep.' I began walking towards the cabin steps.

Joe followed me. 'No! I mean, don't go … stay.'

I turned my head to find him standing directly behind me, and he didn't move away as I slowly stepped back down.

Instead, he whispered, 'I'd like to talk to you too.' And then he kissed me, and it was wonderful. His hands began around my waist, travelling down, grabbing my bottom and pulling me towards him. I responded by linking my arms around his neck and stroking his tanned, muscular shoulders.

We didn't stop kissing as we staggered back over to the seat, and he pulled out the hidden mattress with one hand while the other remained firmly on my bottom cheek. This made me realise two things: first, the fact that he pulled the bed out so swiftly made me think that maybe this wasn't the first time he'd done something like this on the boat, and, second, that my knickers weren't exactly seductive, but I guess he'd bought them so he'd seen them already anyway. But did I care? No, not me, I didn't give a flying banana. This is what I wanted, and it felt so right. I was going to enjoy it, with no more hesitation and free of guilt. Now, who's the purple woodpecker?

The next morning, I had well and truly made up my mind. I sheepishly left the boat to find Mark, but as I arrived at the shed, I realised it was empty. I quickly got dressed and walked up the beach to the camp where I saw him sitting at the table with Rio tucking into the biggest fry-up I had ever seen.

'Mornin'!' he shouted at me with a mouth full of sausage and egg as I approached.

'Morning, Nancy,' Rio said, with a knowing smile. 'Sleep well?'

I cleared my throat before replying as nonchalantly as possible,

'Yes. Very well, thank you.' But I found I was unable to stop smiling.

'I'd better be getting your breakfast, you'll be needing your energy,' Rio said, getting up and going to dish up.

Once she was out of earshot, Mark looked up at me, down at his breakfast, and back up at me with an enormous grin. 'Let's do it,' he said.

Chapter Ten

'Ok right, let's start from the beginning,' I began as the others sat down and hitched their chairs around the table like we'd been assigned a joint geography project. After breakfast, we had gathered everyone around and made our announcement that we intended to help them get the money. The news had been met at first with surprise followed by a slap on the back, a great deal of thanks and a welcome into the den of iniquity.

'What's your current plan? How did you contact Mark's dad? Or did you go straight to the police?' I looked towards Joe, who I assumed would be the brains of the operation.

'Well, we haven't actually decided yet,' he said lamely. *Perhaps I was wrong about the "brains" bit.*

'You haven't decided yet!' I replied rather more loudly than was strictly necessary. 'You've had us here for about a week and you haven't even decided that! Good Lord, this is going to take longer than I thought.' Realising I sounded like the teacher, I calmed down. 'Right,' I said, 'let's discuss our options. First, we could do it in person. I'm pretty sure we can all agree that's a no-no, yes?'

They all nodded, and I continued. 'I guess by post is out unless we want to lead them straight to us. At the moment, they probably assume we're still in England and that's a big plus in our favour. As soon as they find out we're abroad, Interpol will become involved and our chances of success will become much less.'

I wasn't technically sure what Interpol was, but it sounded good. Again, everybody looked at me and nodded as though I was an expert and I began to enjoy myself.

I carried on. 'Email is definitely out as it's too easy to trace and, let's face it, we haven't got a computer.' As I'd been talking, I'd written down all the possibilities on a lined notepad Rio had provided and struck them off in turn with a biro. 'So. I guess that only leaves the telephone option. Does anyone know if they can trace mobile phones?' Blank faces all round. 'Mark? Doesn't your dad own a mobile phone company?'

'Yeah, but I only use mine to text my mates – I've no idea how they work. I doubt whether even my dad knows that.' Then as an afterthought, and perhaps to reprieve himself, he added, 'Although when you go abroad, the phones do say "Welcome to the Seychelles or The Bahamas" or wherever you are, so they must be able to trace the signal or which network you're closest to.'

'That's true.' I remembered receiving such messages on my holidays in Greece. 'So, no to mobiles?' Mark looked pleased to have helped, although this information did not solve our problem.

'I guess it has to be a phone box on the mainland,' someone else piped up. It was Joe. This time everyone looked at him and nodded like a nodding dog convention.

'Hmm,' I half agreed. 'Though I'm not sure if they can be traced back. I mean it used to be that they were able to trace it after three minutes, but I imagine technology has moved on from then. I mean, that's how Thelma and Louise got caught.'

'Yeah, and, 'cause Brad Pitt shagged Thelma and told the police they were going to Mexico,' piped up Frankie, who had suddenly become more interested in the conversation.

'That's an excellent point, Frankie,' I congratulated him. 'We should learn from that and remember that we shouldn't tell anyone about our plan who's not around this table, even if it is Brad Pitt.'

Again, everyone nodded and Frankie beamed as Joe slapped him on the back saying, 'Good point, mate.'

'Of course, there's a lot more CCTV around today, so if we did that we'd have to suss out every angle. Could be tricky.' I looked down at my list to see all our options ticked off one by one. 'There must be another way …'

'How about—' Coultan spoke for the first time '—we write a letter, but get one o' my good friends to post it from someplace else? Another country may be, aye?'

All eyes moved to Coultan and then to me as I tapped my biro pensively against my lips. 'Hmm, that may be a viable option, Coultan. Who would you get to do it and where from?'

'That would take some serious thinkin' about. There are many possibilities, but most would want a cut o' the proceeds.'

'Do you have any friends in England who would do it? Anyone who wouldn't ask questions? We post a letter to them and they forward it on from there.'

'When it comes to friends in England darlin', I would have thought you would have more than me.'

Mark and I looked at each other, racking our brains to come up with anyone we would trust to do it, but there was no-one. 'I think all my friends and family would take a letter like that directly to the police or even worse, to *The Sun* newspaper to earn themselves a few quid.'

'Mine are the same. I don't know anyone who would open it and just do as I asked. Especially, I suppose, as we are planning to rob my dad.'

'Mabel!' Joe slapped his hand on the table with the force of realisation, which made us all jump. 'Mabel would do it!' His blue eyes lit up in excitement as he enthusiastically ranted on. 'She wouldn't ask any questions. She knows me too well. She's so innocent, she'd never put two and two together. She'd just assume she was doing us a favour.'

'That's brilliant!' I joined in his excitement. 'And CCTV or no CCTV who's going to suspect a little old lady posting a letter?' We were all pleased with the breakthrough and started eating some peanuts from a bowl in front of us as Rio fetched another jug of lemonade and topped up everyone's glasses. 'Although, we should probably still consider anything that could go wrong with Mabel posting the letters for us,' I instructed the group in a similar way to my third-year physics teacher addressing the class.

'She might tell the carers at the home,' Rio suggested.

Joe considered this for a few seconds and said, 'Well, I'll tell her it's to do with a plan to get her out of there. I'll just explain that if she tells anyone, or lets anyone else post it for her, it will spoil the plan and she'll have to stay there – which is the truth, to be honest.'

'Good, good,' we muttered in agreement.

'She hates the carers,' Frankie added.

'Yes, yes,' again we all agreed with Frankie, who seemed delighted to have helped.

'In that case,' Mark joined in, 'we should send the ransom note directly to the police. If we sent it directly to Giant ... well, it would make more sense to her if it was sent to the police. If she saw anything on the news about my dad, she'd never connect the two.'

'And, and …' embellished Joe – everyone was getting into the spirit now – 'if I told her what to do over the phone, I wouldn't need to put a covering letter in with it so there's no risk of anyone finding it. I'll put nothing in but the letter we want her to send, so all she has to do is stick a stamp on it and post it. I phone her at the home every week anyway, so it won't be anything out of the ordinary.' *Ah, what a great guy, phoning her every week.*

'This is great, man!' Coultan exclaimed. 'I think we got ourselves the beginnings of a plan.'

Everyone was getting more and more excited and giddy at the prospect of this crazy idea being possible – between us, it seemed we might actually be able to pull it off.

I was busy scribbling down notes. 'I'll burn this later,' I said without looking up, and to no-one in particular. 'This is simply for the planning stage.' *This must be what Guy Fawkes felt like, sitting plotting with his co-conspirators,* I thought.

'Ok, to recap. Stage one, Joe will telephone Mabel. We'll write a letter and post it to Mabel without a stamp – we can decide what to write later,' I added, looking around the table from one pair of eyes to another. 'Mabel sticks on a stamp and posts it in a London post box.Nothing links the letter to us or this island. All agreed?'

I received nods and mumbled assent from the assembled group and, after taking a deep breath, I continued,

'Right, stage two. Assuming they agree to our demands, how do they get the money to us? I'll assume that a cheque's out.'

'Swiss bank account?' Joe suggested. I tell you, it's a good thing he had a pretty face.

'Tom Cruise! *The Firm!*' Frankie exclaimed as if he'd split the atom. I was indeed in a world of crazies.

'Does anyone have a Swiss bank account or know how to set one up?' I asked calmly, as if I was genuinely considering this to be an option.

Unsurprisingly, they all looked at each other shaking their heads.

'What is a Swiss bank account?' Rio asked. 'Why do they always have them on TV?'

Again, blank faces all around.

'I guess, that's that out then,' I said, putting a line through the words on my notepad. I'd only written them down because it had been Joe's suggestion, stupid as it was.

'So, it has to be cash,' Rio concluded.

'Yes, I agree, it does,' I said, writing down *CASH* and putting a tick beside it. 'But not new money as they can trace the serial numbers. I saw that on *The Vice.*'

'Ah, so that's why they always ask for used notes,' Mark interjected 'Like Steve McQueen in *The Day of the Jackal.*'

'Steve McQueen wasn't in *The Day of The Jackal,*' Joe corrected, 'You're thinking of *The Thomas Crown Affair*. *The Day of the Jackal* was that other bloke, what's his name?'

'Is that *Star Wars*?' Rio asked.

'No, that's *Return of the Jedi*,' Mark replied.

'Well, I ain't never seen either one of them,' Rio said.

'Edward Norton?' Joe suggested.

'That little Irish guy?' Coultan asked.

'That's Graham Norton,' I laughed. 'And neither he or Edward Norton were in *The Day of the Jackal*. Although it would have made it more amusing. Charles de Gaulle wouldn't have known what had hit him.' We chuckled a little at the image of Graham Norton on a one-man mission to assassinate the French President.

'Anyway, used banknotes,' Rio said, bringing us back to the task in hand.

'Ah yes. Used notes,' I agreed as I wrote the words down on my pad. 'Although, they might photocopy used notes before they give them away to blackmailers. I saw that on *Crime Squad*.' I was pretty sure I'd impressed them all with my extensive knowledge of effective policing, if not with the obvious fact that I watched too much TV due to having very little social life. I continued, 'But I still think it's our best option. We'll just have to get rid of it quickly. It's still got to be harder to trace than a string of serial numbers.'

'Geez, they don't make it easy for criminal entrepreneurs, do they? It's true, there really is no encouragement for new businesses and creativity,' Mark remarked and everyone nodded. 'So, how do we get the money? The police will have to leave it somewhere.'

Before anyone else had time to make a suggestion, Frankie shouted, 'In a bin! They always leave it in a plastic bag in a bin!'

'Excellent idea, Frankie.' Everyone agreed. 'Now, where's this bin going to be? In England? In Jamaica?'

Apart from Mark, everyone looked at me in utter confusion.

'Jamaica? Why Jamaica?' They turned to each other in wonder, as if it they were missing something, when in fact it was me who'd lost the plot.

'Are we ... not ... in ... Jamaica?' I asked slowly, feeling more than a little foolish but not quite sure why.

The others laughed. 'Why would we be in Jamaica?' Joe asked, still laughing at me, which made me feel even more stupid.

'I dunno. I just assumed … well we travelled for days on a boat and arrived on the island, with palm trees, and the sun, and …' I must have subconsciously looked up at Rio and Coultan.

Coultan caught my eye, and, still laughing, said, 'I see. It's 'cause I'm black.' For a minute I thought he was doing his best Ali G impression until I realised it was Coultan, and I very much doubted that he'd ever seen Ali G in his life. 'You see a black man and assume you're in Jamaica.'

'No, no, not at all,' I stammered, starting to feel as if I might as well have been wearing a white, pointy hood.

'It's ok, girlfriend,' Rio joined in. 'He's only teasin' with you. We are from Jamaica, and it was an easy conclusion to jump to.'

Coultan was still chuckling. 'Yeah, yeah, I'm pullin' ya legs, girl. Jamaica is the homeland, but this is now my home.'

I felt a bit better, but my face was still burning with embarrassment.

'So, where the hell are we?' Mark asked, and I was glad the attention was diverted away from me and also pleased that I wasn't the only one who didn't know. The others stopped laughing and looked across to one another with "we-agreed-we-wouldn't-tell" expressions.

'Ok, fine!' I said in a huff. 'Don't tell us. Work out your own stupid plan, but don't come running to me when you end up back in Wormwood Scrubs.' I slammed down my pen and folded my arms like a spoiled brat, still annoyed at being laughed at.

'Ok, ok,' Joe said. 'Calm down. Frankie go and get your football.' Frankie stood up so quickly he knocked his chair over backwards as he ran to get his inflatable globe. While we waited, Rio went to get more ice for the lemonade and Coultan rolled a joint. We sat in silence, and I sneaked a look at Joe to see if he was disgusted at my childish overreaction, but he saw me looking at him and winked, which would have made me blush had I not already reached my red-faced peak.

'I'm sorry for that little outburst,' I said to the group as a whole.

'I'm just a bit... you know.' Which seemed to explain everything, even though it didn't.

'No, I'm sorry,' Coultan apologised.

'Yeah, me too,' agreed Joe. Rio and Mark also nodded, and we all relaxed again, just in time to see Frankie bounding his way across the sand whilst blowing up his globe, his cheeks puffed out like Thomas the Tank Engine. When it was fully inflated, he dutifully passed it to Joe, who put in the stopper and turned it towards me and Mark.

'Right, we are just about ...' He waved his finger over the countries while he was looking for the island. 'Well, we're not actually on here because we're too small, but it's somewhere about ... there.' His finger finally settled on a bit of blue sea between Sardinia and Minorca.

'No way!' Mark shouted in surprise.

'Yep, this is a Spanish island called Mecinia – one of the Balearics.'

'Bollocks?' Frankie asked in surprise.

'Balearics.' Joe told him. 'That's the name of the group of islands, like Majorca and Ibiza.'

I couldn't quite believe it either. 'You mean to say we're only a matter of miles away from Ibiza, the party capital of the western world?'

'Yep.'

'So how come no-one's been here? I would have expected to at least have seen an inflatable banana boat or a couple of pissed paragliders.'

'No-one comes here,' Joe explained. 'It's a private island, you see, and as there aren't any bars or clubs, no-one bothers to come this far.'

'Well, I never,' I said, sounding more like my granny than was cool.

'So, now you know.'

'Yep, now we know,' Mark agreed. 'Let's go party!'

'Yeah, right. So perhaps we shouldn't send the money to Jamaica after all.' Everyone laughed at my little joke, and we decided it was time to get back down to business. I picked up my pen once again and began. 'Ok, so really we should ask them to send the money in Euros, which makes it better for us because that means we could potentially be in any number of European countries.' Everyone agreed, and it was decided that we would leave the exchange calculation to later on. I added this to my to-do list, which made a change to my usual "buy loo roll and clean out the oven". To throw the police off our Spanish scent, we also decided that we would ask for the money to be delivered to either France or Italy, both of which were close enough to sail to. This reminded Rio that the pizzas and garlic ciabattas she was cooking in the stone bake oven would be almost ready, so we broke for lunch in high spirits, safe in the knowledge that our plan was well underway.

Chapter Eleven

After grabbing a slice of pizza (two in Frankie's case), we all moved out of the shade to sit in the afternoon sun. Although we had agreed to break for lunch, our minds were still buzzing with ideas. Every now and again someone would make a suggestion and we would approve or disapprove with a 'Yes that's brilliant' or 'No that wouldn't work because ...' The mood was one of excitement and anticipation, and no-one needed any persuasion to regroup at the table once the food had gone. After a quick refresh in the sea and a couple of calls of nature, we congregated once more in exactly the same seats as before, me with my pen poised ready for action.

'Right, we've got a bag of used Euros in our French or Italian bin, what next? How do we collect it without getting caught?'

'We tell them "No police or the girl dies!"' Frankie announced out of nowhere, obviously quoting from his back catalogue of 1970s cop shows.

'Ok,' I carried on, not exactly thrilled at the threat of having my head blown off. 'We'll call that Plan B, Frankie. But I think we'd better have another plan, just in case it's not Starsky and Hutch who are dealing with our case.'

Frankie, oblivious to my sarcasm, nodded in agreement before his eyes lit up again '*Cagney and Lacey*?' he asked, although I wasn't sure why or what I should say to that.

Luckily, Joe, who was trying to stifle a laugh, helped me out with.

'Yes them too.' Which, for some reason, seemed to satisfy Frankie, who appeared content in the knowledge that he had made yet another worthwhile contribution.

It was Mark who brought us back to the world of sanity. 'Even if we say "no police", they're going to be there. They'll be swarming all over the place with guns, long-lens cameras, infra-red cameras, snipers, helicopters, the works.' He saw us looking at him, so he added, 'Yes, I watch TV too!'

'So, what can we do?' Coultan asked him. 'Whoever goes runs the risk of getting caught or seen, and as we're all known to the police, it won't take them long to identify us.'

'How about me?' Rio volunteered. 'The police have no record of me.'

'No!' Mark practically shouted before realising what he'd done and following it with, 'Well, there's no point in Rio getting caught. It's obvious – I'll go. They're not going to shoot me. I'll just say you made me do it.' There was a confused murmur. Would that work?

'Thing is—' Joe interjected '—if you go, what's stopping the police just taking you away with them? There'd be no need for your dad to pay up. He's not gonna fork out for Nancy, is he?'

'Hey!' I whined.

'Sorry,' Joe said, and I believed he was. 'But it's true. Mark's the stick on the end of our carrot.' When we laughed, he realised what he'd said and he added, 'You know what I mean!'

'Yeah, we do.' I laughed, still feeling a little put out that I didn't have anyone who would pay a million pounds for me. 'In that case, there's only one possible solution. I'll collect the money.' The prospect terrified me, of course, but I tried to sound brave nonetheless.

To my surprise and indeed delight, Joe declared, 'No, I don't think so.' My heart skipped a beat. *My hero.*

'But what other option is there?' *Thanks for that, Mark.* 'If Nancy goes, gets the money, tells the police she has to do what she's told or I get a bullet, there's less chance of them dragging her back to Scotland Yard and more chance of you getting your money.' Joe looked at me, ready to refuse, but Mark was right. There was no other option.

'Ok. I'll do it,' I said, sounding a lot more enthusiastic than I was.

Joe sighed. 'Only if you're sure. You don't have to.'

'I'm sure.' I nodded, and the others clapped.

'You go girlfriend!' Rio shouted, and I felt like I was a hero, or at the very least a contestant on *The Jerry Springer Show*.

'Ok, worst-case scenario, the police take me anyway. You guys haven't got your money and you still have Mark. What are you going to do then? We'd better have a Plan B.'

'Starsky and Hutch!' Frankie shouted.

'Ok, a Plan C,' I added quickly to keep on track and prevent any further flare-clad crime fighting duos being brought into the equation.

'I propose,' said Joe sensibly, 'if that does happen—' he looked over at me '—if that does happen, we give up everything. We release Mark somewhere and speak no more about it.' No-one had any better solutions, so I jotted this down on my notepad under the heading "Plan C".

'So, recapping plan A: I've got my bag of used notes, what do I do with them?' Before anyone had time to answer, I rattled on. 'Do I, A – run for the hills and spend the cash in a bar in Brazil? B – pass it on to someone else as quickly as possible in case I lose it or get caught with it? C – stash it somewhere so we can go back later and pick it up? Or, of course, D – none of the above?'

It was Coultan who spoke first. 'I say, stashin' it is way too risky, man. They're gonna have swarms of police all over the place. They would lie in wait until one of us picks it up and then wham, they got us right where they want us.'

'Plus—' Joe added '—that would take loads of research. We haven't even decided which country it will be in, let alone where we can safely stash a million pounds.' We all nodded and 'hmmd'.

'So, I need to pass it on to someone and somehow trick the police into believing I've still got it. Then, they'll continue to follow me and not the other person.'

'Yeah, like the briefcase-in-a-lift trick!'

'Yeah.'

We began to get excited again as we threw ideas into the ring. Everyone had suggestions about holdalls, plastic bags, disguises and hotels with elevators. Soon we had the makings of a pretty excellent plan.

'Ok, it's finally coming together,' I said, taking charge again. 'So, what are you going to do with the money?'

'Spend it, man,' Coultan answered, relaxing back into his chair and inhaling from the latest fat joint he had recently finished rolling. Everyone was definitely in agreement with this and cheered and clapped. By now, it had turned into a party atmosphere.

'I didn't mean that.' I laughed. 'I mean, you can't just keep a stash of notes buried in the sand. Every time you try to buy anything with it, whether it be timber or a bottle of rum, you'll run the risk of getting caught. You need to get rid of it as soon as possible. Swap it for clean money somehow.'

'You mean, like put it in a bank?' Joe asked seriously. 'Is that possible? Surely they can check bank accounts, especially if it's large sums like that?'

'Yeah, I suppose,' I admitted. 'I guess it would take a lot of work, getting a fake ID, setting up bank accounts and all that. I'm sure we've all seen *The Shawshank Redemption,yes?*. It would take too much time. It's probably too risky.'

'You could pay it into mine,' Rio put in. 'I ain't on no police file, and how are they gonna prove I didn't win it or somethin'?' We all considered this for a moment. Would that work?

'I think Rio just wants to keep it all for herself,' Mark said, laughing.

'Hey!' Rio laughed too and threw Frankie's inflatable globe at his head. Mark's cheeks flushed a little.

'That's it!' I yelled excitedly, 'Pass me that globe.' Mark picked up the globe that had landed on the floor behind him and handed it to me.

'Where are we again?' I asked myself as I rolled the globe round in my hands. 'There we are.' I indicated the spot Joe had pointed out before. 'Look!' I almost squealed with excitement. 'We're not too far from Monaco! Monte Carlo! Casinos and gambling everywhere! Surely they must have people banking millions every day! No-one would think it the least bit strange if Rio banked it there!'

'Brilliant!' Rio was getting as excited as I was. 'Me and my man here get all dressed up in our finest clothes, play a couple of tables, swap the cash for chips and then, in the morning, go to the bank and pay in our winnin's, yeah man.'

'And—' I embellished '—if you do that, the exact same day that I pick up the cash, from say ... Pisa over here,' I moved my finger a short distance across the globe, 'and I carry around a fake bag for a couple of days, the police won't even think of stopping you, because they'll believe I've still got it! Maybe—' I was getting carried away now '—if you paid it in a couple of transactions, like odd amounts, or even if you open up a second bank account and do it, there's no way they would find it. By the time they even start looking, it will be just a load of numbers on your bank account statements!'

'Wow, girl, you're good! You sure you ain't done this before?'

'No, but I wish I'd done it years ago!' We all laughed and Coultan decided we should celebrate by opening a bottle of rum. He rarely needed an excuse, but the completion of a plan to steal a million pounds was definitely worth a celebration of some kind. Naturally, dates, times and details would need to be configured, and Joe agreed he would go into town to check out hotels, maps, ports, public transport and casinos at an Internet cafe. We figured that in the middle of all these holiday resorts, nobody would bat an eyelid at some guy doing this kind of research.

But now it was time to party. The relief was expressed in a form of giddiness as Rio turned on the karaoke machine for want of background music, rum was poured and we all clinked glasses 'to us', to 'the best plan ever' and to 'a million pounds!' Coultan clinked rather too enthusiastically as rum spilt out of the glasses and all over our hands. As more rum was poured, we decided we'd done enough planning for one day, and after I'd designated various tasks to complete, we ceremoniously threw the notes I'd made into the fire. The sun was now low in the sky and the air was becoming cooler. The general atmosphere around the camp was that we should get drunk, and after a quick dip and splash around in the sea to freshen up, that's exactly what we did.

Frankie stoked up the fire and Rio threw some of her homemade beef burgers on, which filled the air with fragrant spices and a cloud of thick smoke which would have burned our throats were they not already numb from several glasses of Coultan's rum.

I was transformed, a million miles away from the person I thought I was. Not only was I here living like a castaway, with no mascara or daily moisturiser, I had just played a major part in a conspiracy plan to steal and blackmail with people I'd only known for a week but would trust with my life. Who was I? What had I become? Could I ever return to my normal everyday life after this? As I stood gazing into the fire, swaying slightly with the effects of drink, Joe came up and put his arm around my shoulders.

'You ok?' he slurred.

'Oh, yeah, I'm wonderful,' I slurred back, and I was. At that moment, I was wonderful.

'I thought you were about to do a little dance around the fire.' I looked at him and saw the firelight twinkling in his eyes.

'I will if you do.' I dared him. At which point he threw his glass down on the sand, wiped the back of his hand across his mouth like a man who meant business and started drunkenly hopping around the fire, making the call of a Native American with his hand. He looked so ridiculous, I burst into a fit of laughter; so much so, I failed to stand up straight and staggered to try to keep my footing.

'C'mon!' he yelled across the fire. I was unable to speak for laughing and shook my head as he jumped around the fire, grabbed my hand and dragged me along with him. Frankie came bounding over to join in, grabbing Mark on the way. I saw Rio and Coultan look over in surprise, glance at each other, and before long all six of us were dancing, screeching and hollering into the evening air like wailing banshees. We were liberated, uninhibited and, for once, the masters of our own destinies.

We spent the rest of the evening eating, drinking and spilling more than was strictly necessary. Voices were loud and animated as we came up with more ideas to add to the plan, and now and then someone would break into song (usually Coultan) and we'd all join in with renditions of 'Hey Big Spender', and for some reason, 'There's No Business Like Showbusiness' – probably just to continue with the Shirley Bassey theme. Each member of the group considered the tasks I had given them: Joe had his Internet research to do. Rio was to go to town to buy newspapers, envelopes, rubber gloves and a new dress. She said the dress was because she wanted to look the part in the Monte Carlo casinos (Coultan said it was only an excuse to buy clothes). Mark and I agreed we would work on our stories to make sure they matched when we were inevitably questioned by the police (which sounded so easy when you're sitting on a beach drinking rum). Coultan would contact some "associates" regarding the best places to moor boats, while Frankie had the best job of all, which was to locate Huggy Bear and gather inside information.

By the time the sun was halfway below the horizon, the gaiety had ceased somewhat. Rio was tidying, Mark and Frankie had finished playing football with the globe, and Mark was explaining to him which countries Giant Airlines flew to. Coultan was asleep, glass in hand. I sat on the cooling sand looking out to the ocean, Joe beside me; he had one arm around my shoulders again, and the other hand held the dregs of one of Coultan's spliffs.

'What a brilliant day,' I said with a sigh.

'Mmm,' Joe agreed. 'It was a brilliant day. A weird, bizarre and fucked-up brilliant day.'

'Totally,' I agreed back. 'Who would believe it?'

'Not me.'

'No, me either.'

'Definitely not me.' We sat in our pensive stupor, shaking our heads, which was, in fact, more of a lolling. The moment was quiet as I leant my head against his.

'Thank you,' he whispered.

'For what?'

'For today. We all know we couldn't have done it without you.'

'We haven't done it yet.'

'I know, but now we've got a genuine possibility of our dream becoming a reality.'

'Mmm.'

'It's not your dream though, is it? That's the weird thing.'

'It is kind of. I really do want you to get the money too.'

How could I explain it to him? Especially as I was very aware that I was tipsy and liable to spout out any old rubbish.

After a couple of minutes of silence, he said, 'So what is your dream, Nancy Smart?'

'Ah, my dream.' I sighed.

'Go on, tell me about it.'

'My dream is ... my dream is to stay here forever, in the sun, with you guys. But still have the million pounds,' I added quickly.

'That's my dream too.' He smiled.

'No, you can't have that dream. That's my dream. You've got your own dream.'

'So, if I have my original dream, you can't have your dream, even though we have the same dream?' We tutted at the absurdity for a few seconds. We were aware we were talking drunken gibberish, but we didn't care.

'Stay,' Joe blurted out.

I looked up at his face. 'You know I can't.'

'Yeah, you can. Forget the money, just stay.' He looked so sincere I wanted to cry.

'I would if I could but it's just not an option. I'd still be registered as kidnapped, they would interrogate Mark and eventually, you'd be found and locked up. You did kidnap us – that's a serious crime. Even if we told them not to press charges, with your records you'd be put away for years. Then what would happen to Mabel?' It was obvious that I had already weighed this up in my mind.

'Yeah, I guess.'

'It would be nice though,' I said more softly.

'Yeah, we could grow old together in poverty. You could have my coconuts and vine leaves ready on the table when I came home from a hard day digging sandcastles.'

'Yeah, with your flip-flops by the fire,' We laughed at the scene which was preferable to my dreary nine to five existence back at home.

'So, why did you do it? Help with the plan? You're smarter than all of us – you could just leave now. You know we wouldn't stop you.'

'I know.' I did know. 'I did it because when I'm gone, I want to picture you all in the sun, building your retreat, serving your guests; not living in squalor with nothing, returning home, unable to get work. I couldn't bear it if you ended up in prison rotting away. I know that if you needed money badly enough, you'd come up with another criminal plan, and let's face it, without my help, that's where you'd end up.' Although I said this laughingly, we both knew it was probably true. 'And, of course, because …' *Should I say it?*

'Because?' he asked seriously. I looked into his eyes in the glow of the sunset. Surely there would never be a better time to say it? Surely there was nowhere else on Earth that was more romantic, more wholly appropriate?

'Because I think I love you.' *There, I'd said it.* I held my breath for his reply.

'Really?' he said with a half-smile, telling me it was safe to continue.

'Really,' I told him. *Please say you feel the same way,* I willed with my best telepathic eyes.

'I think I love you more.' It must have worked.

'Bet you don't.'

'Bet I do,' he said, playfully hitting my arm. 'I love you more than … anything.' He stumbled for words drunkenly, then he leaned in to kiss me.

'Anything? Like what?' I probed, pushing him back to an upright position.

'Like, like Coultan's rum,' he said, which was obviously the first thing that came into his head (like there wasn't enough of it in there already).

'That much, eh?' I was impressed, but I continued the game. 'I love you more than walking on golden sands and paddling in clear waters.'

'Yeah?'

'And— ' I added as an afterthought '—while wearing Dolce & Gabbana sunglasses, and eating Haagen-Dazs ice-cream.'

He raised his eyebrows and shook his head, clearly realising he was defeated. Nothing could beat that, so he changed tact. 'Ah, but I'll love you the longest.'

'Yeah?' I wasn't so sure.

'Yep.'

'How long?'

He looked out over the ocean and sighed. 'Until the sun sets on our lives,' he answered solemnly, if a little slurred.

There was no way I could beat that.

'Ah,' was all I said.

We were talking crap, but it was wonderful, meaningful crap, and I was sure that no matter how long I lived or how many men there were in my future, I would never experience such complete love as I did at that moment. I also knew I could never talk about it or even write down my feelings, so I committed to memory as much of the atmosphere as I was feasibly able to soak up. The sound of the waves gently lapping the sand, the distant sound of voices further up the shore, the smell of the fire and Joe's sun-soaked skin, the last glimmers of the sun as it bedded down beneath the sea and the warmth of Joe's arms wrapped tightly around me.

Chapter Twelve

The next night, over a dinner of delicious stuffed peppers and roasted vegetables, we all listened as Joe described the events of the afternoon. In the morning we had concocted the ransom note. Rather than spending hours cutting up newspaper letters, we had decided it would work if Mark wrote it in his handwriting, as if forced to do so at gunpoint. To help with the sincerity of Mark's statement to the police, Coultan had held a gun at the table. Although it was completely devoid of bullets, at least Mark would be telling the truth in that detail. The letter laid out the demands of the kidnappers, clearly stating that this was not an act of terrorism, it was merely a request for money. It stated how much money we – sorry they – wanted and made clear that, providing the demands were met, neither Mark nor I would be harmed. The point of exchange would be a bench overlooking the Leaning Tower of Pisa, which we figured was such an iconic structure it could not be missed. As we had no way of receiving communication from the police, we asked for confirmation through the midday news bulletin on the World Service radio station. Further instructions would be provided once we had received confirmation of their agreement.

That afternoon, Joe and Frankie had travelled to the mainland to make their usual telephone call to Mabel, but this time with their unusual request. Joe said it had been very straightforward and that Mabel had asked no questions about the letter. She put all her faith in

Joe; if there was a remote chance of her getting out of the residential home, she had no problem doing what he asked.

 Later on, I saw Joe sitting on the ground by the fire. He was alone, his arms resting on his knees as he held a beer bottle in both hands. He was staring into the whirling flames as they flickered and crackled in front of him.

'Hey, you ok?' I asked gently as I parked myself down beside him, jolting him from his fire gazing trance.

'Hi.' He smiled at me and put his arm around me. 'Yeah, just thinking about today.'

'Are you regretting it?'

'No, no, not at all. It's Mabel, you know. She used to be so feisty, but lately she sounds so dejected, so resigned. She tries to pretend everything's ok for me and Frankie, but I can hear it in her voice like she's giving up. It's just sad, that's all.'

I gave his leg that was nearest to me a little squeeze. 'It won't be long now. She's practically halfway here already. As soon as we get that money, you can get her.'

'But what if it's too late? What if her spirit's already gone?'

'No chance. It takes more than that to keep a woman like Mabel down. From what you've told me about her, she doesn't strike me as someone who's going to give up without a fight.'

Joe smiled. 'That's true enough.'

'And,' I continued, 'Look at this place, if anything will perk her up it will be here. I tell you, this island, with this weather and you and Frankie, it'll be better than Valium.'

'You're right,' he said more cheerily.

'I usually am,' I said, grabbing his beer and taking a swig as he shook his head and rolled his eyes to the reddening sky above us.

We calculated that the letter would not reach Mabel for at least two days, and assuming she posted the ransom note the same day she received it, that meant we had at least three days before the note fell into the hands of the police. During these days, I spent a lot of time with Mark. We lay in the sun and practised interrogating each other, devising every conceivable question the investigators could ask us to make sure we stuck to the same account of what happened. We tried to keep it as close to reality as possible, but obviously we had to bend the truth in some areas, and in others the story was bent so much it was practically perpendicular.

We had established they had tied us up and kept in a wooden hut – truth.

They allowed us out for meals – truth.

The weather was hot (to explain the tanned skin) and we could see the sea but did not have any idea where we were – truth. I shuddered as I'd remembered by Jamaica blunder.

They had guns, and although we tried to escape, we weren't able to – truth.

There were three kidnappers, one of them was black, one was big and they all had very short hair – truth. One was completely gorgeous – truth, but best kept to myself. There was no need to mention there was a women.

We went into minute detail of what happened, what we had seen, even sounds, smells and textures of our surroundings to prevent any slip-ups which would cause suspicion. On the third day, we tried to come up with descriptions of our three captors, but it was difficult to imagine the same made-up faces, and drawing them in the sand just wasn't working.

'Why don't we describe faces of people we are familiar with?' Mark suggested as we lay down by the shore topping up our tans.

'Because the only people we both know are these guys and describing them would kind of defeat the object.'

'No, I mean famous people, stupid!'

'Hey that's a brilliant idea!' I said, surprised as so far Mark hadn't had many.

'It is,' he replied smugly.

'Ok, so who?'

'The Bee Gees?' he suggested.

'There isn't a black Bee Gee.'

'We can make one of them black. How about that one with the long hair. Is that Maurice?'

'I don't know, but I'm not sure the Bee Gees are the best option. What if we have to make up E-fits and they put all three together? Someone might put two and two together.'

'And what? Arrest the Bee Gees?'

We laughed at the notion. 'No, I just think we should pick three unrelated faces.'

'Ok, who should we pick?'

'Ok, what about Will Smith for the black guy? He looks nothing like Coultan, which is ideal.'

'Ok, that's cool, we can do that,' Mark agreed. 'And what about Elton John?'

'Elton John? He doesn't look much like a kidnapper. I reckon we need someone more thuggish. Like Grant Mitchell.'

'Grant Mitchell? From Eastenders? Ok, that would work. So, we only need one more – the man with the plan, maybe someone with a bit of bandit stubble?'

'Like Desperate Dan?' I suggested.

'Yes, but maybe more three-dimensional.'

'George Michael?'

'I met him once. He was doing a promotion for my dad … nice bloke.'

'Really? That's cool! But could he pass for a kidnapper?'

'Yeah, sure, why not? Ok, that's it. Officer, it was Will Smith, Grant Mitchell and George Michael that kidnapped us!' Mark jokingly confessed, and I clapped my hands together like a seal in excitement.

'C'mon let's celebrate our breakthrough with a nice cool dip in the ocean,' I suggested, and that is exactly what we did.

While we spent the days "learning our lines", playing games on the beach and sunbathing, the evenings were spent chatting and laughing round the fire. My nights were spent with Joe.

On the eleventh day on the island, we were all at sea. Rio had packed up a picnic and we clambered aboard the little boat. We headed out to sea until we managed to get a signal on Coultan's little transistor radio. It took a while to find the right spot, but after approximately an hour of sailing round in concentric circles we found a spot with a half decent signal and dropped anchor. During the morning we listened to a music station. I hadn't realised how much I'd missed music, and it was great to hear some old songs and some new songs by artists that didn't begin with the letter "B". Coultan showed me how to cast a rod, and we all sunbathed on the deck with our lines dangling in the water, waiting for a bite.

Just before midday, Coultan turned the dial to find the World Service station, and we all gathered round the little radio, listening intently. We heard the headlines, but there was no mention of us. We listened to the main news stories, but still nothing. We continued to listen for about half an hour, but still nothing.

'They must not have received the letter yet,' Rio suggested.

'Yeah, either that or they're not going to bow down to our demands,' I added.

'Or they don't need to communicate with us because they're near to finding us.' Joe looked worried, and we all subconsciously looked into the sky to search for helicopters or any sign of a raid.

We continued to listen to the radio while we ate our lunch before heading back to camp, a little crestfallen after the joy of the musical morning and all a little more unsettled. In the afternoon, Joe helped me fix up my hammock and I helped him build a second one next to mine for him to sleep in. It was agreed that Mark could use the one he had used previously next to Frankie. We both felt the same uncertainty of not knowing how much longer we would be together. It was inevitable that, one way or another, we would soon be separated, and, although neither of us spoke about it, we needed to share more moments, whether it be having a laugh, trying to build a hammock or sleeping side by side.

Joe gently woke me by tugging on the side of my hammock until I started to swing.

'Morning,' I whispered as I saw his face appear over the side of the canvas.

'Look,' he whispered back, nodding in the direction of the sea. The sun had begun its daily ascent, and the layers of pinks, oranges and golds were reflecting in the still waters. It was more beautiful than I had ever seen it, if that were possible, but maybe that was because of the company I was sharing it with.

'Wow!' was all I could say. I looked back at Joe, who raised his eyebrows.

'Shall we?'

You try stopping me, but Joe was already up and helping me out of my hammock. Before long we were jogging down to the water's edge, his hand in mine as he pulled me into the icy cold water behind him. It was glorious. Freezing, but glorious. Just me, Joe and the morning. With the warmth burning inside of me from his kisses, I barely felt the cold of the water.

After our dip, we watched the remainder of the sunrise, sitting there on the sand, snuggled up in the same blanket, arms around each other. It was transient; it couldn't possibly last forever, but we had to soak up every second until the day arrived and 'normality' ensued once again.

After breakfast we were back on the boat, circling and trying to find the same spot as the previous day. Again, a few minutes before twelve, we switched to the World Service and assembled around the radio. The headlines came and went as we sat biting our nails. And then it came. The news we had been waiting for. I began to sweat, and my heart hammered so hard I thought it would explode. The voice introduced itself as an Inspector Mildred of the Metropolitan Police. He said he had a message for the kidnappers in the Mark

Cheriton abduction case. He agreed that the demands would be met, providing that the two hostages were set free as promised. After a plea to give themselves up, explaining that this would help their case when they were, inevitably, found and eventually tried, he conceded that he would await further contact and provided a telephone number directly to his office. After the broadcast, we sat in shocked silence, just looking at each other.

'What?'

'Did he just say ...?'

'Have they ...?'

We were stunned. We had only gone and done it! None of us could actually comprehend that our little hare-brained scheme had worked. They had agreed to give us the money!

Coultan laughed his deep laugh and, one by one, we joined in, still in a state of some disbelief. Mark high-fived Frankie and soon we were hollering and woo-hooing into the air, our rapturous cries swallowed up in the mass of ocean which surrounded us.

'I think we need to have us a party!' Coultan bellowed and turned the dial back to a music station.

We stayed out on the boat for several hours, fishing, singing along to some of the songs and trying to dance to others which was not easy due to the overcrowded conditions and the ever-present rocking nature of the vessel. When our bellies needed feeding and we'd caught enough fish for supper, we reeled in the anchor and headed for home.

Back on the island I found myself subdued. After the exhilaration of the success of the ransom note, the realisation of what lay ahead suddenly hit me. Not only was I solely responsible for five other people's futures, I would have to survive on my wits and fool the authorities. Fool a Force that was thoroughly trained in catching criminals and outwitting ne'r-do-wells, like me. I was suddenly panic-stricken. Not only was I scared of being caught, I was scared by the realisation that I would have to leave the island and never return.

In this unlikely place I had found a home, I'd forged unexpected friendships and found a love I had never known existed. But by its very nature of this predicament I now had to leave it all behind, for good.

Joe must have sensed my mood and asked if I wanted to take a stroll with him. We walked across the sand in silence, heading towards the waters edge. When we reached the ocean, he took hold of my hand and steered me leftwards, amidst the shallow waves.

'You're quiet,' he began, 'Are you worried about the plan?'

'Yes.' I admitted. 'I'm not sure I can pull it off and I don't want to let you all down.'

'What? The only reason that we've got this far is down to you. Just the fact that you're willing to give it a go, means the world to us, to me. And if for any reason it goes wrong, there's no way we'll blame you. We can't thank you enough for stepping up and agreeing to help.'

'Really?'

'Yes of course! Whatever happens, we will be forever in your debt.'

'But you could wind up back in prison.'

'True, but that is more likely to happen without your help. I just pray that you're ok. Listen Nance,' he stopped and turned be to look at him. 'If it does go wrong, promise me you'll do whatever you can to save yourself. Lie, throw us to the wolves, whatever it takes, we deserve it for getting you into this, you don't. I can't bear the thought of you doing time. Not for us.'

'But…'

'I mean it, promise me.'

'Ok, I promise.' I conceded, praying that it would never come to that. He kissed me on the forehead before turning once more and we continued walking.

It was now time for the conversation I had been dreading. The one where we agreed we could never see each other again if we wanted to make it out of this situation unscathed. I wasn't sure how to begin but even thinking about it started a steady stream of tears. As I sniffed the tears back, Joe looked up at my face.

'Oh no, Nancy, please don't cry.' We stopped and he held my face in his hands, wiping the tears from my cheeks with his thumbs.

'I just hate the thought of never seeing you again.' I blurted in broken breaths.

'Hey, of course we'll see each other again.' He reassured me.

I looked up into those beautiful blue eyes, searching for an explanation. Some kind of scenario I hadn't considered as to how I could open the box and keep the money.

'You know that's not possible right? If it fails we'll both be in prison. If it succeeds and I come wandering back here, I will lead them straight to you. If they never find the 'kidnappers' the case will stay open and there will be an ongoing investigation. I can't see Max Cheriton giving up on finding whoever fleeced him and kidnapped his son.'

'You think?' Joe asked naively. Had he really seen a future for us?

'Yes, this is it. This is all we get. One way or another I have to leave this island, for good.' A new set of tears sprang forth.

'Well maybe I can come and visit you? You know, when everything dies down a bit.' His eyes pleaded with mine for affirmation.

'I don't think so. I wish there was a way but it's too risky. If you send me so much as a text or a postcard it could be found and traced. We can't afford to take that chance. Not if we've got that far.'

'So that's it? Never?'

'I don't think so.' I spluttered through my tears that were now flowing freely down my face. 'I think we have to see it for what it is, a once in a lifetime meeting, a memory that will stay with us forever.'

'But I love you, Nancy.' He too had eyes brimming with tears now.

'I love you too.' I sniffed, as he pulled me into his chest, holding me so close my tears left wet marks on his t-shirt. We stood there for a while, holding each other close, shoulders shaking as we tried to control our sobs. Eventually we pulled apart. We had to face reality.

'There's nothing we can do.' I looked up at him, my blotchy red face, hot from crying. 'We have to accept it is a love that can never be.'

 That night we threw our days catch on to the barbecue along with jacket potatoes and peppers wrapped in tinfoil. While we washed the delicious food down with cold beers, we agreed it was a fine night to get out the karaoke, and it wasn't long before Frankie was hooking the machine up to the generator and Coultan was handing out rather enormous glasses of rum. Frankie's version of 'Lip up Fatty' by Bad Manners seemed to warm up the party. This was closely followed by Joe's rendition of 'You're Gorgeous' by Babybird, in which he pointed at me and made me turn all gooey and girly. Coultan's version of Bob Marley's 'One Love' had us all joining in, and I followed it with a Blondie number. Rio joined me in 'Venus' by Bananarama before her solo of Betty Boo 'Doin' the Do'. Then Mark rather surprised us all with his attempt at the high notes of 'Small-town Boy' by Bronski Beat, which was hilarious.

 As the songs kept coming and the rum kept flowing, we sang and we laughed. We even danced to renditions of The Beach Boys, The Bluebells and Blur. When Coultan sang Ben E. King's 'When a Man Loves a Woman', it sent shivers down my spine, and when Joe put his arm around me and squeezed my waist, it sent them right back up again. When we'd run out of energy, we finished the night – in fact, the early hours of the next morning – with a joint attempt at 'Hey Jude' by the Beatles, drunkenly waving our arms *almost* in time with the music and na na na na-ing along at the end. As I recall, it would have put the original version to shame.

 In the state we were in, there was no hope of us clambering into hammocks without sustaining multiple injuries, so while Rio and Coultan turned into their hut and Frankie and Mark made make-shift beds on the floor – i.e. crashed on a pile of blankets by the fire – Joe and I headed down towards the boat. Joe pulled out the little bed, and I snuggled in beside him as he crashed beneath the covers.

Chapter Thirteen

It was my last full day on the island and I didn't want to get up. Half because of the wooziness in my head, and half because I was in bed with Joe and I loved to hear him breathing next to me while he slept. I didn't want to wake him, but didn't want to waste a second of this last day by sleeping. While contemplating what to do, he stirred beside me, and as I checked to see if his eyes were open, he pulled me to him and we snuggled back under the covers. *Ok, maybe I won't get up for a little while yet.*

It was almost lunchtime before we finally emerged from the depths of the boat. The sun was already high in the sky and bodies were busying themselves around the camp. We spent the afternoon going over the plans for the next day. Mark wrote the instructions for me to read out to the police, Rio made sure the clothes I had worn on my arrival – my denim skirt, greying T-shirt and old hoodie – were washed and ready for me to wear. We were all upbeat, as if we hadn't realised the enormity of the situation. To help myself get through it, I tried to tell myself that it wasn't happening and took my mind off it by playing football with the boys and helping Rio with her cooking.

At my final supper we decided that no-one would mention the events of the following day. It was also decided that, as we couldn't afford to have hangovers in the morning, we would all leave off the rum and abandon the karaoke machine. We'd had our last party together.

While the others cleared up, I wandered off for a walk to clear my head. I walked down to the sea as the sun was beginning to set. Luckily, it was still quite warm. I strolled along the water's edge and looked back up towards the camp. Everything was so familiar to me now. Rio and Coultan's hut, the fire, the trees to the left from where my hammock hung, the beach beyond where Joe chopped his logs. To my right, there was the hut where Mark and I had slept in those first bewildering days, and further along I could see the tree I'd sat under crying after I'd burnt my feet. Over the last two weeks this little place had transformed from my prison to my home. It was a lot to get my head around.

The reddening sun dipped its bottom into the water and I sat staring out to sea, pondering everything and nothing all at the same time. I lay back on the cool sand and looked up into this magical corner of sky for the last time. I sensed someone sit down a little way away to the side of me, followed by another at the other side. It wasn't long before all six of us were lying down along the sand, several feet apart. No-one spoke, no-one said a word, we just lay there in the quiet of the dusk, listening to the sound of the waves as they stretched up the shore, reaching out for us. Lying there, the churning in my stomach ceased, and I was overcome with a real inner peace, a contentment that was alien to me. It felt wonderful. We were a picture of contradictions; we were alone and yet together, enemies and yet friends, safe and yet frightened to death.

Later we gathered round the fire, some with hot drinks, some with cold beers. We made polite idle chit-chat and while we were comfortable in each other's company, there was also a sense of uneasiness, as though no-one wanted to say what they were really thinking for fear of upsetting the group. I knew if I stayed there, I would end up in tears; saying my goodnight farewells seemed too hard to contemplate. Instead, I decided to make it quick, like pulling off a plaster.

'I'm going to go to bed now, it'll be a long day tomorrow,' I announced, more sombrely than I had meant to. Everyone said their goodnights and Joe got up to walk with me,

'Do you want to stay with me on the boat?' he asked. Yes, forever, I wanted to say, but I had to start cutting my ties before it became too difficult to do so.

'No, I think I'd like to spend my last night in my hammock, looking out over the sea,' I told him.

'Do you want some company over there?' he offered.

'Yes, I'd like that.' I smiled at him, and he took my hand as we walked to the trees. And there we lay in our hammocks, holding hands across the divide. As I tried to drift off to sleep under the stars, tears fell silently from my tired eyes.

That night I hardly slept. I tossed and turned as much as you can in a hammock, as my brain churned over the past two weeks, my future and the day that lay ahead. It was like the night before the worst interview ever; an entire day event where every word, every gesture, every move would be scrutinised and analysed. But it wasn't for a job, or something with no purpose to be forgotten in a few days' time, with a lot of "better luck next times". There were lives at stake – not only Joe, Frankie, Coultan and Rio's, but Mark's and mine too. This day had the potential to change all of our futures, and it was all dependent on me. There was no-one to fall back on, I couldn't just walk out and have another go next year – it was now or never. I had to lie and deceive people all day. I would become a thief, a fraud and a criminal. Could I do it? Should I do it? Would I do it? Would anyone? Would I be at home on Thursday catching up on gossip with Steph, or would I be in Holloway catching up on a life sentence?

And, of course, there was Joe. This would be the last day I would ever see him. There would be no absent-mindedly bumping into him buying groceries in Tesco, no accidental meeting on a train, and worst of all I hadn't even got a photograph. Nothing to keep by my bed or hidden in a box of secret treasures. After today, I would never again look into those blue eyes and shiver as they looked back into mine. This is what frightened me most about the forthcoming day, the day that was almost breaking, the last day of my life as I now knew it.

I rose with the sun and headed over to take a shower. The camp was quiet and peaceful and I felt terribly alone; it was like no feeling I had ever had before. The birds were singing and the crickets were chirping as they had been doing every day, unaware of the unique day that was to come and the uneasy nausea that had taken over my body. As I stood under a cool shower, I let the water soak into my skin and wash away the sweat and weariness of the uncomfortable night I had spent. A breeze swept through the cubicle, and the welcome coolness reached every nook and cranny of my body with a refreshing revitalisation.

I wrapped myself in a towel and wandered through to the kitchen area, where I saw Rio had got up and was already cracking eggs into a frying pan. She looked up and smiled as I walked towards her.

'I heard you get up, so I've come to make you some eggs, darlin',' she said as she reached for a loaf of bread and sliced it.

'Thanks, Rio,' I said as I pulled up a chair and sat down opposite her. I couldn't think of anything appropriate to say. I wasn't yet ready to talk about the day, but to discuss something mundane seemed pointless.

'So, how are you this morning, sweetheart?' Rio asked me, as she flipped bubbling fat over the egg yolks.

'Ok,' I lied. If I admitted to her I was scared shitless it would achieve nothing other than to make me, and her, feel even worse. Rio sensed I didn't want to talk about it so simply nodded and carried on with cooking the breakfast. It was at that point I realised how much I would miss Rio. She was an exceptional woman. She seemed to instinctively know what to do in any situation and maintained a sense of peace and calm wherever she went. She really would do anything for anybody who asked. Sometimes she would do it without needing to be asked, just to make life a little easier for those concerned, like getting up early to cook my eggs. She had treated me with nothing but kindness and respect since I'd set foot on the island, cooking my meals when she thought I might be hungry, lending me her best clothes when I had nothing to wear and knowing what to say when I needed another woman to talk to. I admired Rio for her beauty, her serenity and her wisdom, and I made a pact with myself to become more like her in my everyday life. She was a genuine friend.

'I really admire you, sister,' she said as if speaking my thoughts.

I looked up sharply. 'You admire me?' I asked in disbelief.

'Yes. You are so brave to do these things. You have guts, girlfriend.'

I was truly shocked to find that Rio admired me, of all people.

'You know what you want to do and you just do it, no worries. You got your head right screwed on. I think you are amazin'. I wish I was as brave as you.'

I wanted to cry, but I realised that wouldn't make me appear very brave. 'I'm not brave, see,' I said, holding out my hand to show the fingers shaking uncontrollably.

'Ah, but that's only temporary nerves, and, despite that, you'll still have a go and do it. That's what makes you brave.'

'How little you know the real me.'

'But I do know the real you. I've got eyes and ears. I see what I see and I hear what I hear.'

'I'm not just nervous, I'm terrified,' I admitted.

'Well, who wouldn't be? But hey, even if something goes wrong, we'll still all be grateful to you for the rest of our lives, for trying. We admire you greatly.'

Tears welled up in my eyes. No-one had ever admired me before. I was the colourless chameleon who was incapable of making a decision about anything. Was this the real me? Perhaps Rio had to point it out before I could recognise it myself.

'Hey, girl, I'm sorry. I didn't mean to make you cry. Here.' She handed me a piece of kitchen roll, and while I dabbed my eyes, she took the eggs from the pan and put them into sandwiches. She handed one to me before sitting down on a stool as she tucked into hers.

'I know,' I sniffed. 'Only I was just thinking how much I admired you!'

We laughed as we ate.

'Well, it looks like we got ourselves our own little mutual appreciation society, doesn't it?'

'I guess so. We could've been great friends,' I added sadly.

'We already are.' She squeezed my hand. I was a little cheerier now as we wolfed down our breakfast. While we were sitting there, I spotted Joe heading our way. He stretched his arms up over his head, picked up a towel and made his way towards us. *Good God, how could he be that beautiful when he'd just got out of bed?* As he approached and saw us, he waved his towel in our direction before disappearing behind the shower cubicle. Unwittingly, I let out a deep sigh, forgetting Rio was sitting next to me, lost in my own little Joe world until she spoke again.

'I'm sad for you two,' she said, dragging me back to reality. 'I see he loves you so much.'

Tears sprung to my eyes again.

'Uh-oh, I've done it again.' She handed me more kitchen roll. 'Hey, don't worry, sister. The future is an unknown thing. No-one knows how it's gonna work out.'

'Yeah, but Joe's not going to be in my future. He can't possibly be.'

'Why not?' Rio asked innocently. *Oh, poor, innocent Rio. She was as deluded as Joe.*

'Because if I ever came back here, I'd lead the investigation straight to you.'

'Things have a way of working out. Nothing is impossible if we want it badly enough.'

'This is. We've agreed to forget all about each other after tomorrow, move on with our lives.'

'Well, if you've agreed ...' she said, rolling her eyes.

'What? That's it. The end. Finito.'

'Maybe you two should have a little chat, to work things out.'

'No, I don't think so. We've said all we need to, anything else and my brain will explode.'

'What if *he'd* like to say something more about it?'

'I'd rather not give him the opportunity. This is difficult enough as it is. I'm not sure I could cope if he tried to change my mind. It might help if you didn't leave me alone with him between now and when we go. I can't afford to crack up, not today.'

'I understand. I will do what I can.'

'Thanks, Rio. That's a real help – it's for the best.'

'We'll see,' was all she said. She really was deluded. I wished with all my heart that she was even a little bit right, but to hold on to even a glimmer of hope would be dangerous. There was no room here for wishful thinking. That never did anybody any good. We had decided to never look back and imagine what might have been. The decision had been made and I had accepted it. *Well, almost accepted it*, I thought as Joe came round the corner, dripping wet, his hair all spiky, his chest glistening and looking more tanned than ever against the whiteness of the towel wrapped around his waist.

'Hi,' I said with too much enthusiasm.

'You ok?' he asked.

'I am now,' I said, checking out his body as he pulled up a chair and sat down. 'I mean, after my chat with Rio here.'

'Yeah?' he asked, turning towards Rio.

'Ah-ha.' Rio smiled back. 'We've been havin' a little chat, sister to sister. Eggs?'

'Please,' Joe replied unnecessarily as Rio had already cracked one into the pan and was in the process of cracking another.

'Well, I'd better get dressed,' I said, standing up. 'Big day ahead,' I added to show how much I was taking all this in my stride. I looked at Rio who smiled and at Joe who winked as I scuttled off to collect my things together. As I walked away, Rio and Joe's muffled voices continued behind me.

Chapter Fourteen

As the boat pulled away from the shore for the last time, I felt an overwhelming sadness, like the end of an enjoyable holiday or leaving a home full of happy memories that I knew I could never return to. I watched as the hut and the camp, became smaller and smaller as we headed off into the blue horizon which was wide open and waiting for us. I continued to watch until they were too small to see and, eventually, they disappeared into the backdrop of the island, which itself was shrinking to a small blob … and then it too was gone. Ahead of us, there was nothing but sea. Below us, all manner of ancient life forms busied about their daily routines, but above the surface, there was nothing but calm as we steamed our way onwards.

The day was becoming hotter, but the breeze created by the boat's movement kept us cool, and once I'd adjusted to the jerky motion of the waves, it was easy to relax and forget about the worries that lay ahead of me. As I stretched out on the deck lazily, I drifted off to sleep as I was rocked gently from side to side.

I must have been asleep for some hours, as when I awoke Rio and Joe were unwrapping a picnic lunch and laying it out on the deck beside me.

'Ah, Sleeping Beauty's woken up,' Joe said, smiling. 'And just in time for lunch, I see.'

'Crikey, how long was I out for?' I asked, hoisting myself up to a sitting position and rubbing my eyes to wake up, hoping upon hope that there had been no unsightly drooling going on while I was asleep.

'Only about two hours.'

'Two hours! We must be nearly there.'

'No, not yet.' Rio came through carrying cooked chicken legs wrapped in tinfoil and some cold rice salad. 'Methinks you must have needed your sleep today.'

'Yeah, I didn't get much last night,' I explained drowsily. Coultan turned off the engine and came to join us for some food. I was starving, and it was clear the others were too as the six of us tucked in, heartily eating our fill and more. Perhaps it was nerves, but everyone seemed to be hiding it well as we sat chatting and laughing about the last few weeks, which now already felt like the good old days. Six old friends sat reminiscing over lunch, bobbing gently up and down in the middle of nowhere. Had there been any onlookers, they would have presumed we had known each other for years and none of us had a care in the world.

Once the minimal leftovers were cleared away, Joe restarted the engine and soon we were back on course, speeding across the waves, heading straight for Italy. Mark and Frankie sat together, watching the waves over the side of the boat. Coultan and Rio sat discussing their plans for when they eventually arrived in Monte Carlo – which casinos they would visit, when they would pay the money into the bank and the clothes they would wear. I was sitting further down, on the other side of the deck, for my part of the plan I was on my own. Once I had passed on the money, I had to fend for myself, play it by ear. Had I genuinely got enough nerve and initiative to pull this off all on my own? Surely it was impossible for little old me to fool the entire British and probably Italian police forces and convince them I was a victim? As I considered it, I started to panic. I couldn't do it. It was wrong. It wasn't just some naughty game, this was a criminal offence and I would have to pay the consequences. Throughout my life I'd never stolen so much as a pencil, and now here I was committing fraud and deception on such a huge scale no-one would believe it. I could scarcely believe it myself. Was it too late to call the whole thing off? I'm sure they would understand. I turned to watch Rio and Coultan who were musing over whether anywhere in Monte Carlo would do an exceptionally hot chilli, and I wondered how they would react if I told them I had changed my mind.

During the past few days, I had tried to convince myself I was capable of this, and now suddenly I wasn't so certain. Deep down I knew the real reason my mind was changing, and he was currently steering the boat. I was able to see him from where I sat, shirtless, leaning on the boat's wheel, arms folded, looking straight ahead. I loved him. I could tell him I had changed my mind. Mark would be released and I would stay. I was sure he wanted me to; he'd said as much. He would hold me in his arms and we'd weep with joy. When it came to men in my past, I'd been pretty unlucky – yes, there had been some weirdos, but there had been some I believed I'd genuinely fallen in love with, only for them to up and leave like rats down a sewer, some for other girls, some for apparently no reason at all. But I had never felt for any of them what I felt for Joe. He would never leave me for an ex-girlfriend that he had never truly stopped loving, or go off to university and never be heard of again. Joe would be forever.

I was a good person – apart from the lying, blackmail and plans to defraud – didn't I deserve a bit of happiness for once? A bit of luck? Now I had found true love, shouldn't I do anything to keep hold of it? Why should I be a martyr? Was it my turn to be selfish? Love like this, with a man so beautiful my heart melted whenever his name was mentioned, didn't come along every day. It might well be my one chance of genuine happiness, I had to take it. To hell with everyone else. I wanted to be with Joe, with or without the million pounds. I would get a bar job in Ibiza or Majorca and support us both. I was going to do it. I would announce that this was the end of the road. 'Turn the boat around!' I would say dramatically, 'We're going home!' I decided that the next time I was alone with Joe, I would tell him my decision. *Let the hugging and the weeping commence.*

'Shit, get down!' Joe's voice boomed down the length of the boat as the five of us threw ourselves down flat onto the floor. We heard the sound of a speedboat close by as it passed us, people laughing and shouting above the sound of the engine. It had been so long since I had heard anyone other than the six of us speak, the unfamiliar voices were strange to my ears.

'It's ok, they've gone,' Joe shouted the all clear, and we recomposed ourselves. 'Nance, Mark, you'd better keep your heads down in case any more come past.'

We did as we were told, although it seemed completely unnecessary as we were miles away from land, and surely we would see any boats coming anyway? I wondered what the speedboat had been doing all the way out here. Perhaps it was lost. Coultan walked over to speak to Joe at the front of the boat, and soon Joe returned in his place and sat down beside me. Rio caught my eye and gave me a knowing, don't-worry-I-won't-leave-you-alone-together look. I smiled back but inside I was shouting, *no, leave us alone! I want to tell Joe I'm staying so we can do the hugging and weeping thing. Piss off, Rio!* But, bless her, she had no idea of my shifting thought patterns and started a conversation.

'So Mark, Frankie, are you two going to be ok on your own on the boat while me, Coultan and Joe drive to Monaco?'

'Yes, karaoke!' Frankie, beamed excitedly.

'No, no karaoke, Frankie!' Rio laughed, and then added more sternly, 'You have to keep a low profile. You have to stay quietly below deck so no-one knows you're there. You understand?'

'Yes, we understand.' Mark confirmed, stressing the levity of the situation. 'We have a pack of cards so will stay well hidden downstairs until you return. Won't we Frankie?' Frankie nodded.

'Good.' Rio wagged her finger playfully in their direction. 'And once we're back from Monaco it'll be time for Mark to leave, so you'd better make the most of it. Ok?'

'Ok.' Mark and Frankie replied simultaneously, looking at each other with exaggerated frowns.

'So, are we nearly there yet, Joe?' Frankie asked.

'Yeah, not long now,' he answered. *Not long?* That meant I hadn't got long to tell him my new plan. I'd decided that I needed to tell Joe alone first and then break the news to the others. Oh, why did Rio have to be so nice and keep the promise I had asked her to this morning? What did I know this morning? *Jack shit, that's what*. Being on this boat had changed everything.

We had several conversations about the plan, the future and, believe it or not, the weather. I sat and listened, providing the occasional 'mmm' or one-word answer, biding my time for the right moment to drop my bombshell and well and truly rock the boat.

Eventually, Joe offered to get us some lemonade, and I took the opportunity to tell Rio casually, 'Rio, I think I would like to have a quick chat with Joe after all.'

'You sure, girlfriend?' she asked me gently.

'I am. Very sure.'

'Then consider me gone.' She smiled as Joe returned and sat back down, climbing to her feet and going to keep Coultan company at the wheel. This was my chance.

'You know, I'm so nervous I haven't been able to shit for three days,' Joe announced. He may have looked like a Greek god, but he was still a bloke. It wasn't quite the mood I had hoped for, but then beggars can't be choosers. How should I begin? When I didn't respond to his toilet remark, Joe turned to face me.

'You're very quiet,' he said. 'You ok?'

'Yeah, I was just thinking.' Here I go ...

'Yeah, big day ahead right?'

'Indeed. About that …' I began.

'You must be very nervous. Don't worry, you'll be fine. We all believe you can do it.'

'Oh, I don't know about that ...' I began again.

'Yeah, we were just saying before, when you were asleep, you're really brave. There's no way we'll ever be able to thank you properly.'

Good grief! It was like those stories on *EastEnders* when one character is trying to confess something, and everyone they meet down Bridge Street tells them "I know you would never let me down" and "at least you're always so honest, treacle," so they end up keeping their trap shut, making it snowball into some explosive episode shown at Christmas. But I didn't want to keep quiet, I just wanted to get a word in edgeways. This wasn't a soap opera, it was my life, and if I didn't say my piece now, it would only be me who suffered.

'Hey, Joe,' I said rather sternly, surprising him. 'Sorry, I just really need to say something.' I had finally got his undivided attention, but not for long.

'Joe!' Coultan shouted down the boat.

'Yeah, in a sec,' Joe shouted back, lifting himself to his feet and crouching beside me. 'What is it?' he asked, looking intently into my eyes.

'Er, I just have to tell you, that, err …' *Go on*, I willed myself, *go on, say it.* I took a deep breath. 'I, well, me and you, I don't want to …'

'I know what you're going to say,' he told me. Somehow, I didn't think he did.

'I was going to say that I've changed … well, I mean, I've realised …' This was even harder than I'd thought.

He smiled down at me. 'I love you too, Nancy Smart,' he said, taking my hand in both of his. 'This entire experience has changed me too, and I'll never forget you.' He kissed me on the lips and then held me close to him while I wept. Not the tears of joy and elation I had hoped for, but tears of parting and desolation.

'Joe!' Coultan shouted again, completely destroying the tender moment. 'We're nearly there and I need your help up here.'

Joe gave me one last squeeze and then pulled away, 'We'll be ok,' he said to comfort me. 'Just not together.' He now had tears in his eyes too. 'Yes, just not together,' he repeated, looking down at the floor. 'I've got to go.' He nodded towards the front of the boat, 'And you'd better hide,' he added, standing up with his hand out to pull me up next to him. He squeezed my hand before letting me clamber down to the cabin beneath where it was stuffy and airless. Frankie and Mark followed closely behind as I opened one of the small windows and sat down to wait, watching the Italian skyline edge nearer and nearer towards us.

I cast my eye around the cabin. It held so many memories. The day I arrived, sitting over there gagged and tied, terrified at the unknown and in fear for my life. The days of boredom and uncertainty that followed. They all seemed so long ago now. I'd wanted to escape the boat so badly back then, but now I wanted to stay on it for as long as possible. Since that first experience with Mark, I'd sat many times on this boat, talking and laughing, falling in love. I remembered coming down those wooden steps in my old T-shirt, being with Joe, kissing Joe, sleeping with Joe. It felt like I had grown up on this boat, and once it docked, my innocence would be gone and things would never be the same again.

As we drew near to the docks and the ants in the distance became people, I closed the little curtain next to where I was sitting. Rio came down to sit with me and told what was going on. We had temporarily docked and Coultan had disembarked to find his friend Stefano, who would apparently point out where we were able to moor more "safely". I heard people talking above my head. It was Coultan, Joe and a voice I didn't recognise, which I assumed was Stefano. The engine started up once more, and the boat chugged along for a matter of minutes before we stopped once again. I sneaked a peek through the window and watched as Joe and Coultan tied the boat to a small jetty where there was only one other boat. I assumed that this was perhaps Stefano's own private landing.

I heard the voices again, and then Coultan shouted down to us that it was all clear and we climbed back up on deck. Saying goodbye to Mark was more difficult than I had imagined. During all the worry about leaving Joe I hadn't thought about how unbelievably sad it would be to leave Mark. True, there was a chance we could see each other again but it would never be the same. The experiences we had shared since the fateful day at the airport, the terror, the hope, the fun, it was all so unexpected, so unique.

After saying goodbye to Mark I was propelled into such a tight bear hug by Frankie, I was lifted two feet into the air. Oh how I would miss Frankie. The big guy with the big heart, we'd had such fun times it was hard to believe they were at an end.

I picked up my bag and Joe helped me clamber off the boat for the last time and onto the wooden planks. In front of us, way up on a hill, was a picturesque villa-type house with a terracotta roof surrounded by fruit and olive trees, and acres and acres of land. I saw a man walking away from us, along the long winding path towards the house. That must be Stefano, intentionally unaware of what he had been a party to – the less he knew the better for all concerned, but we were silently grateful to him all the same. At the end of the jetty, he had left an old maroon estate car, and Coultan was merrily jangling the keys as he walked towards it. There was no more stalling. I had to accept that I had missed my chance to tell Joe, and now we were on our way to Pisa. We had chosen Pisa in Italy, both for its proximity to the Italian coast – and our island – and because of its one obvious landmark, which we had selected as an ideal spot to make the cash transaction.

Coultan jumped in the driver's seat of the car and Rio climbed in beside him. Joe and I sat in the back, hunched down in the seats so as not to be seen as we made our way towards the main road. It took a while for Coultan to get the hang of the controls of the car, and we bounced around in the back seat. For some reason we found this incredibly funny and started giggling like children, releasing some of the nervous tension inside us and relieving the pain of another bruised knee. It was like being kidnapped all over again, only this time I was in on it – I was one of the bad guys and I had to admit it was kind of fun.

Rio and Coultan gave us a running commentary of the journey across the junctions and along the dual carriageway towards Pisa. All too soon we had reached the city, and the traffic became louder as people hustled and bustled in the late afternoon. Using a printed map, Rio was trying to navigate Coultan to the San Marco Hotel where Joe would be dropped off. After a couple of wrong turns and one-way streets, Coultan managed to park just a few roads away. When it was all clear he got out of the car, grabbed Joe's bag out of the car boot before opening Joe's door. Joe squeezed my shoulder before stepping out of the car.

'Good luck,' he whispered loudly and winked. 'See you soon.' And with that, he was gone. It all happened so quickly. I didn't dare poke my head up to see out of the window, so relied on Rio and Coultan to watch him go. We waited there for about five minutes before pulling away and driving around the block to make sure he was safely inside the hotel.

'Yep, he's in,' Coultan reassured us, and from my dead-legged crouching position I saw the multi-storey hotel looming up above us, so high I was unable to see the sky. This building was just another innocent bystander, yet so crucial to our plan.

Next, it was my turn. We drove a little way back out of Pisa in the direction of the airport. Shortly before getting back onto the main road, Coultan pulled into a deserted back alley before letting me out of the car. The street was empty and silent as Coultan grabbed me and hugged me so close to him that I wanted to cry again. Rio joined us for a three-way hug and I didn't want to let either of them go.

'I'm going to miss you two so much.' I muffled into the hug. To which a tighter squeeze came in response. Yes, these people had kidnapped me and without them I would not be in this position of jeopardy, but ultimately it had been my decision, and if it came to it, I would make the same decision again if I had to for these two, for my friends.

All too soon they were back in the car pulling away, and the street was deserted once more. Except for me.

I stood there for a few minutes, not sure what to do. I had never felt so totally isolated. I was alone in a strange city, in a strange country, with nothing but the clothes I stood up in, a few Euros and some blackmailers' instructions in my bag. I didn't even have a passport. I was already illegal. I shivered, maybe from fear or maybe because the place they'd dropped me in was devoid of all sunlight and eerily cold.

I cautiously walked towards the end of the alley, towards the light, and stepped out into a busy street and the warmth of a summer evening. I turned left in what I had been told was the direction of the airport. After being on the island for so long, my ears were not accustomed to the noise of endless cars as they thundered up and down the busy road, screeching and revving, stopping at traffic lights and loudly beeping at crossing pedestrians. People arged and barged around me, some stopping abruptly in front of me to browse in shop windows while others raced past in tailored suits as they made their way back from work. I found myself suddenly jealous of these people. People who belonged here, who were familiar with these streets from walking up and down them day after day. People who were nearly home, looking forward to relaxing after another un-extraordinary day.

No-one gave me a second glance. I was just another nobody in the crowd, weaving in and out of the other pedestrians – yet I felt like a madwoman as I stumbled my way through, being bumped and jostled and carried along with the tide. It reminded me of a rock concert I had gone to in Wembley Stadium in searing August heat, where I was wedged into the row fourth from the front and was forced to jump up and down constantly, fused to the group of leather jackets that surrounded me.

As I was carried away on my pedestrian wave, I grabbed onto some driftwood in the form of a wooden kiosk selling cigarettes and an abundance of faded postcards of the Leaning Tower. Fortunately, it was also selling cold drinks and maps of the town, so I bought one of each. My Italian was limited to the point of non-existence, but by pointing at the map and shouting 'Coke, *per favore'*, I purchased the said articles.

I crisscrossed my way back along the pavement and towards a

large, imposing church where I perched on a small wall to catch my breath. I opened the map and found the street I was on from what Rio had described, and by locating the big Catholic church I was sitting by.

The airport didn't seem to be too far away, which was lucky as I had no choice but to walk there. We had decided I should ring the police from the airport to throw them off the boat scent and broaden their search. It had seemed like a splendid idea at the time, and looked so easy on paper – such a short distance on the map. Now I was actually on my way in the sticky heat, feeling stressed, along with the increasing tiredness of my flip-flopped feet, I realised I may not have thought this through. As I walked on and on, the noise of the traffic subsided and the number of people I met became fewer and fewer until I was the only one left, walking like an escaped lunatic past green fields with occasional glimpses of the ocean. My hair was once again unruly and gone to frizz, and my clothes were wrinkled and sweaty. The only consolation was that the airplanes were getting lower and lower over my head, indicating that I was heading in the right direction. Steadily, buildings were coming into view, first out-buildings and hangers, some small bi-planes in a field and then the cold wreck of a plane put out to pasture. What a mess that was. I turned away and carried on past the long and short stay car parks and beyond, towards the terminal building and control tower. When I arrived, I half expected to be congratulated and receive a medal for being the only person ever who was stupid enough to walk to the airport.

Now what do I do? I was becoming exceptionally nervous as I stood a little way away from the entrance. Do I want Departures or Arrivals? Well, neither, if I was perfectly honest, but what I did know was that as soon as I stepped through those automatic doors I would be on CCTV. As yet, no-one was there looking for me in PIsa, but once I'd made my call to the police, every tape would be collated and scrutinised.

Ok, you can do it, I told myself but stood rigidly to the spot. *Come on*, I argued with myself, the sooner you do it, the sooner it will be all over. All over. Did I want it to be all over? Did I have a choice? No, you don't have a choice, one voice said, *just do it. Ok, ok,* a second voice was getting stroppy at the first as I straightened my clothes with shaky fingers and took a deep breath.

Chapter Fifteen

Before I knew it, I was walking on jelly legs towards the doors, making my way over the pedestrian crossing along with travellers and their bouncy children and bulging suitcases. Once I was through the automatic doors, I walked towards the bright blue telephone kiosks at the end of the long departure hall. I had to queue. I couldn't believe it. *This never happened in films, queuing to deliver a ransom speech.*

I stood fidgeting nervously, looking every bit the agitated terrorist. I tried to act nonchalant by looking around the hall. Noisy families queued alongside young Italian lovers holding hands and kissing each other at regular intervals. Behind them, a group of five or six girls of about my age chatted and giggled while fanning themselves with their passports. I found myself so envious of these girls. I wanted to be one of them – normally, I would have been. They were excited about their trip, their little wheeled cases obediently at their heels, just room for some stylish shoes, some summer clothes and their make-up. I felt so dowdy just being in the same space as them. As their queue crept forward, I looked up to see where their plane was going. *LONDON GATWICK*, it read on the screen. Tears welled in my eyes and began running down my cheeks. I hadn't realised how much I'd missed England until I saw *LONDON GATWICK DEPARTURE 19:34, ON TIME.*

I was nudged out of my trance by the phone booth door opening and as a man in a suit stepped out, I stepped in, closing the door firmly behind me. I looked into the adjacent booth where a sizeable woman dressed all in black stood with her back to me, and although she was gesturing animatedly with her free hand, I could not hear a word she was saying.

I picked up the receiver and balanced it between my head and shoulder while I opened my purse, took out my instructions and started ploughing coins into the slot. After another deep breath, I dialled the number that was written down in front of me. As the dialling tone beeped, I glanced over at the London queue. The last few people were being checked in and lugging their luggage on to the weighing machine. *How I just wanted to get on that plane …*

At last it was my turn. I dialled the number for Scotland Yard.

'Oh hello,' I stammered as a lady's voice answered the telephone. 'I need to speak to Inspector Mildred.' My voice was shaking.

'Who's calling?' the woman asked breezily.

'Er, Nancy Smart, I'm—'

'Oh yes, I know.' The woman became flustered and shouted away from the phone. 'It's her!' she yelled, 'Nancy Smart!' I heard muffled voices in the background as she attempted to cover the mouthpiece with her hand.

'Nancy?' A man's voice came onto the phone.

'Yes,' I replied. 'Is that Inspector Mildred?'

'Yes, it is. Nancy, are you ok? Are you harmed in any way?'

'Yes, yes, I'm ok,' I stammered, continuing to shake uncontrollably. I turned my back to the glass of the booth so no-one could see the complete and utter terror that must have been on my face.

'Where are you? Are you free?' he asked, inappropriately reminding me of John Inman.

'I-I have something I have to read to you,' I continued.

'Ok, ok, I'm listening Nancy.' I could picture all the other officers in the room, crowded around the phone, taping the call, trying to trace the number. 'Ok.' I started to read …

Inspector Mildred, listen carefully. These are our demands.

The girl and the boy are unharmed and will remain so providing our demands are met. As requested, the sum of one million pounds is to be delivered to us. The money must be converted into the equivalent of used Euro notes. These notes are to be placed inside a plain white, untraceable plastic carrier bag inside a zip-up holdall bag with no tracking device.

You must then wait in your office by your phone at noon tomorrow to await further instructions regarding location. The money must not be traceable in any way. Only when we are satisfied that this is the case, will we release both hostages.

I paused as I folded the piece of paper up and put it back into my pocket. 'Inspector?' I asked, suddenly worried that I'd been speaking to an empty room.

'Yes, yes, I'm here, Nancy. Tell them I understand and it will be done.'

'I have to go now,' I told him and hung up the phone. I struggled to push the heavy door of the phone booth open and stepped back out into the noisy, bustling hall. I noticed that the London flight now said *CHIUSO*, which I assumed meant "closed", and I was suddenly overcome with a pang of fear. I scoured the room, pretending to look for someone, and then proceeded to tie my hair back in a ponytail – a supposed signal to my captors – for the benefit of the CCTV cameras.

Outside in the fresh air, I felt immediate relief that it was all over and I could relax. But then I realised it wasn't really all over at all. This was just the first rung on a very long ladder, and the hardest part was yet to come. I was tired and drained as I prepared for the long walk back into town. It was already dusk and the impending trip worried me. My feet were killing me, and I may as well have been wearing paper plates on my feet for all the comfort my flip-flops gave me. I decided to risk it and take a taxi. I clambered into one waiting at the taxi rank before realising I had no idea where I wanted to go. We had agreed that I would find a small hotel in the town for tonight, but how did I relay that to a grumpy Italian taxi driver?

'Speak English?' I asked, hoping that was a possibility, but the taxi driver just rolled his eyes to the roof of his cab and spouted something long and irritable in Italian.

'Town?' I tried, pointing out the window in the general direction from whence I came. No response. 'Hotel?' I tried. *Surely this was universal?* He asked a question in Italian, which I assumed was "Which one?" but I only knew the name of the San Marco, and I couldn't stay there, or even mention it. What if the police interrogated this crazy Italian taxi driver about where he took me? Instead, I tried option three. 'Tower?' I asked. He still looked blank. 'Leaning Tower?' I pleaded, creating a crude impression of the tower with my hands. *For God's sake, this is bloody Pisa!* I'm sure he knew what I meant but still pretended not to understand clearly just to annoy me, the scruffy English idiot. He succeeded.

It's not as if I exactly had time to study the intricacies of the Italian language before I came! I wanted to shout. I was just about to give up and get out of the cab when I remembered my map. I dragged it out of my bag and pointed to the picture of the tower on the front in luminous Technicolor.

'Ah, Torre!' he said, pretending it had just clicked in his brain and he sped off like a man possessed, jolting me backwards in my seat. It took us just a few minutes to travel the distance that had taken me hours to climb about half an hour earlier. Past the fields and down the busy dual carriageway, screeching and beeping past the formidable church where I had rested, which was now illuminated with large footlights. The shops were closed and the people now strolling down the road were in their best clothes, laughing and enjoying the evening air. I opened my window and the sounds of normal life rushed in. I longed for the time when I would once again share a carefree drink with friends on a summer's evening. The air blowing up in my face was wonderful, and I felt pleasantly cool for what seemed like the first time in days. I closed my eyes to breathe it in for just a second until the taxi lurched to a halt.

'Here, Torre,' said the driver without turning round. Attempting to find the right fare in my foreign money got me all flustered again, and I eventually gave him a 20 Euro note, muttering something about keeping the change and clambering out as quickly as I could. *Hang on a minute*, I thought, *I can't see any tower*!

'Here, Tower?' I asked him through the open window. He again pretended not to understand, although he had certainly seemed to understand 'Keep the change'.

He drove off again at breakneck speed, beeping and screeching for no apparent reason.

'*Bastardo*!' I shouted after his tail lights to make myself feel better, which it did a little. So, where the hell is this bastard tower? I asked myself as I turned around 360 degrees, looking over the top of the surrounding buildings. *Great, he's dropped me in the middle of nowhere*. I knew we hadn't passed the tower so, with absolutely no desire to flag down any more taxis, I ambled down the road in the opposite direction from which I'd come. With no idea of where I was or where I was going, I became increasingly nervy. Nobody in the world knew where I was; not my parents, my friends, Mildred, not even Joe. I could be murdered right here on this strange street and no-one would ever know. It was a scary thought, so I began to walk warily and a little faster, my flip-flops click-clacking conspicuously along the empty street. And then, with a glance down a narrow side street, I saw it. *The Tower*. The street was quaint and cobbled, lined with closed cafés and tiny tourist shops. As I reached the end, it opened out into a large square expanse of grass and directly in front of me, stood the Leaning Tower of Pisa.

I slowly walked towards it as it drew me closer. I imagined it in the daytime, swarming with tourists all eating ice-creams, having their photos taken with the tower, gaily pretending to support it and prevent it from toppling over. I imagined me and Steph here, making jokes, asking some friendly stranger to get a photo of us both, the Tower in the background. I could see the photo now on my wall at home, next to us at the Parthenon or in front of the Pyramids. We would then probably have a picnic on the grass, munching sandwiches we'd just bought from one of the tiny delis while reading our guidebooks.

But now the sun was setting and I was all alone. I came to stop on a bench in front of the Tower, still far enough away to see it in all its quirky glory. I wondered if any other error in engineering had ever been photographed as much as this one.

It was a lot cooler now as the sun dipped lower; the sky turning from blue and orange to pink. I pulled my hooded top from around my waist and wrapped it around me while I drank the last of my Coke and thought of Joe. How I'd like him to be sitting next to me right now, his arm around me, feeling safe and loved. I wondered what we'd have talked about, if anything at all. It was one of the most romantic places I'd ever been, every girl's mini-break dream, and I was alone. Alone and scared. I wanted my bed, I wanted my life back and I wanted Joe.

But he was here, here in this alien city. I could almost feel him near me. I whipped round as a chill ran down my spine, but of course he wasn't there. He would be laying low at the San Marco Hotel, so close and yet so far apart. It was agony.

What the hell had I done? I had lied to the police and then travelled the length and breadth of a strange city on my own in the dark. Who was this person? It couldn't be me. I would never do anything like that. Perhaps it was some drunk nutter who had taken over my body. That's no doubt what the man out walking his dog thought as he passed by me, huddled on a bench, swigging out of my bottle.

By now the sun had disappeared completely, and I headed back towards civilisation. After about ten minutes of walking with no luck of finding a hotel with vacancies, I gave in on my no-more-trying-to-talk-to-Italians resolution and asked a young couple directions to the nearest hotel.

'Hotel?' I tried in my best Italian accent, eyebrows raised to show I was asking a question. This time I got lucky.

'Ah, a hotel,' the girl replied, 'Yes, please,' she said, pointing down a road to the right, bending her fingers at the end to indicate a left turn at the next corner.

'*Grazie,*' I volunteered, pleased that I was making progress, as the couple nodded and continued down the road. I headed in the direction that the girl had directed me, and, sure enough, round the next corner stood an old, but rather grand looking, hotel: a big white, brightly lit building with broad stone steps leading up to the door. *Shit, how much is this gonna cost?* I thought, knowing I only had about 60 Euros on me. As I was thinking twice about entering, I noticed a price list in the window. The lowest price I could see was 40 Euros, and I assumed, rightly or wrongly, that this would be for one night. I closed my eyes briefly. *Please God, please God, let me find a room. I know I'm a sinner but I'm a knackered sinner. Please don't make me sleep on an Italian bench.*

I breathed in deeply and, trying to look as if I belonged there, I marched through the doors and over to the mahogany reception desk. 'One room, *per favore,*' I requested, holding up one finger to assist me.

'Ah yes,' said the tidy looking, bald man behind the desk. 'That will be 40 Euros, please,' he responded in his Italian accent. I scrambled for my money and straightened the notes out neatly before handing them over to the man who was smiling kindly at me.

'Any luggage, madam?' he asked, kindly.

'Er, no, sorry,' I replied, apologetically for some reason. Luckily, he didn't seem to think this was odd, and when he gave me the key and directions to my room, he continued to smile so much, I had to resist the urge to hug him and kiss his shiny head.

'Mucho grazie,' I thanked him heartily before turning towards the lift which he had called for me. The lift was old and rattly with those metal fretwork gates that you had to pull manually across. I'd always wanted to travel in one of these lifts – odd that I was doing it now in this strangest of situations.

When I was absolutely sure that the lift had stopped and would not jerk itself any further, I yanked back the double doors and stepped out on to the empty landing. My room was halfway down the corridor. I turned the key, stepped inside and closed the door firmly behind me.

I woke up to shafts of sunlight streaming through the curtains and wondered where the hell I was. The room looked kind of familiar, and then I remembered – the white hotel, the smiley concierge and the rattly lift – and my heart slowed down to normality again. I looked at my watch. *Ten o'clock, good, I'd got a couple of hours yet.* The night before I had just taken off my clothes, laid down on the oh-so-comfy bed and dropped straight to sleep. I hadn't even had my longed-for shower or ordered anything to eat. I now swung myself heavily out of bed and crept towards the window. As I was still just wearing my pants, I only opened the curtain enough to stick my head out and wrapped the rest around me to preserve my modesty. I threw open the window to let in the fresh morning air.

The light was bright, and lots of people were milling around in and out of tourist shops and drinking cappuccinos in pavement cafés below. As I looked up, I could see the Tower looming up from beyond the rooftops, it's white stone gleaming in the sunlight, and ant-like people swarming around the uppermost balcony. *I bet they are hot*, I thought, but still wished I was one of them on their free-and-easy holidays, all the same. I watched the picturesque scene in front of me for a while longer before peeling myself away and heading into the bathroom. I could still hear the chatter and bustle of the world outside and although I still felt alone, these sounds of life comforted me. As the shower trickled onto my skin, I became more invigorated, positive and ready to face the task ahead. *I'm not alone, I thought. I'm an independent woman. I'm on a mission, and ... I will see Joe later*, I added, which made me smile to myself. I even began a rendition of 'That's Amore', which I'm ashamed to say was the only semi-Italian song I knew, barring 'Just One Cornetto', however stereotyped that was. I sang because I was full of confidence, because I had proper shampoo and because I didn't want to think about the fact that seeing Joe later today would mean it would be the last time ever that I would.

I was slightly disappointed to note that there was no hairdryer in the hotel and that I would have to let it dry naturally yet again, but I guessed it was for the best to look rough, so I dried it with a towel and raked my fingers through it, exactly as I had done for the last two weeks.

I checked my watch. *Eleven o'clock.* I still had an hour. I made myself a cup of coffee with the little kettle and coffee sachets in my room and pulled the comfy chair up to the open window. I sat wrapped in my towel, drying naturally in the gentle summer breeze and drinking my coffee. I liked it here – in fact, I would have loved to stay longer, had it not been for the little bit of business I had to take care of and the knot that the thought of it caused in my stomach.

After a second cup of coffee, I finally dragged my clothes back on and tried to smooth out some of the wrinkles. If I'd been more with it last night, I would have stuck them in the trouser press – although, knowing me, I would have burnt them to a crisp and been forced to wander the streets of Pisa in a hotel sheet or, even worse, stark naked. But at least I was dressed and, once again, ready to face the day and all the unpredictability it would bring. The beauty of being a kidnap victim on your own in the middle of a foreign country was that you could pack light, and it didn't take long to stick my purse and my map in my bag. This was it – the day of reckoning was upon me. I took a deep breath and reached for the door handle just as there was a knock on the other side of the door. I froze, my heart pounded and my mouth went dry. Shit, was it the police? Had they found me? What to do? I looked at the window but quickly decided against Spiderman-ing it down the drainpipe. Instead, I decided to face whoever it was. I took a few steps back before answering as casually as I could, '*Si?*'

The door opened slowly and a young Italian chambermaid peered round with a basket of cleaning products and an armful of fresh towels. 'Ah, *si, si.*' I gestured for her to come in as I made my way out behind her and through the door, breathing an enormous sigh of relief on the other side. I bumped and jolted down in the old rattly lift and emerged back in the marbled foyer. I looked over to say goodbye to the smiley concierge, but he had been replaced by a sour-faced but beautiful woman who looked me up and down as I put my key on the counter, before continuing what she had been doing on her computer.

Back down the stone steps and out into the bustling alley I went, turning left towards the main street in search of a phone box for the next part of my mission. I didn't have to walk far before I could see a cluster of them on the corner of a major shopping thoroughfare.

They were all empty, so I chose the one furthest away from the crowds, on the edge of the pavement. The cars were as loud as ever, but inside the booth the noise was drowned out enough to make my call. Again, I took my instructions from my purse along with several coins, which I slotted into the phone. I dialled the number, and almost as soon as the ring started someone picked up.

'Nancy?' It was the voice of Inspector Mildred.

'Er … yes … yes, it's me,' I spluttered.

'Are you ok?' he asked, clearly concerned.

'Yep, I'm fine,' I answered, sounding a bit too chipper, so I added a little more wearily, 'I'm ok.' Well, at least I hadn't followed it with something like, 'Just fine and dandy, and how's you?' like I normally would have done.

'I have the money right here, Nancy,' he continued. 'A million pounds converted into used Euro notes. What do you want me to do with it? Where do you want me to take it?' He was kind of stepping on my lines a bit, but I decided not to hold that against him.

'Erm, I'm in Italy,' I said. 'In Pisa.' I detected movement and scuffling down the other end of the phone as if a team of officers had already sprung into action. 'I have to tell you to get the next plane out here and meet me at five-thirty English time, in front of the Leaning Tower, just you and the money. They said to tell you that they'll be watching, and if you bring anyone else or have any surveillance, well then, me and Mark, well … me and Mark …' I didn't know how to end it without sounding silly. *What should I say*? 'Will get it,' or 'will die,' or should I go with *The Godfather*'s, 'will be sleeping with the fishes?' It all sounded wrong, so I was relieved when Mildred jumped in.

'I understand, Nancy. I'll be there on time with the money.'

'Ok,' I replied.

'Where are you going to be for the next few hours, Nancy?' he continued, but I immediately hung up the phone. I didn't want to exchange more pleasantries than I had to, plus I didn't actually know what I was going to be doing for the next few hours. *Well, I guess I can start by getting something to eat*, I thought, feeling a tad peckish. By now I had got some of my bearings, and I headed back towards the tourist shops and cafés I had passed on my way to the phone. On the way I stopped at a newspaper stand where an British red-top newspaper caught my eye. I bought it and tucked it under my arm. Then I found a a small café which still had some empty tables outside. The menu was in Italian and English, so I ordered myself a pizza and Diet Coke without too much trouble, and I settled down to read my paper and wait for it to arrive.

Reading through the headlines, I felt a pang of homesickness: a popstar had been caught with cocaine, some crazy one-hit-wonder was storming the charts and a man from Battersea swore he had seen tiny aliens landing in his birdbath. It was enjoying reading trivia like this that made me English, and I smiled at the thought of being home soon. But then I turned the page and gasped – because staring back at me was a very familiar face. It was me! Well, the me of about five years ago anyway. It was my graduation photo – me in a mortarboard and gown, holding my degree. Next to my picture was one of a thin and weedy boy of about sixteen, in what seemed to be a school photograph. It was Mark. But this was the miserable, pale-faced boy I had met at the airport, not the lithe, tanned, laughing Mark I had seen emerge over the past couple of weeks. Above the photos, the headline read:

GIANT HEIR & NANCY SMART – WORRIES DEEPEN AS NO NEWS RECEIVED

Chapter Sixteen

The article underneath went on to say that as no demands had been made and no further news had been received, the police were fearing the worst for our lives. I checked the date. *Two days ago.* I wondered if anything had been printed since then about my phone call and the demands made for the money, I also wondered why my mum had given them that picture of me – surely they had a more recent one, a nice one of me tanned on holiday, perhaps?

I was reading the article for a second time when the waiter arrived with my lunch, and I quickly turned the paper over as if there was any possibility whatsoever that he would make the connection between the smiling graduate on the page and the dishevelled British girl at the table in front of him. I very much doubted it but kept my sunglasses on and my head down just in case.

My pizza tasted good. Whether it was because it was an authentic homemade Italian pizza eaten alfresco at a pizzeria or whether it was because I had barely eaten anything since I'd arrived in Pisa almost twenty-four hours ago, it was hands down the best pizza I had ever tasted. What I needed was a nice bottle of Italian red to wash it down with, but decided getting pissed was probably not a good idea at this juncture in time.

After I'd wolfed it down, I let my stomach settle and scanned the rest of the paper. My horoscope read: *Life seems a little dull for you at the moment. Treat yourself to some new shoes and buy some sensual massage oil to perk up your man.* This only proved further to me that horoscopes were full of shit. Then again, it was hardly going to read: *You'll find yourself in Italy this weekend after spending a couple of weeks kidnapped on a Spanish Island. Try to keep your spirits up by lying to the police and helping the man you've fallen in love with build a holiday condo with the ill-gotten gains.* It would have been accurate, but unlikely all the same.

I still had some time to kill and needed to stretch my legs. I wandered over towards the Baptistery, a church on the same site as the Tower, doing my best to blend in with the tourists, although very aware I looked different because I had no camera to take photographs with and because I seemed to be the only person on my own. Every so often I peered round, craning my neck to pretend to be looking for someone. I was trying to make it appear that I was being watched by my perpetrators and did not have the liberty to roam free and talk to strangers.

Inside, the church was cool and dark in the places that the sun streaming through the many windows didn't reach. It was nice to stroll around its walls quietly, away from the excited throng outside. Although there were people present, it was lovely and peaceful, with the respectful silence and whispers you only find in churches. The tablets and plaques were all written in Latin, which emphasised the age and prominence of each piece. I stayed in the Baptistery for a while, enjoying its serenity and comforting presence before dropping a few spare coins into the collection box and re-emerging into the bright sunlight and bustle of the crowds.

I walked the perimeter of the tower but decided against climbing its three hundred steps. Instead, I retreated to one of the cafés nearby where I was able to observe the braver souls attempt the climb from the comfort of a wicker chair with a cappuccino in my hand. I whiled away the rest of the time at the café. With my dark hair and tanned skin, I wondered if anyone would think I was a real Italian, looking demure and cosmopolitan drinking my coffee. But then I realised that no self-respecting Italian would probably come anywhere near this tourist trap unless they worked here, and if they did, there was no way they would dress as shabbily as me, with no make-up and wind-dried hair.

At about a quarter past five I paid my bill and found the bench I had sat on the previous night. There was an old man with a cane sitting at one end, and I smiled at him as I sat down at the other end. He gave a small salute to acknowledge me, and I immediately put him down as an old war hero. He wasn't there for long as a lady of about his age arrived carrying two ice creams, and then they walked away, licking as they went. So, I was alone on my bench once more. It was still late afternoon, so it wasn't as dark or cold as it had been the last time I had sat there, and I hoped I would be easy for Mildred to spot. I was far enough away from other people so they wouldn't hear our conversation, but near enough that my story about being under surveillance was plausible.

I scanned the surrounding scene, looking for anyone who could potentially be Mildred. I was expecting a shirt and tie and maybe a leather jacket to be smart, but still attempt to keep a semblance of cool youth vibe. I was right about the shirt and tie, but there was no jacket. I spotted him immediately after he came around the corner. Holdall in hand, big and sweating in the heat of Pisa sun and no doubt the pressure of the situation he now found himself in. As far as I could see, he had come alone as requested, but I suspected there would be more than one undercover officer submerged somewhere amongst the crowds. I had seen enough cop shows to understand the possibility that I was being filmed by some long lens surreptitiously sticking out of a bush somewhere. It was now time to start acting my ass off.

I sat up straight and tried to look impassive as Mildred advanced.

'Nancy?' he asked as soon as he was within earshot.

'Yes. Inspector Mildred?'

'Yes, yes,' he replied as he caught his breath and sat down on the bench next to me. I moved away slightly to leave a gap, to show I was nervous and a little edgy.

'Are you ok?' he asked.

'Yes, yes, I'm fine,' I answered wearily. 'I'm glad you came.'

'Of course. I'm sorry you've been put in such an awful situation,' he said sympathetically.

'Me too,' I replied and made myself sound so miserable, tears actually sprang to my eyes. Fantastic. I turned to face Mildred and gave him the full benefit of my acting skills.

'Are you on your own?' I asked, nervously looking around.

'Yes,' he replied. 'I did everything as you said. I have the money in a plastic bag in used notes in this holdall, and I'm definitely alone.' After a slight pause, he added, 'Are you wired?'

'Me? No.' I shook my head. 'But they are watching, they said they would be. They could be anywhere.' I brought my legs up to my chest on the bench and hugged my knees to prove I was scared, like a hedgehog balling up against the outside world.

'It's ok, you're going to be fine, Nancy. You'll be just fine.' He continued to talk while he lit a cigarette and offered me one. I shook my head. 'Thing is Nancy …' he said, not looking at me but staring straight ahead. 'Thing is, I want you to come back with me now, so you're safe.'

Luckily, we had planned for this. 'No. I-I-I can't, what about Mark? They said that if I didn't do exactly what they said, they'd … well, they'd …' I was all fidgety because of genuine nerves, which I hoped was adding to the authenticity.

'I know, kill him,' Mildred finished, which shocked me and I shot him a look. 'Sorry, sorry Nancy, I didn't mean … Mark will be just fine.'

'How do you know that?' I asked.

'Well, if you come with us, it'll only be a matter of time before we pick Mark up.'

I felt a rise of panic. 'Do you know where he is?' I tried to sound more hopeful and less worried.

'No, I've got to say not yet, but I have my best officers on this and we have a few leads. Once you give us some information, I'm sure we'll find him without too much problem.'

'I can't take that chance, sir.' I added the "sir" to show him I respected him and to confirm that I was just the innocent victim in this. I checked my watch. 'My time's nearly run out,' I said quickly. I needed to hurry things along and get myself out of this situation as soon as possible before I blew it. 'I have to do this. I'm too scared not to, you understand?' I pleaded with my worried looking eyes but didn't want to mention the money until he did for fear of looking too eager.

'I do understand, Nancy, I do. And I want you to know that you're no longer alone. We'll be with you every step of the way.'

'That's good news, thank you. Does the money have some sort of bug or tracking device?' I asked innocently, as if I'd never thought of it before.

'No, we didn't want to risk that, but now we have confirmation of where you are we won't let you out of our sight until we catch these men, ok?' he said, patting my shoulder. My eyes filled up again and I nodded in relief, wiping the tears away in an obvious way with the heels of my hand, hoping I looked as convincingly wretched as I was trying to. 'It'll all be ok. You'll be home soon enough.'

I continued to nod as if unable to speak without crying. 'And Mark?' I spluttered. 'Yes, Mark too. We won't do anything to jeopardise him.'

'Promise?' I pleaded with what I hoped was my little-girl-lost face and it seemed to work.

'I promise you that, Nancy.' He pulled the bag up to the bench and put it between us. He unzipped it and pulled back the carrier bag inside. 'See? Exactly as you said: used Euro notes, untraceable, no indelible ink, no tracking device.'

I peered inside and saw wads of money, more money than I had ever seen in one place at any one time in my life, and tried desperately not to smile. Instead, I covered my emotions with an enormous sigh and wiped some non-existent sweat from my brow. I stood up and picked up the bag that was heavier than it looked.

'I'm to keep the money with me at all times and you are not to contact me until I am released. They will be watching.' I tried my best to sound convincing.

'Ok, Nancy. I hear you. We'll stay at a safe distance, but will be here if you need us. You still have my number?'

'Yes, thank you. I have to go.'

'Can you tell me anything to help us before you go, Nancy?' Mildred urged.

I looked up sharply and scoured the surrounding scene. 'I don't know much,' I said hurriedly, then by putting my hand casually over my mouth as if coughing, I continued. 'Staying here tonight, train to Venice tomorrow,' I mumbled to show I didn't want anyone reading my lips.

'Good girl, Nancy, good girl.' Mildred stood up to watch me go. I tried to smile with my mouth while keeping my eyes sad and desperate. He smiled sympathetically back at me. I turned my back and off I walked, desperately trying to repress the sense of relief inside me when I really wanted to skip with delight and shout woooo hoooo! *What an acting performance*. Steph could learn a thing or two from me.

I hoiked the bag with me back down the alley that had become so familiar to me, past the café where I'd had my lunch, past the stone steps of the hotel with the smiley concierge and back out into the main street with all the day-to-day hubbub of Italian life. Many of the shops had now closed and most people were heading for home after a day's work or looking for a place to eat. I checked my purse to see if there was enough money left for a taxi, which was ironic considering I was carrying a bag holding over a million Euros in cash. I had seven Euros and some change, so figured this would be enough to take me the short distance along the main road to the San Marco Hotel. I hailed down a taxi like a native and told the driver my destination as he sped off into the line of traffic. Out of the back window I checked to see if Mildred was behind me, but I was unable to spot him. I guessed I was being followed covertly just the same; they were experts at this after all.

The familiar sight of the San Marco Hotel loomed up in front of us, and the taxi pulled right into the hotel driveway. I thanked the driver and emptied my purse into his hands. He didn't argue, so I assumed it was enough and climbed the hotel steps as he U-turned out of the drive. Staring up at the myriad of windows above me, I thought I saw a figure several floors up, looking back at me, but I couldn't be sure through the reflection of the sky and the pinks and golds of the setting sun.

Inside, the hotel was not as homely as my last one, but just as clean. At the desk, I mentioned the name that the room had been booked under a few days earlier and hoped that this would be enough to get my keys. Luckily, the smart-looking lady behind the counter didn't seem to be of the chatty variety, and without further ado I had the keys and was heading in the direction of the elevator. My heart was beating so hard I thought I was having palpitations, my hands were sweaty and my whole body was shaking. The police would be hot on my tail behind me, and I hoped Joe was in front of me; it would be the first time I'd seen him in what felt like weeks or months rather than days … and the last time I would see him forever.

The lift arrived – thankfully, it was empty – and I pressed the button for the top floor and my room. As the lift ascended, I tried to smooth my hair, but it was no good; there was no time and no hope of making my appearance any better. On the sixth floor, the lift stopped. I could hardly breathe, my chest was so tight. The doors slowly opened and there was Joe. He was dressed in tennis shorts and T-shirt, a white sweatshirt slung over his shoulders like a pro. He looked good. He saw me and smiled before jumping into the lift beside me.

'Hi,' he said almost shyly. 'Everything go ok?'

My throat was dry. 'Yeah, yes, fine, like clockwork,' I croaked.

He gave me the smile I had fallen in love with, and I pressed the button to hold the doors open to stop anyone else calling the lift, keeping an eye out down the corridor. Joe quickly unzipped the holdall and swapped the contents of cash over to his sports bag, shoving the pillow from his bag into mine. 'Almost forgot,' he said. Before closing his bag, he grabbed a handful of cash and shoved it back into my holdall for expenses as planned. 'There, done,' he announced, slinging the sports bag full of cash over his shoulder and jumping out of the lift.

'Ok.' I stepped back in. I didn't want to leave, but as time was of the essence, we had to go.

'Good luck,' he said, giving me the quickest of pecks on my hot cheek, and then he seemed to think better of it and kissed me on the lips. It was all too brief and over in a second.

The lift doors closed.

'Nance—' I heard just before the doors sealed shut, preventing any more sound, and, once again, just like with Danny Greenslade in the library, I was left not knowing the end of an enormously crucial sentence. Wow, I was shocked to realise I hadn't thought about Danny Greenslade since I was at the airport, that now seemed another world away.

My lift carried on its merry way up to floor twelve where it stopped, and me and my holdall turned left towards room 1212. I was glad to get inside the room and lock the door behind me. My last mission for today was to place the holdall in the window in full view of the outside world. I walked over to the other side of the room where the window was and placed the bag on the windowsill for all to see.

I saw through the window that I had a small balcony, but I decided not to go out – just in case. Instead, I observed the activity out of the window. People were coming and going about their business – some of the comings would be undercover police, and as several cars arrived from all directions, and information was swapped over mobile phones and walkie-talkies, nobody battered an eye at the tanned Italian-looking man, dressed in white tennis clothes as he jogged casually out of the hotel gates, giving a quick glance back before turning left down the road, his sports bag slung casually over his shoulder.

I still had a long way to go on my journey of deception, but for tonight I had a temporary reprieve. With the bag firmly wedged on the windowsill, I closed the curtains behind it. The hotel room bathroom was all in white and had a bath with complimentary toiletries. I turned on the taps and sat on the edge pouring in the bath oil, watching the bubbles sparkle. While I waited for the bath to fill right up to the top, I quickly rinsed my underwear in the sink. There was no way my skirt and top would dry in time, but I hoped at least my smalls would dry in tomorrow's early morning sun.

I stepped into the bath, and the warm water felt wonderful after the dust and heat of the day. As I immersed my sticky body, I felt more relaxed than I had in days. I ducked my head under and let the clear water cover me, listening to my heart beating in my ears – now back to a nice, steady normal rhythm. I lay in the bath until my fingers turned wrinkly, relaying the day back through my mind. It was unbelievable that so far everything had gone according to our crazy, haphazard amateur plans. I felt guilty at having goodness knows how many British and Italian police running around after me, although I figured they would be getting paid after all. It might even make a nice change for the British police to come over to Italy – they might even have time to pop over and see the Leaning Tower while they were here. It would be a nice story to tell their friends.

The main thing I felt bad about was what my family and friends would be going through. My parents would be in agony waiting by the phone twenty-four hours a day for any news, and Steph would be worried sick, crying and eating too much comfort food. If she got fat, it would all be my fault. I tried to lift my mood by imagining their faces when they found out that their worst fears were not realised after all, that I was safe. I visualised us hugging and crying when I arrived home. The end was near and that, at least, was a comfort.

The only knot I had in my stomach now was the one tied around the memory of Joe. He was gone for good. What I'd experienced with him was so unexpected, but in the face of adversity we'd found something we hadn't been looking for. The days we had shared we could never get back, and I wouldn't even be able to tell anyone about them. Eventually, they would fade in my memory as if they'd never really happened at all. I lay a cold flannel across my face to cool the burning tears on my cheeks. Snapshots of him flooded into my head: the first time I'd seen his blue eyes when he brought in our supper and I'd acted like a right stroppy little madam, him and Coultan drunk and disorderly, the time he thought I'd drowned and our many conversations down by the shore, the nights we'd spent together on the boat and in our hammocks, and then just now in the lift. No proper goodbye, no time for tenderness, no time for "I love you". He was so familiar to me now; his puzzled frown, his smile, his laugh. I knew I had to snap myself out of this and be back on track by tomorrow, but tonight I let myself wallow in my sadness and thoughts of what might have been. *And wonder just what was it that he'd wanted to say before the lift doors had closed?*

Chapter Seventeen

The water had become cold now, and I dragged my prune-like body out of the bath, wrapping myself in a big towel and using another one to wrap up my hair. It felt good to be cool and clean again. I now just had to do something about my hunger; it seemed a long time ago since I'd stuffed myself with pizza and thought I'd never have to eat again. I found a room-service menu and called down to order a tuna sandwich to prove I wasn't living extravagantly with the ransom money. The woman on the other end seemed a little wary and spoke with hesitation, as if she was being told what to say. I guessed the call would be taped or at least have police listening into it, so I spoke quickly and with no emotion. While I waited for my sandwich, I found a hotel dressing-gown hung up in the wardrobe and wrapped it comfortably around me before arranging my washed undies over the back of the chair, ensuring it was pointed towards the curtained window. *Hooray, I'd even found a hairdryer! Hello Mr Hairdryer, I've missed you!* What a luxury it was to dry my hair into something resembling a style. There was a knock at the door. I took a deep breath, put on my nervous face (which under the circumstances was not difficult) and opened the door only slightly.

'Room service,' said the woman outside, who had dark hair but a distinct English look about her.

'Thank you,' I said as I reached out to take the plate from her hand.

'You're welcome,' she replied slowly, her eyes darting past me into the room as if looking for something.

'Thank you,' I said again, signalling for her to leave so I could close the door again. She gave me a last quick once-over, and then left me to re-lock the door as she no doubt returned to report her findings.

It seemed wrong to watch television, but there was a TV set, and I felt I needed it on for a bit of company, to engage my brain and stop the turmoil going around in my head about Joe. I turned it on and flicked through the channels until I found something in English. Alas, all I could find was a back-to-back rerun of the old sitcom *Last of the Summer Wine*. I hadn't seen one of these in years, and I snuggled under the covers to watch while munching on my enormous plate of tuna sandwiches. I wondered if all the guests got that much tuna or if it was just the ones under police surveillance.

After seeing Compo get "broomed" by Nora Batty for the umpteenth time, I finally turned it off and lay down to get some sleep. As I lay there with my eyes closed, the only sound the muffled noise of traffic on the road outside, I pictured the scene miles away. As I hadn't been "rescued" or arrested yet, I could only assume that everything with the other guys was going according to plan. Coultan and Rio would have picked up Joe and swiftly driven down the coast road towards Monaco, the bag of money stashed somewhere between them. They would be laughing and, if I knew Coultan, desperate to crack open a bottle of celebratory rum, commenting on how they couldn't believe they'd got away with it and rejoicing in their newfound wealth.

It had been over four hours since I had seen Joe disappear with the money, and by now they would be well on their way. They may even be there by now. Coultan would get dressed in all his lavish colours and Rio would look like an exotic princess in her new dress. They would gamble high in one, maybe two, casinos before splitting the cash and banking it in their various bank accounts. With the bag of pretend ransom money sitting in full view on my windowsill, the police had no reason to look in the direction of Monte Carlo, let alone suspect the wealthy Jamaicans with their broad smiles and infectious laughter. They would be ok, I knew that; I had no doubt they would pull it off, raising no suspicions, charming everyone they met.

While they were gambling, Joe would be alone waiting for them. The plan was he would act the part of their chauffeur. He would have changed out of the sportswear and dressed in a smart grey suit, wishing he was back in his old comfortable shorts and T-shirt. Maybe he'd be sitting in the car listening to the radio, or maybe in a hotel room, getting ready to leave for the casino. Maybe he would be thinking about me. Seeing him today was fantastic and torturous all rolled into one. Close enough to touch but no time for a proper kiss or even a hug; he was right there in front of me but might as well have been a million miles away.

I must have been tired because I didn't wake up the next morning until 9:30. *Shit! They'll all be wondering what I'm doing, having a lie-in as if I'm on holiday.* I got up quickly and dressed in my clean, but still slightly damp, clothes, sinking half a cup of sachet coffee as I went. *Right, I have to go now.* I opened the curtains wide and was nearly blinded by the sun, already bright in the sky and reflecting off the expanse of winding river in front of me. I grabbed the holdall and, feigning its heaviness, heaved it down off the windowsill. I stashed the money that Joe had given me into my purse and left the room, hurrying back towards the lift.

I had the lift to myself again as I descended to the ground floor, and who knew what was waiting for me there? In the foyer there were several people milling around, some reading newspapers, others standing casually at the pay phones. *Which ones are watching me?* I scanned their faces for signs of recognition, but they were giving nothing away. At the check-out desk, I handed over my keys and was presented with a bill for my room and the tuna sandwich, like any other paying guest. And, like any other paying guest, I handed over my cash and left. Back down the steps I went, hailing down yet another cab, hoisting my "heavy" bag into the back seat with me and instructing the driver to take me towards the railway station. Behind me, several more cars kicked into action and soon we were leading a discreet cavalcade along the carriageways of Pisa.

At the station, I bought a one-way ticket to Venice and headed towards the listed platform. In the twenty minutes I had to wait, many people joined me: tourists, Venetians and, I assumed, more undercover police officers. I stood, nervous and fidgety, the holdall firmly wedged between my feet. Eventually, the train arrived and I clambered aboard with the other passengers. I found a seat next to the window and dragged the bag onto my lap, wrapping my arms around it, holding it close. The journey to Venice passed through such beautiful scenery, it was easy to forget why I was there. We flew past farms and villages, olive trees and vineyards, children playing and waving at the train as we flew past. Tuscany was stunning, so green and fertile. The lull of the rhythmic wheels on the tracks, de-dung, de-dung, de-dung-ing along, made me sleepy and more than once I felt my eyes close against the sun and my head droop till it was almost resting on the bag. *I must not fall asleep!* I told myself. What if the police thought I was too relaxed? Or even worse, I missed my stop at Venice? Or worse still, someone nicked my bag?

After a long six hours and one quick change over we reached Venice station. I was dying for a pee but hadn't dared to leave my seat during the journey to go to the loo. Instead, I prolonged the agony. I just had to get rid of the bag once and for all.

Another day, another Italian city where I didn't belong. Another hail to another taxi and another request to take me to yet another hotel. This time it was the Hotel Cavalieri which was just a hop, skip and a jump from the station. Here the nice taxi driver offered to carry my bag. I very impolitely declined in no uncertain terms, which I felt bad about, so tipped him an extra ten Euros. I strolled into the hotel to make sure that the police had time to catch me up. Lo-and-behold, I heard cars screech to a halt behind me but I kept walking forwards towards the check-in desk.

This time it was a young boy behind the counter who seemed more interested in the Italian soap opera on the TV than in me. He just gave me the room key and continued what he was doing. Yet again there was a lift – four of them to be precise. I pressed all the "up" buttons, but it was the one on the right that reached me first. This time it was the tenth floor, and the room was down a winding corridor which seemed to end up in the bowels of the hotel. At last, there was my room, tucked away in the corner. It had seemed a long way to pretend to carry my heavy bag.

The Cavalieri, like the San Marco before it, had been meticulously researched to ensure there were no signs of CCTV, and, as far as I could see, this was luckily the case. The booking had been made over the telephone with top-floor rooms requested to accommodate our plan.

Inside the room, I quickly pulled the pillow out of the bag and shoved it on a high shelf in one of the wardrobes. I left the bag unzipped and open and the door on the latch. I then ran out of the room, down in the next available lift, and back out into the small car park at the front of the hotel. Adrenaline was buzzing inside me, and I ran and ran until I reached the front road entrance. There I doubled over while I tried to catch my breath.

I looked around to see if I could locate Inspector Mildred. Sure enough, there he was, red-faced and running towards me. I cried with the relief of it all. I'd gone over this moment many times in my head and it all felt strangely unreal.

'Nancy, are you ok? What happened? Where's the money? What have they done to you? Are you ok?' he was asking question after question, as I tried to get my breath back.

'They told me to leave the bag … in the … in the room.' I handed him the key I still had clutched in my hand. 'They said once I'd done that I was free to go.'

Mildred shouted orders in various directions and swarms of undercover police officers appeared, some seemingly from nowhere, and ran towards the hotel. 'It's ok, it's ok, it's all over now, it's all over now.' He put his arms around me and rocked me gently from side to side to comfort me as I cried genuine tears of relief. He was so nice and soothing, I cried even more for deceiving him the way I had. I was a bad person and he was nothing but kind to me.

A voice came over his walkie-talkie. 'Inspector?'

'Yep?' Mildred replied.

'Inspector, we've found the bag, but it's empty. We've sent agents to cover all the exits and entrances, but as yet there's no sign of them or the cash.'

'Well, keep looking!' he bellowed back, before apologising for shouting in my ear. After I had calmed down and my tearful convulsions had reduced to mere sobs, Mildred put me in a police car with a female detective who, judging by her Millets-style couture, was more English than Italian, and spoke to me as if I were a five-year-old.

'Now then, we're just going to take you back to the police station, ok? And then we'll get you something nice to eat, ok?' She was nice and meant well, so I nodded my thanks and continued to stare out of the window. *So, this was Venice, huh?* From the window of a speeding police car, it looked delightful – pity there was no time for sightseeing.

We wove down narrow streets and over bridges, the canals beneath us stretching into the distance, and round corners between the classical Venetian townhouses and hotels. This unique city had been the centre of art, culture and deviant pleasure for centuries, her hedonistic opulence had been the chosen home of the likes of Lord Byron, Shelley and Casanova, inspiring poetry, painting and theatre, and today she still attracted culture hounds and romantics to ride in her gondolas and explore her piazzas.

Of course, I missed all this as I was escorted by Venice's Finest to the local nick. Despite being a police station, it was in keeping with the rest of the Venetian buildings; it's yellowing stone walls and classical architecture could be mistaken for a small theatre – a far cry from the square concrete buildings usually associated with the British cop shops. I was guided down hallways and into what appeared to be some sort of interview room which was nicer than any I had pictured – no plastic chairs and lone swinging light bulb. Perhaps they kept those for the worst Venetian "perps".

I had forgotten for a moment that, as far as they knew, I hadn't committed a crime; I was innocent and they just wanted to ask me some questions. While we waited for Inspector Mildred, I asked if I could go to the toilet. In the excitement at the hotel, I had forgotten how desperate I was, but it had now returned with full force. The female police officer from the car quickly guided me to the ladies', and I felt the relief that only going to the toilet with a full bladder can bring. I was now ready to face the world once more.

As I washed my hands in the small basin, I checked out my reflection – blimey I still looked rough despite the obvious tanning and the use of a hairdryer the previous night. The heat, the busy train and the tears had once again taken their toll. I guessed that was for the best in the long run, avoiding the whole glamorous Bond girl/gangster's moll stereotype. Nevertheless, I couldn't wait to be reunited with my faithful eyeliner and my good old hair straighteners.

Ok, this is it, I now have to lie through my teeth, yet again. I can do this, I can do this. It'll be just like phoning in for a sick day at work. It's uncomfortable at first, but so worth it in the end. I straightened up and took a deep breath. *Bring it on, I'm ready for you!*

Back in the little room, Mildred was waiting for me. They had brought in some real Italian coffee and some pastries that smelled yummy and comforting. I sat on one end of a leather sofa and tucked in greedily like I hadn't eaten for weeks, and the Inspector and Police Officer looked at each other sympathetically.

'So, Nancy—' Mildred sat down in the comfy chair opposite me '—how are you?'

'I'm ok,' I said with a mouthful of something flaky with chocolate in it.

'Yeah?'

'Yes, really, I'm ok now … just tired and a little shell-shocked. I'm just glad to be here and safe.' I put down the pastry. I added that last bit to stop me from sounding too glib.

'Good, good, that's good.' Mildred sat smiling and nodding at me. His English cheeks were rosy where he had gained a little colour from the sun as he'd scampered across Italy in pursuit of me and my pillow.

'Have you spoken to my mum and dad?' I asked.

'Yes, yes, they've been informed that you're safe and well. They're obviously very relieved – you can speak to them yourself shortly, and you'll see them tomorrow when we take you home.'

Tears welled in my eyes. *My poor parents. What on earth had I done to them?*

'Have you found Mark yet?' I asked, almost forgetting that I was supposed to be fraught with anxiety about his well-being.

'Not yet, but don't you worry – I'm sure it's only a matter of time now,' he said, trying to calm me.

'I hope so,' I said. 'I guess the kidnappers have got what they wanted, so they've no reason to hold him any longer.' I looked into Mildred's eyes while I said this to see if I could uncover any indication as to what he knew.

All he said was, 'Yes, that's right, I'm sure he'll be fine, one way or another.'

At least I knew that if they hadn't found him yet, they hadn't discovered the boat or the island and the others were safe.

'Ok, Nancy, I know it's been a long day for you, but we need to ask you some questions. We want to make sure we get Mark home safe, and we need to catch these bastards. Are you up to it?'

'Yes, sure,' I said. It seemed preferable to get it over with and avoid another night of worrying.

'Ok, now I need to set this tape recorder running,' he said, starting a little 80s-style tape recorder on the coffee table in front of us. 'It's nothing for you to worry about, it's just so we don't miss anything, ok?'

'Fine,' I answered.

Just then there was a knock, and a baby-faced officer stuck his head around the door. 'Inspector?' he asked, and Mildred got up to speak to him.

'Sorry, Nancy. I won't keep you a minute,' he said before disappearing out of the door behind the young officer.

I was left with the British police woman. 'He won't be long,' she told me, switching off the tape recorder and pouring out more coffee.

'Thanks,' I said as she handed me a cup.

'I'm Barbara,' she added.

'Thanks, Barbara. I'm Nancy,' I responded rather stupidly 'But of course you already know that.'

She smiled at me. 'I think everyone in England knows your name, and probably in Italy too for that matter,' she said, sipping her coffee.

'What?' I said, taken aback a little.

'You've been the talk of the town, on every TV programme, in every newspaper.'

'Really? How did they know?' Had I actually been stupid enough to assume it would have been a minor story, resigned to the middle pages of the paper?

'What? Do you think Max Cheriton's son could get kidnapped and no-one would find out? This is England we're talking about, you know what the papers are like.'

'And they know all about me?'

'Of course. You'll be a real-life celebrity when you get back home.'

'But I don't want to be.' I panicked. I didn't like the idea of being the centre of attention. That was Steph's domain.

'I'm pretty sure you won't have a choice, love. You'll be on *Richard and Judy* before you know it.' She smiled knowingly, as if this was her idea of the pinnacle of fame. All I had were images of me being one of those sad, unfortunate celebrities who had been flung into the limelight after having an affair with a Premiership footballer, and, through terrible advice, had ended up on a TV talk show to prove how nice they were.

The door opening and Mildred coming through it broke this hideous image. He looked flustered as he came back to sit beside me.

'What's happened?' I asked, concerned that something had thrown a spanner in my well-planned works. 'Is it Mark?'

'Kind of.' Mildred visibly tried to calm himself by pouring more coffee. 'Mark's father is here and is demanding to speak to you.'

Chapter Eighteen

'What?' *Shit, I wasn't expecting that – facing the man I had scammed out of a million pounds.*

'It's ok, don't worry. I've told him you're not ready to meet with anyone yet, and we need to talk to you first.'

'Thank you.' I breathed a sigh of relief, before adding, 'Not that I mind talking to him, I just have nothing to tell him, and —' I felt I needed another reason '—and I need to get everything straight in my own head first.'

'Yes, I know, that's what I told him.' *Phew, good answer.* 'Ok, where were we?' Mildred pressed the record button again and settled himself back into the chair. 'Right, let's get this over with.' *I couldn't agree more.* 'Now, this will be just like an informal chat. I want you to be open and honest, I want you to tell me everything that happened as you remember it. Some of it may be a bit uncomfortable, but it's important – and once we've got it on tape, you can get over it and start forgetting all about it, ok?'

'Ok,' I answered. He wouldn't make the greatest of counsellors, but he meant well.

The questioning seemed to go on forever. I was glad I had prepared for some answers, but other took me by surprise. The transcript of my evening went something like this:

MILDRED: Let's start at the beginning. Why were you at the airport on Saturday the twenty-first of August?

NANCY: I'd driven my parents there. They were going on holiday to Tenerife.

M: Why didn't you just drop them at the door?

N: I helped them in with their bags and joined them for a drink in the café while they waited.

M: But you were still there after they had gone to the departure lounge?

N: Er, yes. I still hadn't finished my drink, and I didn't want to get stuck in rush hour traffic, so I decided to wave off their plane from the viewing area place.

M: And it was here you met Mark?

N: Yes, I sneaked through a fire exit to get some air and he came out to tell me off.

M: And had you met him before that day?

N: No.

M: Were you aware who he was?

N: No, I had no idea, I assumed he was a cleaner. Which I suppose he was, but I didn't know he was anything to do with Max Cheriton. Why would I?

M: So, what happened then?

N: I heard a noise and turned round to see these two masked men with guns and this guy, Mark, with his hands in the air.

M: And?

N: And I almost shat myself.

Mildred tried not to laugh at this point

M: And then?

N: They forced us down the steps and into a blue transit van. Didn't you get any of this on CCTV?

M: We got some, but we need to hear your side of things. Now you say they forced you. Was this physical force?

N: They pushed us a little, but they had guns, so we did what they said.

M: I see, and did they say anything to you during this time? Any reasons as to why they were doing this?

N: No, not really, I got the impression that I was some kind of accident. That I hadn't been in their plan and that they were really just after Mark.

M: That makes sense. Did they bind you in any way?

N: Yes, they tied our hands with rope, blindfolded us and stuck duct tape over our mouths.

As I was describing this, it all now seemed like light-years ago. How could there ever have been a time when I had not known who Mark was? How could I have been scared of Frankie and Coultan, and not been in love with those piercing blue eyes shining out from beneath Joe's balaclava?

M: It must have been horrifying for you.

N: It was.

M: Where did they take you?

N: I've no idea. I tried to remember the directions we moved in, but we seemed to travel for so long I lost track.

M: Do you know how long you were travelling for?

N: No idea I'm afraid. It felt like days but could have been a few hours, I'm afraid I lost all concept of time. Although I know we did go on a boat at one point.

M: A boat? That's interesting. What sort of boat?

N: Sorry, I know very little about boats.

M: Ok, but can you remember if it was a big boat, like a ferry, or a small fishing boat kind of boat?

N: Oh, I see, no, it was a small boat with an engine, and there was an inside to it with seats and a toilet.

M: Can you tell me where the boat was going or how long you were on it for?

N: At least two days, maybe more. I slept a lot, so lost track of time. Whenever they took our blindfolds off, it was either night time or we could see nothing but water, so we had no idea which direction we were going in. I'm sorry, I'm not helping much, am I?

M: It's ok, I know this is difficult for you, just remember what you can. The piecing-it-together part is what the police are here for.

FOR THE TAPE: OFFICER FAIRCLOUGH ENTERS WITH COFFEE AND A PLATE OF SANDWICHES.

M: So, they took you on this boat and where did the boat end up?

N: I'm afraid I don't know that either. They blindfolded us when we were taken off. I remember walking down some kind of jetty and hearing that clinking noise that boats make, so assumed we were in some kind of marina or harbour.

M: And then?

N: Er, in some kind of car or van again, I think. There were proper forward-facing seats this time, but it had quite a loud engine, so I'm not sure which it was.

M: And how long did you drive for this time.

N: Not sure. An hour, maybe two.

M: And throughout this entire journey did these men talk to you or to each other?

N: Occasionally, they spoke to us to tell us to do things but not really what you would call a conversation. They sometimes spoke to each other, but it was in a foreign language so we didn't understand them.

M: What language they were speaking in? Was it Italian?

N: No, not Italian. It sounded like Eastern European; it was quite a harsh language, if you know what I mean, like German, but not German – I did that for my GCSEs and so I would have recognised that – more like Polish or one of the Baltic states or something.

M: I see. So, it was nighttime. Where did they take you in this van?

N: I don't know where we were, but they put us in this shed type of hut, which is where we spent most of the rest of the time while we were there.

M: And were you still tied up?

N: Not at this point. They untied us while we ate and slept.

M: Were any of them in there with you?

N: No, just me and Mark.

M: Did they feed you?

N: Yes, they gave us some kind of stew with bread.

M: Did you have a window?

N: Yes, it had wooden slats over it, but it was dark through the gaps.

M: And in the daytime, were you able to see through?

N: Yes, there was some grass and sandy patches where there was no grass, like a wasteland.

M: And beyond that? Could you see anything else?

N: Yes, I saw some kind of wooden structure, like a fence.

M: At any point, did you try to escape?

N: Yes, that first night. Mark and I managed to get the door open and ran off.

M: Really? And what happened, did they find you?

N: Well, we obviously had no idea where we were going, they knew the area much better than us and brought us back.

M: Did they use force?

N: They did a bit, but not excessively as they still had their guns and we were too knackered to run away again.

M: Did they punish you?

N: No, they just locked us back up and I guess had someone guarding us after that.

FOR THE TAPE: OFFICER FAIRCLOUGH ENTERS THE ROOM TO SPEAK WITH INSPECTOR MILDRED

The tape recorder was turned off again and I welcomed the breather. I was exhausted, and my brain ached from trying to say the right thing. So far, so good. I hadn't had to tell any whoppers, only one or two exaggerations, nothing to arouse any suspicions.

'Is this going to take much longer?' I asked Barbara, who had been sitting quietly listening in.

'No, I shouldn't think so. It's getting late, and we're all quite tired now. How're you doing?'

'Not too bad.' I sighed. 'Just looking forward to a nice warm shower and a good night's sleep. It's getting quite chilly in here.'

'It is a bit, isn't it?' she said, rubbing the tops or her arms like people always do when they say they're cold. She didn't, however, accompany this with a "*brrrrrrr*" which I believed was customary.

She stood up and poked her head out of the door. 'Can you get us a couple of blankets in here, please?' she asked someone outside in the corridor.

'Sure,' came the reply from beyond the wall.

After a few minutes, Mildred still hadn't returned, but they had given us some blankets – they must have been standard-issue police blankets, judging by their grey colour and frayed edges, no doubt used to cover the heads of Italian serial killers on their way to court. But they were warm and welcome and helped to reduce my growing number of goose pimples. I checked my watch, *10:30 pm*, no wonder I was tired. I hoped they hadn't called Mildred out to meet with Max Cheriton again; I was way too knackered to do battle with him tonight. My head was resting against the back of the sofa, and I so wanted to close my eyes and go to sleep. I was almost nodding off when Mildred burst back through the door, beaming from ear to ear.

Shit, what's happened?'

'We've done it!' he announced, very pleased with himself.

Shit! What have they done? Caught them? Found the island?

'We've had the call, it's all over.'

'Wh … what call?' I tried to pretend I was as excited as he was.

'It's Mark, he's safe. They've released him and my colleagues are on their way over here with him!'

'Was he alone?' I asked tentatively.

'Yes. Whoever was holding him let him go alone like they said they would. I'm afraid we still haven't located your kidnappers or the money, but don't you worry, we've got a few more leads to follow up. We'll find them soon enough.'

'That is excellent news!' I agreed, and I meant it. 'I'm so glad he's ok.'

'Yes, and it's all thanks to you, young lady.'

You don't know the half of it. I rubbed my face tiredly to hide my smile.

'And of course, it's possible that when we have time to question Mark, we may well get even more information to help us find them.'

I wouldn't bank on it, I thought, but replied with just a smile and a nod.

Mildred asked Barbara into the hallway for a quick chat before they both reappeared.

'Ok Nancy, it's been a long day and you're looking tired out, so I'll finish my questioning there for today. I'll probably need to talk to you again in the morning though, ok?'

'Sure, and thank you, Inspector, you've been very good to me.' This would have normally sounded creepy but I was sincere. Mildred had been nothing but kind to me and had unwittingly made my deceit so easy.

He left, closing the door behind him, and I eased myself off the sofa. Barbara put her hand on my arm and spoke softly.

'Hang on a minute, Nancy. I need to have a little chat with you.'

Uh oh, what does she know? 'What about?' I asked nervously.

'It's all right, it's nothing to worry about, it's just something I have to do before you go. It's routine, I'm afraid.'

I sat back down and covered myself back up with the blanket. 'Ok.'

She started the tape recorder again. 'Routine, I'm afraid,' she repeated. 'Now, Nancy, I need you to tell me if these men hurt you in any way,' she continued the soft, sympathetic tone.

'Not really. As I said.'

'Did any of them touch you, Nancy?'

'Only to move me from place to place, they didn't beat me up or anything.'

'Ok, that's good, but did any of them touch you … inappropriately?'

'Oh, I get it, erm …' I had to cough to stop myself smiling at the image in my head. 'No, nothing inappropriate.'

'And they didn't make you do anything, you know, against your will? Sexually?'

I wanted to shout, "Against my will? You must be joking!" But instead went with, 'Certainly not.'

'They didn't force you into anything?' she implored.

'No, not at all.' I bit my lip.

'Ok, that's good.' Barbara sounded relieved and celebrated by turning off the tape recorder once again.

Outside it was now raining as well as dark, and they guided me towards a *Polizia* boat waiting on a nearby canal which took us the short distance to the hotel where we were being put up for the night. It was freezing cold on the water, and I wrapped my blanket around myself tightly, my feet wishing they were in socks and not still hanging on to the thread-bare flip-flops I'd been wearing for weeks.

Thankfully, it was only a short journey. I was desperate for sleep. Another day of lies over with, another crime committed and, yet again, another Italian hotel. I reckoned by now I could have given the Italian Tourist Board a run for their money. I stood in the quiet lobby with Barbara, while an Italian police officer did the necessaries at the check-in desk, both of us too weary to make conversation, me still wrapped in my old police-issue blanket, my eyes trying their level best to stay open.

'Nancy!' It was a voice I recognised, but it took me a few seconds to register who it was. 'Nancy!' It called again as I watched a figure attempt to break free from the bustling group who had recently entered the lobby.

'Mark!' I yelled back, cupping my hands over my face in surprise, trying to stop the tears that had already started to well up.

Tired as I was, I ran towards him, dropping my blanket for the first time since they had given it to me, and we collided in a hug in the middle of the room.

'It's ok, everything's ok,' he whispered in my ear, and I held him tighter, not wanting to let him go. 'How're things with you?' he asked into my hair.

'So far, so good,' I sobbed back to him.

To all our spectators we were two released captives, relieved to discover we were both alive and well – to us, our words meant much, much more. They meant that everything had gone according to plan, that Coultan, Rio, Frankie and Joe were safe, that Mabel would join her boys in paradise, and that so far no-one was any the wiser as to our part in the whole thing. I wanted to stay there with Mark; I wanted to talk about everything we had been through – the laughs, the rum, the karaoke. I wanted to hear about what had happened since I'd left, how they'd all celebrated, and I wanted to tell him about what I had been doing. I had kept it in for so long now that I was desperate to talk to someone, and he was the only person who would understand. I also realised that I had missed him. We had been through so much together, I felt closer to him now than to anyone else from my previous life.

After several minutes, our respective parties came to drag us off one another. I had Barbara who gently pulled me by the arm saying, 'Come on now, time for bed,' in such a motherly tone I wouldn't have been surprised if she'd added "up the wooden hill".

On Mark's side, there were several Italian police officers and a bunch of strangers I had never seen before except for the bearded face and puffed out belly of Mark's father, Max Cheriton, recognisable from the television and newspapers. He was a formidable figure, and I was a little panicked to find him heading in my direction.

'You must be Nancy,' he almost bellowed, thrusting his hand towards me. 'I understand it's you we have to thank for getting Mark back, little lady.'

I felt a little guilty about shaking his hand, but I realised that it would look odd if I didn't respond, so I tentatively stuck mine out to meet his. I'd stolen a million pounds from this man, and I wasn't really sure how I should act – plus I was really too exhausted to think straight anymore.

'What the hell!' he boomed and pulled me to him, bear-hug style.

Unable to help myself, I whispered 'I'm sorry' into his enormous chest, but whether or not he heard me, he either thought nothing of it or put it down to my disorientation. Eventually, he released me and I wobbled back to Barbara, who led me away towards the stairs. I took a last look back at Mark who I noticed was back in his Giant cleaning overalls, which now seemed so alien and out of place. He winked at me and I couldn't help but grin back.

Chapter Nineteen

This time my room was on the second floor, up a marble staircase. Thankfully, I had it to myself, although Barbara reassured me she was in the room next to me; there would be a police officer on the door if I needed anything, so I had nothing to worry about. I found this slightly ironic, given that the only thing I had to worry about was her and the rest of the police. It felt good to close the door. It must have been the longest day of my life. It seemed far longer than twelve hours since I'd got up this morning at the San Marco in Pisa. How time flew when you were breaking the law and crapping yourself.

My room was beautiful, very opulent, very Venetian. With all the drama of the examination and then seeing Mark, it hadn't really sunk in that I was in Venice – but this room brought it all cascading back to me. The bed was a high four-poster with bolster cushions matching the tapestry of the bedspread and the swagged curtains surrounding the bed and up at the window. In the tidy en-suite there was a free-standing roll-top bath with gold taps which matched the fittings for the washbasin, toilet and bidet. *Very nice!* I thought as I turned on the taps and emptied in the complimentary bubble bath. *Very nice indeed, especially as I should by rights be in a prison cell.* I laughed to myself at how different it all could have been, and could still be.

Although it was already late, I didn't want to get out of the bath. It was so relaxing and it was wonderful to wash the dirt of the day away. As I languished in the tub, I checked out my tan and wondered why it hadn't been commented on; I guess it wasn't as prominent as it had been a couple of days ago, and they must have just assumed it was from before I left. I'm sure it hadn't even crossed anyone's mind that I may have been lying on a beach sunbathing like a desperate tourist. It amazed me that not only had I succeeded in not giving anything away in my actions, but that my body itself had not caused suspicion. The cuts and bruises lied for themselves. I had mentally and physically fooled everyone, and while I wasn't exactly proud of this, there was a strange sense of achievement.

After dragging myself out of the bath, I pulled the plug on all the grime and the dust of the day and watched it disappear down the plughole along with the swirl of lies I had told and the last dregs of deception.

Wrapping myself in a clean white, cosy robe, I slipped my feet into comfy slippers and padded around the room, checking out the pictures in their ornate frames. Yes, this was very nice. I could never afford anything like this by conventional means. I assumed they could claim it all back on expenses, so I helped myself to a bottle of wine from the mini-bar. I chose a small bottle of Italian (*naturalmente*) white, filled one of the glasses provided and went to check out the view. I drew back one of the heavy curtains but could see nothing but my reflection, so I carefully unlocked and opened one of the thin balcony doors and stuck my head out. I don't know why, but it surprised me to hear noise way down below in the streets. The sound of music, of voices, the sound of Venetian life going on as normal just as it should be.

The rain had stopped, but the pavements were wet and bright with reflections of ornate street lamps and restaurant fairy lights. I peered over the edge of the balcony and saw a small piazza bar below, waiters buzzing around like apron-wearing flies from table to table, its de-coated customers enjoying the last of summer evenings by the beautiful Grand Canal on which my hotel stood.

In my head I pretended I was an independent tourist, here on my own. Perhaps I was on business in Italy to write about the beautiful city of Venice. If I wasn't so tired, I would have liked to have popped down to that bar and joined them. I vowed that once all this mess was over, I would come back to this hotel and enjoy a glass of wine from that little bar – but for now, I raised my glass and went back into my room, locking the door behind me.

Once I'd scaled the north face of the bed, I turned off the lamp and lay there like the Princess and the Pea. It was by far the grandest, comfiest bed I had ever slept on, yet I would have swapped it for my hammock next to Joe in a heartbeat.

I must have slept like a log because I didn't even hear Barbara coming into my room the next morning with a tray of continental breakfast. I woke to find her shaking me gently.

'Nancy, Nancy,' she was saying as I came to. She seemed in a good mood as she flung the curtains wide and opened a window. I also noticed that she was being risqué enough to leave the top button of her slightly manly looking shirt open – maybe the *esprit d'Italiano* was permeating her skin.

'Isn't it a beautiful day? I've brought you some breakfast,' she announced gaily, pointing to the tray. 'And here are a few bits and bobs we've picked up for you. You've been wandering around in those old clothes long enough. I hope they're your size.' She smiled again, before telling me she would be back in an hour and then almost prancing out of the room, which, although I'd only known her a day, seemed quite out of character for Barbara.

Oooh goody, new clothes! I scrambled out of bed, donning my complimentary towelling gown and grabbing for the bags that Barbara had left. *Please don't let Barbara have picked them out, please don't let it be some sort of checked shirt and overalls,* I begged the heavens, but I was pleasantly surprised. Inside the bags was a black dress, semi-fitted at the top with short sleeves and a full knee-length skirt. I was impressed. Before I dressed, I sat eating my breakfast on the little balcony, the busy canal below me rolling along like it had been doing for hundreds of years. The piazza bar was now closed but people were milling around; couples holding hands, singles on mobile phones, some carrying paper bags full of groceries, objets d'art or tourist nick-nacks. It looked like a painting, and I had just about as much of a chance of being part of it if it were actually one.

After breakfast, I couldn't wait to try on my new outfit. As I slid it on, my thoughts returned to Joe and the day he'd brought me the bag of hideous clothes; he'd clearly never needed to buy for a woman before and he had no idea what to get me. *Ah, he was useless at shopping – but I loved him anyway.*

Right now, I was looking and feeling good in my new Italian dress and sandals. I felt like Sophia Loren as I posed in the mirror until I was rudely interrupted by Barbara bringing me back down to Earth. She was looking a little flushed and had even removed the waistcoat she'd been sporting earlier. *Cor, the Italian heat must be getting to her.*

'So, are we back off to the police station?' I asked, believing I already knew the answer – but I was wrong.

'No. In fact, they've set a couple of rooms aside for us in the hotel so Inspector Mildred will do the questioning here. They thought they might as well question both you and Mark together,' came the unexpected, but most agreeable, answer.

Not only could I stay here in the lap of luxury, but they would also question me with Mark. *Hooray!* I started to fold up my own raggedy clothes and stuff them in the bag my new clothes had arrived in.

'I'll take those for you,' Barbara said, making a grab for the bag, but my reflexes swung it out of her reach and she looked at me in shock.

'Sorry, I-I … er, I'd like to keep them,' I managed.

'Really? Why?' She looked a little taken aback.

Good question. What could I say? Sentimental value from a harrowing ordeal? I knew why I wanted to keep them, and it was sentimental. They were full of reminders of the island, full of sand, full of sea, full of smoke, full of memories where nothing else tangible remained. They were washed by Rio and touched by Joe.

'Erm, I'm not sure,' was my answer. 'I just don't feel ready to give them away yet. Does that make any sense?' I asked hopefully, playing on my distressed, traumatised victim role.

'Ok, ok, Nancy, that's fine,' Barbara reassured me, 'Whatever you want.' She smiled and I sighed with relief, although she was probably making a mental note to book me into a psychiatrist as soon as our feet hit British soil.

With my old clothes in the bag safely at my side, we took our leave of the lush room and clip-clopped down the marble stairs, closely followed by the Italian police officer who had been standing guard all night. In what looked like a conference room, I was met by Mildred and Mark, who was all spruced up and looking as fresh as I felt. They both stood up and smiled as Barbara and I walked in. We could have easily been mistaken for two couples on holiday, were it not been for the files and tape recorder laid out on the table.

'Hello, Nancy, Barbara,' Mildred said when he saw us, and Mark just grinned at me. I discovered they had been questioning Mark for the last hour, and, so far, his story pretty much tallied with mine, which surprised no-one, especially not me and Mark. We spent the next couple of hours going over how we spent our time at the camp, what we ate, how often we were allowed out for exercise, any clues or hints as to where we were held etc, etc. They asked me about my time after I'd been dumped in Pisa, about the instructions of where to go and what to do, about the fact that I was constantly being watched and what would have happened if I hadn't carried out the exchange. They asked Mark about the time after he'd been let go in Pisa too, and we answered everything just as honestly as we could and just as we had planned.

When we didn't have a set answer to a question, we just made something up, and Mildred, Barbara and the little tape recorder took it all in. Being there with Mark made the experience so much easier. Gone was the worry that he might say something different to me, or that either of us would let something slip. We backed each other up so much we almost convinced ourselves.

The hardest part was compiling the "photo fits" of our captors.

This took a while, and Mark and I tried not to laugh when we ended up with George Michael, Grant Mitchell and Will Smith staring back at us from the table, with Mildred poring over them as if they were "nasty pieces of work".

Then that was it. The pictures were filed away for distribution and the tape recorder was turned off. Remarkably, we were free to go.

Inspector Mildred asked us to sit and wait in a small café bar on the ground floor of the hotel while he checked the arrangements for our imminent departure. The floor to ceiling windows were pulled open and the breeze of the early afternoon fluttered round the tables, ruffling hair and rustling shopping bags. Mark and I sat with Barbara, sipping our cappuccinos and nibbling at the various pastries in front of us.

'You see …' Barbara patted my arm. 'It's all over now and it wasn't that bad, was it?'

I didn't know if she meant the whole kidnap ordeal or just the interview session, but either way, it hadn't been as bad as I had first thought, so I smiled and nodded back at her. Just as she opened her mouth to say something else, she was interrupted by someone calling her name in a thick Italian accent.

'Ba-baro!' came the voice, and we all turned to see a young athletic lad of about twenty-five heading towards us in light linen trousers and smart striped shirt open at the neck, his suit jacket slung casually over his shoulder.

'Ba-baro, you are still here, I am glad,' he announced as he approached, causing Barbara to turn the colour of the scarlet cotton tablecloths. She jumped up in a panic, scraping her metal chair on the floor as she did so, and made her way quickly towards the young man. Mark and I watched her initial fluster metamorphose into the kind of shy embarrassment usually reserved for teenage girls with a crush. We looked at each other with confused expressions.

'Who's that?' Mark asked me.

'I've no idea.' I looked back at the man, who was gesturing emphatically. 'Hang on a minute, yes I do!' His face started to look familiar. 'That's the Italian police officer who was patrolling outside my room all night.'

'Not all night, by the looks of it. Apparently, his truncheon was out elsewhere.' Mark laughed at his own schoolboy joke.

'No, I don't believe it, not Barbara?' I was amazed that this had happened right on my doorstep and I'd missed it. With my nose for gossip, this was not like me at all. 'No wonder she had a spring in her step this morning!' *Good for Barbara*. It was nice to know she was a passionate woman under those shapeless shirts and pleated slacks.

'Hang on a minute—' It had just occurred to me '—they were supposed to be protecting me last night. What if I'd been killed while they were getting their jollies?'

'Killed? By whom?' Mark smirked.

'You know, by the ...' *Kidnappers*, I was going to say, but then realised just before I said it. 'Shit, I've got myself believing all this rubbish now!'

We laughed and laughed, and I felt the most relaxed that I had since I left the island. It was great to be back with Mark, feeling like we were two old comfortable friends. He was wearing new trendy jeans and a white T-shirt which helped to show off his tan, his skin had all but cleared up and he was the picture of health – a different boy to the spotty little lad I'd bumped into less than three weeks ago at the airport.

We relaxed back in our chairs, facing out towards the sun. 'We did it,' I whispered, so only Mark could hear me.

'Yep, well you did most of it,' he said under his breath. Neither of us could help smiling. I had the urge to ask him loads of questions about that final day, but I didn't have much time.

'So how was ... so was everything ... I mean ... did you ...?' I began, wanting to know everything but asking nothing.

'Yes, everything was fine.' Mark checked around him to make sure no-one was listening and that Bar-baro was still engrossed with the Italian before continuing. 'Frankie and I stayed on the boat until the others returned, which to be honest was a bit scary. We were waiting down in the cabin for police helicopters to come and take us away, to be honest. We sat there for hours, talking nonsense – you know what Frankie's like.'

I did know. I loved talking nonsense with Frankie, and it made me sad to think that he was out there talking nonsense and I wasn't there to hear it.

'And?' I urged Mark to go on.

'Oh, and then the others came back, Coultan and Rio.' He paused and I raised my eyebrows at him. 'Oh yeah, and Joe, and they told us what had happened, you know with you and when they were in Monaco, which was pretty cool. We waited there a while and then, Coultan drove me to Pisa where I phoned the police, and voila, Roberto's your uncle.'

We were prevented from saying more as we spied Barbara walking back over to us.

'I'm so sorry about that,' she said sheepishly as she approached. Mark and I smiled knowing smiles at her.

'Is that who I think it was?' I asked her.

'You know him?' she asked, surprised.

'Well, no, I don't know him but I recognise him. He's that young copper from last night, isn't he?'

Barbara flushed again. 'Erm … yes … that's right. Frederico and I just got talking last night and … erm …' She sat down at our table.

'It's ok,' I reassured her. 'He's well tasty, good on you.' I elbowed her in a cheeky nudge-nudge-wink-wink manner.

Barbara exhaled a breath she'd clearly been holding in. 'Well, he was very nice,' she managed, looking down at a scrap of paper in her hand on which I noticed a phone number written in curly script.

'Yep, and we won't tell anyone what you were up to while you were on duty last night, eh?' Mark added, and I nodded, giving my complete approval. Barbara looked visibly relieved, but then jumped out of her skin as Inspector Mildred appeared at her shoulder.

'Right kids, ready to go?' he asked, and Barbara shot up to her feet saying, 'Yes, yes, of course, Inspector.'

It was nice to be called a kid again; it had been a few years since anyone had called me that, and I realised that was how Inspector Mildred must see us: two kids he'd helped save from harm who he'd now keep under his protective wing. Mark and I followed them out of the hotel, me clutching my carrier bag of old clothes. Frederico was getting into his car outside and waved as he sped out of the hotel driveway. Barbara hid her embarrassed face from the rest of us.

'All right, Barbara?' Mark teased out of earshot of Mildred, and she smiled back at him as she climbed into the front seat of a police boat. 'Hey, we all have our little secrets,' he whispered so only I could hear. I looked at him as I scooched my way along a seat in the middle of the boat and he winked back.

Soon we were speeding away, back along the canal and over to the mainland. We swapped the boat for a car and travelled through the outskirts of Venice towards the airport. As I watched the historical buildings and canals whizz by, I was glad that this romantic city had whipped up passion in the heart of at least one of us.

An advantage of being kidnapped with the son of an international mogul-millionaire is that when you fly back to England, you can do it in style in a private jet with cream leather seats and an open bar. As I walked across the tarmac towards the jet in my Italian dress, I pretended I was in a film, walking in slow motion, the breeze in my hair, wafting it gently in my face as I turned to see our party striding forwards purposefully, happy to be going home. As I ascended the carpeted metal steps, I was reminded of the line from the Green Day song, 'Good Riddance (Time of Your Life)'. Well, it certainly had been something unpredictable, and yes, I concluded that I had indeed had the time of my life. Things would never be the same again. It had been a once-in-a-lifetime experience; it could not have been planned, it would not be repeated.

I spent most of the flight curled up on a comfy sofa, looking out the window as we left the leg of Italy behind and soared over the sparkling Mediterranean and the jagged landscape of the Alps. Mark sat on the other end of the sofa, but because of the close proximity of his family, Inspector Mildred, Barbara, two other uniformed police officers and the serving staff, there was no opportunity to talk, so we barely spoke at all. I wondered if we were both thinking the same things – that it was ridiculous that just a few weeks ago it had taken us several days to do this journey in a little boat, and now we would make it in just three hours. Was he wondering what Rio, Coultan, Joe and Frankie were doing back on the island? Was it all spinning around so fast in his head that he didn't know which memories to think about first, so it was all a hodge-podge of gaffer tape, bonfires and police officers, of laughter and lies? Maybe he was just thinking how nice it would be to return home to the rest of his family and his friends, trying to imagine adjusting back into real life as if all this had never happened.

After a three-course meal and declining plenty of offers of cocktails and bar snacks, we began our descent towards English soil, and my stomach turned in excitement and apprehension. As the wheels touched the tarmac, it was over – both the journey and the adventure.

We disembarked and were shunted through some corridors and into a private lounge. I could see my parents and my brother at one end. They were all standing up, wringing their hands and craning their necks to spot me. As soon as I could free myself from the herd, I ran towards them, breaking down into convulsive tears at the pure joy of seeing them and understanding the immense relief they must have at the sight of me and the end of their nightmare. My mother was crying uncontrollably while dabbing her eyes with a tissue, even my dad and brother were sobbing into my hair as they held me close to them for a good ten minutes as photographers snapped and flashed away, no doubt trying to get the best picture for tomorrow's front pages.

After a while, Inspector Mildred came over and I introduced him to my parents, but, of course, they'd already met. Out of the blue, he told me that there would be a quick press conference, but it was nothing to worry about.

'What?' I yelped, 'I don't want to do a press conference! I don't know what to say.'

He looked at me sympathetically. 'Just answer their questions, Nancy,' he told me. 'And don't worry – if it gets too much, we'll be there to pull it.'

'But I don't want to,' I whined, pleading to him with my eyes. It was one thing lying on a one-to-one basis when I was relaxed, but making something up in front of all these people, press and goodness knows how many viewers and readers? What if I let something slip and became the world's most infamous phoney, despised by my family, laughed at by the public, and more than likely locked up by the police? I scanned the room and eventually found Mark, talking to an old lady in pearls who I assumed was his gran. He saw me, made his excuses and came over to see what was going on.

'They want us to give a press conference,' I told him.

'What?' he yelped in the same manner that I had, which made his father look up and come striding over.

Inspector Mildred tried to explain. 'It really is just routine. While you've been away there's been a lot of coverage of this case. Everyone in Britain has heard about you, they've been following it in the papers every day and have been waiting for news of your safe return. There have even been vigils! I'm not sure you understand how big your story is. If you take my advice, I think it would be nice for you to say a few words, now that you're back and safe. Everyone likes to see a happy ending.'

Mark and I looked at each other, still a little unsure. Max Cheriton stepped in.

'The Inspector's right, kids,' he said. 'I agree you should do it – but I tell you what, I'll do it with you. That'll take some of the pressure off you two.'

I looked at Mark and he made a compromise. 'Ok, look, we'll do it, but we don't want to talk about what happened over there. We'll just tell them that we're ok.'

'Yes, we're just not ready to talk about all that yet,' I added for sincerity.

'Well, I think that sounds fair, don't you Inspector?' Max Cheriton boomed at Mildred.

'Sounds good to me,' Mildred replied 'I'll be there too, of course, so I can answer anything you don't want to.' He smiled at me, my saviour once again.

After a quick freshen up in the ladies' room, we were on. We sat down at a long line of tables. On my left was my mum and dad, who were there to hold my hand rather than answer questions. On my right sat Mark who whispered, 'It'll be fine' in my ear, amidst the noise of shuffling feet and arguing over seats. Next to Mark sat his father, unphased and relaxed with the media attention, and next to him Inspector Mildred, spruced up in a clean suit and tie, his face newly shaven and his hair combed. In front of the table, a forest of microphones was aimed at us, randomly stuck together with duct tape, ready to catch our every word.

Chapter Twenty

Cameras rolled and flashes rebounded around the room as the mass of press quietened down, ready to begin. The first question was directed to Max Cheriton.

'Max, how good is it to have your son home?'

'It's wonderful, Jim. These last few weeks have been a nightmare for us all, and we're completely delighted it's all over,' he announced, before adding, 'I'm very proud of him.' He patted his son on the back and Mark beamed.

'But what about the money, Max? How much did you have to pay?'

'I'm not prepared to talk about the money, Jim, just to say that it's worth every penny to have both my son and young Nancy here, home and safe. It's priceless, Jim, priceless.'

'But will they retrieve the money?' asked a woman in a suit and glasses. 'What are you doing to find these criminals?'

Mildred jumped in on this one. 'I can assure you that the Met are doing everything in their power to find these people and bring them to justice. Thanks to Mark and Nancy, we have some fresh leads and we have officers out there as we speak following them up. We have every confidence they will be found, and when they are I assure you that Mr Cheriton will have every penny returned to him.'

'Thank you, Inspector. I have every confidence in you and your team.' Max Cheriton shook the Inspector's hand and the flashbulbs sprang into life.

'I would like to ask Nancy a question,' piped up a young lad in an anorak.

Ok, this is it, I thought. Taking a deep breath, I nodded. Mark squeezed my clammy hand under the table.

'First of all, I'd like to ask how're you are doing?' *Well, that was ok.*

'Er, I'm fine, thank you,' I answered politely. 'I'm ok, very glad to be home.' I looked at my mother, who started crying again.

'What do you think about being seen as the innocent party in all of this?'

I wasn't sure what he meant so answered carefully. 'I think we're all the innocent party in this.'

'Yes, yes, I know. I just meant that they took you in error. You weren't supposed to be there. You're nothing to do with the Cheritons,' he continued.

'Oh, I see. Erm, yes, I was taken accidentally, and I wasn't prepared for anything like this. It was certainly traumatic, and I think it will take a while for me to get over it … if I ever do.'

Mark joined in to help me out. 'I would like to say that, although I'm sorry that Nancy got caught up in all this, it made it a lot easier for me. I truly believe that if it wasn't for her, I might not be here now.' He squeezed my hand again, and I leant in towards him to show my appreciation of his words while some people clapped and both our mothers cried.

As promised, most of the other questions were answered by the two old pros, Max Cheriton and Inspector Mildred. While they talked, I squinted around the room, around the sea of faces and cameras, barely listening to what was being said. To the side of the crowd, next to my dad and brother, I could see Barbara back in her waistcoat and shirt, smiling back, as if she was proud of me. Of all my recent experiences, this was by far the most surreal. It was like one of those dreams where you're naked in a crowd, or all your teeth fall out – possible yet impossible all at the same time. I was glad when it was all over.

Several hours later I woke up to find that I had rather embarrassingly been leaning on the shoulder of a plain-clothed police officer in a rather un-demure and unladylike fashion. 'Oh my God, I'm so sorry,' I said, surreptitiously eyeing his pinstripes for any signs of unseemly spittle.

'That's all right,' he said, giving me a wink which I expect was meant to reassure me but instead made me a little more uncomfortable. I sat back in the car seat and turned towards the window, where to my surprise the everlasting motorway view had become wet urban streets and buildings. These streets and buildings that I'd driven past for years had a sense of familiarity, but now they also had a sense of strangeness and foreboding – like a déjà vu in a place that was once mine, but where I no longer belonged.

At last, we turned into my road. The signposts, the shops, even the people, were identical to before everything happened. It felt like a lifetime ago when I left for the airport on that boiling hot day. I almost expected to see new buildings and developments that had sprung up, but, of course, in reality it was only a matter of weeks. *Home*. There it was, the flat above the shop on the corner. The balcony we were drinking on the day before I left was deserted. The bright, flowery curtains Steph and I had hung were closed, and I longed to be on the other side of them, home and safe, back to normality.

'Oh bollocks,' the driver almost shouted, and I peered through the front window to see a mass of people with cameras and notepads outside my door.

'What the hell are they doing here?' I asked rather naively.

'They're waiting for you, love,' one of the police officers replied. 'Don't worry, we'll get you through them all right, we're used to this sort of thing.'

Yeah, I bet, I thought, not entirely reassured. It was bizarre. I'd seen the press on the telly, waiting outside Liz Hurley's house or Jordan's, but I'd never expected them to be waiting outside of mine. I was no-one of any importance. All too soon the car stopped, and I was soon flanked by two burly coppers and Mildred's second-in-command, who I'd nick-named Scruffy McGuffy, who led the way through the crowd.

'Let us through. C'mon now, lads. Make a bit of room here, will you!' he was shouting as I was jostled and cajoled through the crowd, amongst flashbulbs and shouts of, 'Nancy! Nancy! Over here, Nancy!'

Oh my goodness, I'm Julia Roberts in Notting Hill and Fred West all rolled into one! With my key poised in my hand, I charged forwards with it like a lightsaber until I reached the door. It took several attempts to get it in the lock, like a drunkard who finally gives up and crashes on the doorstep.

Luckily, Scruffy McGuffy took the key from me and let us into the dark hallway. As the door closed the noise of the press mercifully ceased.

'Now, do you want us to stay with you for a bit, love?' he asked loudly.

'No thanks, I'll be fine,' I replied, unconvincingly peering into the gloomy darkness.

'Are you sure? Do you want us to give the place a quick once over?'

'No really, I'll be ok. I'd rather be by myself for a bit.' I did so much want to be on my own.

'Ok, but we'll be staying in town for a few days, so if there's anything you need, anything at all, you only have to give us a ring, ok?' He told me as he handed over his card. I wanted to cry again but resisted the urge and instead answered with a vigorous nod.

'Right then,' he announced. He looked at the door and back at me. He seemed reluctant to leave, like a parent leaving their firstborn at school for the first time. Either that or he dreaded the thought of wading through the paparazzi again. They looked at each other in the manner of the three musketeers before making their way once more into the breach, and I closed the door solidly behind them. I leant back against the wood, listening as the muffled shouts of the press dulled as they followed the police officers back to their car.

I stood there for a while, not sure what to do, but with a sense of aloneness and things being noticeably still. The light from the street lamps seeped in through the top window above the door outlining the gloomy stairs in front of me, which I slowly climbed, one hand on the banister, the other clutching my bag of things the police officer had carried in for me. I made my way along the landing and into my bedroom, where I dared to turn on the light. The room was too tidy and some things were in the wrong places, giving me an uncomfortable sensation of someone having been there. I dumped my bags on the floor and moved a few things around, putting them back in their rightful places. I flopped down on my bed – *ahh*, the bed I'd yearned for nearly every night since I'd left it – and realised exactly how exhausted I was. I wanted to sleep and sleep for days until I could wake up when things were normal again.

Just as I closed my eyes, I was jolted upright by a noise – was it a laugh? – from somewhere close by. I was unsure if I'd dreamt it or not. I sat, my heart beating fast, listening for another sound. Maybe it was Steph. *Steph! That's a point, where the hell is she?* Surely if she'd heard me come in, she would have come to see me? Maybe she'd had enough of the press loitering outside and gone to stay somewhere else, but it seemed odd she hadn't come back tonight.

I stood up warily and crept back out onto the landing where I switched on the light. There was no-one there. I knocked on Steph's bedroom door before entering, but it was dark and empty. Next stop along was the kitchen, but there was no-one in there either – a few empty wine bottles, nothing unusual in that. I turned back towards the living room. By now, along with my pounding heart, my body was shaking. I could sense a presence of some kind beyond the living room door, yet no light was creeping out from under it. I slowly turned the handle and gently pushed the door. Something was moving; I could hear it breathing. I slowly put my hand out to turn on the light and then …

'SURPRISE!!!!'

'F***ing hell and shitty f***ing bastards!' I ungraciously screamed as my legs buckled and I fell backwards into the doorway. There were gasps and a few sniggers.

'Oh shit!' Steph rushed forward to help me up and give me a reassuring hug. 'Look everyone's here!' She grinned at me as the light came on, and I saw about thirty or forty people crammed into our living room, some of whom I recognised, some of whom I didn't.

There was Steph with a new haircut, a few other close friends, Shelly Babcock, even Nobby Stiles. And there, in the middle, looking as cool as ever was Danny Greenslade who raised a can of Stella in my direction before coming over and surprising me with a kiss on the lips.

'Great to have you back,' he whispered in my ear, before turning around and shouting, 'Oi, Pete, put some music on.' I was completely blindsided and not at all sure what I should do next.

'I don't know what to say,' I said, running a hand through my hair and re-adjusting my clothes to an almost presentable state, thankful that I hadn't taken my dress off already.

'Come on, let's get you a drink.' Steph laughed and took my hand to guide me through the crowds to our old folding table, now piled high with bottles and cans of all descriptions. I absentmindedly went straight for a bottle of Captain Morgan's and unscrewed the cap.

'Since when do you drink rum?' Steph looked at me, surprised.

'I-I er …' *Shit*!

'You're all over the place, aren't you?' Steph took the bottle out of my hand and handed me a glass of white wine. 'Here, have this.'

I gladly took it and gulped it down while I surveyed the room. Some people were dancing, some were laughing, and all seemed to have a look in their eyes that said how thrilled they were to be here, to share in this experience. They were probably already thinking about how they could brag to their friends that they'd been to the welcome home party for "that girl who was kidnapped". They must have picked out their clothes specially and visited the hairdressers. And here was I, the guest of honour, in no make-up and wearing my now crumpled Italian dress, wishing I was on my own, tucked up in bed. I figured the next best thing was to get drunk, so I dispensed with the glass, picked up a bottle of wine and knocked it back.

The next morning, I awoke with a banging head and a mouth as dry as a camel's sombrero. Again, like too many times of late, I had the familiar notion of not knowing where I was. I tried to think back: *police station, the journey home, party.* Ah yes, I was home in my own bed. I stretched out my arms and legs like a starfish to make doubly sure I really was back in my old familiar space. It felt good to be home. What wasn't so good was the churning in my stomach as the excesses of the previous night rolled around inside my belly. This wasn't helped by the sudden wave of nausea washing over me as I tried to piece together my memories of the evening. I remembered being shocked as hell, dancing with Steph and … *oh my God, did I snog Danny Greenslade?* What did I do that for? How did that even happen?

Oh hell, I couldn't even remember how I got to bed. How on earth was I going to remember what I was saying to people? What if I've told everyone the truth? What if I just blurted out the entire story I'd spent the last few days lying my ass off to hide? *Shit, shit, shit and bugger!* Did I mention Joe? It was the sort of thing I'd tell Steph all about under normal circumstances. This was definitely the worst "I-hope-I-didn't-do-anything-stupid-last-night" experience ever, and I'd had my fair share of those. Never before had my drunken antics had the potential to change so many people's lives, including the possibility of landing me in prison. All it needed was one person I'd blabbed to go to the police, or even worse the papers, and it would be enough to start a full-scale investigation. *My word would never be trusted again.* I had been kidding myself thinking that I could keep something like this a secret for the rest of my life, when the reality was I'd been home for not even twenty-four hours and could have jeopardised everything and let everybody down.

I felt truly sick. I gingerly dragged myself out of bed and staggered to the bathroom where I promptly threw up in the toilet bowl. With the dreadful combination of worry and alcohol, I started to cry and grabbed at the toilet roll to wipe my face.

'Nancy?' It was Steph tapping on the bathroom door. 'Nancy, are you ok in there?'

'Yeah,' I sniffed, obviously lying.

Steph tried the door. I hadn't locked it before I spilled my guts, so it opened and she wandered in.

'Ah, mate,' she said, coming to kneel next to me and flushing the toilet. She handed me more tissue and rubbed my back like she was trying to bring up wind.

This made me cry again.

'Feeling a bit rough, eh? I'm not doing so great myself. Especially now after seeing your chunks,' she added, trying to make me smile. 'C'mon, you wash your face and I'll cook us a hangover fry-up. Then we can sit down and have a chat.'

I did as I was told, and as she pulled out the frying pan for the world's unhealthiest breakfast, I stepped into the shower. What was done was done, and there was no choice but to face the music ... whatever song was being played.

Chapter Twenty-One

When I'd returned home, autumn was just beginning, and in no time at all winter was upon us. I had not been back to work since I left on that day in August, and although they kindly left my job open for me, I had absolutely no intention of returning. How could I go back to such banal normality? My bank manager was overjoyed with me; my account had never looked so healthy in all the ten years of being with the bank.

Although I'd refused the "thank you" money offered by Max Cheriton, I did accept some compensation money from the airport, and it was much more generous than I'd expected. No matter what happened afterwards, I had been abducted on their premises and their incompetent security services had failed to do their jobs.

I also got a bit of cash from the minimal media exposure I agreed to. I seemed to be one of the few people left in the country with no desire to become a celebrity, and while I protested vehemently against any kind of press coverage, I took advice and did one or two shows to satisfy the nation's curiosity, hoping that they'd eventually let me be – and, quite frankly, a girl has to eat.

I agreed to a special pre-recorded interview with Sir Trevor McDonald, providing Mark was with me. We had the final say on what questions were asked and could prepare our answers in advance, which suited us. We also accepted the invitation for a five-minute slot on *Richard and Judy*, as we were both huge fans and agreed we couldn't pass up an opportunity to meet the king and queen of daytime TV. Barbara would be so proud.

As for the press, I actually wrote a piece for *The Times* which they published on the front page. From the tabloids, I chose *The Sun* who I discovered had been supporting us and gunning for our release every day while we were away, so I felt we were obliged to give them something now that we were free.

Their monetary offers were all very generous, which meant I was lucky enough not to need to work for a while. Strangely though, the bank account full of money didn't excite me in the way that I used to think it would.

Although we were still living together, Steph and I were drifting further and further apart. More by luck than anything else, I found out that I'd kept my mouth shut at my welcome home party and not told anybody anything I shouldn't – apparently, I'd actually left the party early. The secrets I couldn't tell Steph caused a gulf between us, and I felt like a fraud not being able to tell her what was permanently on my mind and exactly why I had changed. We both grew tired of the attention I received whenever we left the house. At first we laughed it off and ran away from the baying crowds and straggle of photographers, but after a few months it became exhausting, and I made a concerted effort to avoid events and parties so she could retain some semblance of a normal life, without me unintentionally stealing the spotlight. Inevitably she made new friends who I didn't know, and while we remained friends, we were never the same again.

Christmas came and went, and at New Year I sang that I would forget all my old acquaintances and n'er bring them to mind, but still, my island friends were all I could think about. They were in my thoughts every day: what they were doing, how things were progressing with the business, memories of the times we'd spent together. Occasionally, I took out the plastic Italian carrier bag from the bottom of my wardrobe so I could touch and smell the contents, careful not to spill the last grains of sand within the folds of the clothes.

It was like returning from a fabulous and well-loved holiday. It was always impossible to recapture those happy days, and, eventually, the memories fade along with your suntan, the faces become blurred, the stories are forgotten, and it becomes just a place you visited once, years ago. You get over it and move on.

I still hadn't got over it. I didn't even have a photograph.

The winter was a long one. I tried all sorts of things to keep me busy. I tried temping in various places, but as the work was futile and I didn't need the money; I gave it up. I tried volunteer work at the Cats Protection League, but I cried when they brought the cats in and cried again when they left, and soon realised it wasn't right for me. I began a distance learning course in creative writing and penned a few bits and pieces, but they all seemed to end up being about the same thing: loss, unrequited love, no-one living happily ever after. I even made *myself* depressed with my writing efforts. I was asked to pen a book about my time away and realised that it would be a book of fiction, so I declined for reasons of self-preservation and self-incrimination.

I spent a lot of time with my parents, with my brother, and of course Atlanta. She was growing up fast and was always blunt and straight to the point with her questioning: 'Why are you sad Auntie Nancy?' and 'Why haven't you got a boyfriend, Auntie Nancy?'

The most annoying thing was that I was disappointed in myself. The world was my oyster. With a bank account full of money, plenty of time on my hands and the freedom to do whatever I pleased, I could start a new career, follow my dreams – whatever they were. But I had fallen back into my indecisive ways, unable to make a decision or carve out a path for myself in the world. After everything I had been through, the immense courage I'd shown and the stories I'd convincingly told, I felt I should be out there trying, doing, living.

The truth is, I thought I was going crazy; I couldn't shake the thoughts and feelings I knew I should have been over by now. I wanted to talk about Joe, the way you always did when you've first met someone you know you truly like. I wanted to tell my friends everything about him, and experience that lurch inside when someone else said his name in passing. I wanted to tell everyone I was in love, but that very fact and its inevitable failure were too much to keep me from going insane with inner turmoil. I'd even remembered that it was Edward Fox in *The Day of The Jackal*, but there was nobody to tell. I was constantly fidgety and wanted to physically slap myself to snap out of it. I knew I must be annoying everyone else as I wallowed in my sadness and tried desperately to get a grip. I felt guilty about bringing everyone else down with me and sorry for those around me. Because of that, I spent a lot of my time alone taking lengthy walks. It was easier that way.

Occasionally, Danny would take me out to a party, a day at the zoo or to the local pub. Since my return, he had hung around quite a lot. I discovered that while I was away, he and Steph started a campaign to get me back. They did lots of press interviews and had their photos taken tying yellow ribbons around trees, urging my safe return. Steph had made a scrapbook of the coverage of my case, and I read it and re-read it many times over. Some of it was heartbreaking – I didn't know how my parents and friends got through it. At first, it had all been about Mark, Max Cheriton's son, and an unknown girl who had both disappeared from the same airport. When I was identified, they tracked my parents down in Tenerife and brought them home. In the weeks that followed, it turned out everyone I had ever known seemed to crawl out of the woodwork with a story about me. Most were good, some were not so good and a little embarrassing, many were entirely untrue from people I didn't know or who I had met once in passing and barely said two words to. Even Poncho Pete got his two-pennies' worth. I wondered how much these people got paid for their tawdry lies and felt sadly let down at what people would do for money.

In one paper, Danny was interviewed about how he was coping without me. He seemed to be very upset considering I'd only met him a handful of times, totalling approximately five minutes' actual conversation time. It turns out that one of the reporters had "misquoted" Danny in an interview where he stated he was my boyfriend and the other publications had jumped on the "Missing girl's sexy boyfriend's campaign for her freedom" bandwagon. Apparently, he'd thought it would make him look foolish if he denied it all, so went along with it – oh and, of course, he had ALWAYS liked me anyway, so thought it would be ok. The fact that he also made a lot of money in the process seemed to ease the pain of his deceit. He'd almost started to believe it himself, so when I came home, he continued to hang around and said it was his duty to give the papers their "Lovers Reunited" headline. I was so disorientated at that time I didn't care that much and saw no reason to speak up and deny anything; I couldn't see what good could come of that. I assumed it would just phase out as the press interest died down.

I now felt nothing for Danny Greenslade. I no longer fancied him or saw a future with him in it. Mostly I just got used to having him around, plus he still hadn't found a job or made it big with his band, so he was around in the daytime. In public he put his arm around me to get me through the crowds – I think he enjoyed the attention, the taste of notoriety. I, on the other hand, didn't, and preferred to stay in watching videos or playing computer games. I wasn't in love with him, he wasn't in love with me, we barely knew anything about each other. We were merely friends, and having someone to play with took my mind off other things, even if just for a short time.

Chapter Twenty-Two

It was almost the end of May when Steph dropped her bombshell. It turns out she and Danny had become "close" while I was away, and it had become more serious now that I was back. They didn't want to hurt me, but they had been seeing each other for a few weeks. This was perfectly fine by me, and I told Steph so. After all, we all had our little secrets. She cried a lot and thanked me for putting on a brave face for her. She rambled on about how terrible she felt, how she felt like a crappy friend and how could I ever forgive her.

Honestly? It annoyed me. I was annoyed that she hadn't told me. I was annoyed that, even though I didn't have feelings for Danny, she'd believed I had and said nothing. I was also annoyed that she didn't seem to know me at all. I couldn't care less that she and Danny wanted each other. It was all fine by me, but I had to tell her many times before she was eventually convinced. By the end of June, Danny had moved in and I had moved out.

I went back to my parents for a few months but, despite loving them dearly, I couldn't stay there long and had to decide what to do with the rest of my life. I phoned Mark. We'd spoken several times over the last months, but he had his own life and I didn't want to keep dragging him back into the past with me. He always sounded pleased when I called though, and it was always nice to hear his reassuring voice. He was like my therapy – he should have charged me by the hour. Mark's life had transformed considerably since our return. Now nineteen years old, he had his own penthouse suite overlooking Hyde Park and could be found on most Saturday nights mingling with the jet-set at some trendy nightclub, some restaurant opening or a film premiere. He'd done a couple of TV shows and now co-hosted a popular music entertainment show that was going from strength to strength. He was earning megabucks, had glamorous women falling at his feet and was loving every minute of it. To be honest, I was a little jealous; not of his lifestyle, but that he had moved on so defiantly. He had used his notoriety to his advantage and carved out a brand new life for himself, while I seemed to be stuck in limbo, trying desperately to find my niche but finding only the odd scratch with no purpose or direction. These days he was not always easy to get hold of, but if I left a message, he always made sure he made time to call me back.

One day I agreed to pick Atlanta up from school for my brother, and on the way home she pleaded with me to stop at the corner shop for some sweets. Well, I guessed that's what aunties were for, so I agreed and off she skipped happily towards the large array of sweets, chocolates and pick 'n' mix to make her choice. As I waited by the counter, a newspaper caught my eye. *DITCHED FOR BEST FRIEND* read the headline. *Poor cow*, I thought and turned away, but something made me double-take at the picture below the story – it was ME! I was the poor cow!

'What the hell …?' I exclaimed as I reached for a copy and started to read the small print.

'Do you want to buy that one love?' The counter assistant asked. I wasn't sure if I did or not, but as it was already scrunched up in my clenched fist, I decided I'd better.

'Oh, yes, and those,' I replied as Atlanta dropped a pile of sweets on the counter next to me, no doubt pleased that I was so distracted I hadn't noticed the huge number of sugary, E-number filled delights she had chosen. As Atlanta merrily skipped along, happily munching on a week's supply of additives, I turned to page five where the story continued. Sure enough, there was a picture of Steph and Danny walking out of a popular bar together; Steph, looking fabulous, half-heartedly trying to hide her face, Danny with his arm around her making a vain attempt to wave the cameras and their flashbulbs away. Who the hell had told the press about that? It was such a non-story. There was nothing to report. I read on, "our sources reveal …" it said, while "one insider" told them something else. I was being totally humiliated by something that wasn't even true!

'What are you reading, Auntie Nancy?' Atlanta piped up with a mouth full of something that was bright yellow.

'Erm, just the paper,' I replied.

'Why is it making you angry? You look like Mummy does when Daddy's left the washing out in the rain.' For a little girl, she was very observant.

'Oh, it's nothing. Just something about my friends, Steph and Danny, that's all.' I tried to calm down for her sake.

'Isn't he your boyfriend anymore?' she asked.

'No, he is not.' I replied curtly, aware I shouldn't be taking this out on a five-year-old.

'What are you going to do?' she asked innocently, as if she understood.

'I don't know, sweetie,' I replied. 'But I have to do something.'

I phoned Mark. On this occasion, his advice was to get away, use some of the money to go on holiday, see the world – but before I left, I had to promise that I would visit him in London. He told me I was welcome anytime, day or night, I could just turn up and he would be there for me. I thanked him for his offer and promised to think about what he'd said. Where would I go and would I be brave enough to go it alone?

A few days later, I found myself in the revolving doors of an apartment block overlooking Hyde Park, wheeling a small suitcase behind me. I entered the lift and pressed the very top button. The door opened, and I rang the bell in front of me. A short bald man in pinstripe trousers and a garish tie opened the door. Behind him, I could see and hear the evidence of some kind of party. I wondered for a second if I'd got the right apartment.

'Yes?' snapped the impatient little man.

'Oh, yes, sorry I was looking for Mark?' I asked sheepishly, caught off guard by his abruptness.

'Are you on the guest list?' he asked quickly, as if I was keeping him from something very important.

'I very much doubt it.' I tried a small laugh.

'Who are you?' he asked rudely.

'Who are you?' I snapped back at him. Luckily, Mark appeared before the finger poking and hair-pulling could start, which was just as well, judging by the state of the man's shiny forehead.

'Nancy!' he shouted as he saw me, pushing the little Hitler out of the way to come and hug me. 'Come in, come in!' he said eagerly as he wheeled my case inside for me. I followed him in, giving the baldy man a sickly-sweet smile as I sidled past him. I walked through the party scene and into a bedroom where Mark parked my case.

'Come and have a drink, and I'll get rid of them,' Mark said, gesturing to the people in the open-plan living room.

'No, no really, I don't want to interrupt your party, I'll just get some sleep and we can talk tomorrow or something,' I ventured.

'No way. Just give me a second, ok?' And with that, he disappeared out the door. Within seconds, the music stopped and I could hear Mark's voice ushering people out the door. I peered out of my room just in time to see the little bald man closing the door behind the departing guests.

'You can go too. Thank you, Malcolm,' Mark told the man, who glanced over at me before flouncing out of the door himself.

'Who's he?' I asked Mark as soon as the door was closed.

'Oh, that's Malcolm, my personal assistant-come-agent.'

'Come-dungeon master,' I added.

Mark laughed. 'He's ok, really.'

'Hmm,' I said, not convinced.

'He is!' Mark said, laughing at my face. 'He's very good at his job. Hey, he found me this apartment.'

I looked around and had to agree that little baldy Malcolm had come up trumps in finding this lovely place.

'So, what can I get you to drink?' Mark asked.

'Whatcha got?' I asked at which point Mark flashily opened the door to a mirrored bar, containing what looked like every drink conceivable.

'Rum?' he turned to me, smiling, and picked up a bottle of dark rum, flipping it from one hand to the other.

'That'll do nicely,' I agreed, and he filled two glasses with ice, bringing them and the bottle of rum over to the sofa where I was sitting. While I poured, he put some music on the stereo before coming to join me, flopping down next to me with an enormous sigh.

'I'm knackered,' he told me.

'Join the club.' I rested my head back on the headrest of the sofa. 'But you can't be tired. You're the male Tamara Beckwith of the London social scene. Shouldn't you be just heading out to a club opening or something?' I teased.

'Haha.' Mark smiled, and I noticed his teeth were slightly whiter and less natural-looking than when I'd last seen him. 'Well, you know how it is, daaarrrlin',' he drawled.

'No, not really,' I admitted. 'But you obviously do. You're looking fantastic, Mister Cheriton. You've really got that Leonardo di Caprio thing going on.'

'Why, thank you.' He beamed, stretching one arm out along the back of the sofa as if he took looking good all in his stride. His skin was practically clear and he had a healthy glow, I assumed from a combination of working out and some sort of spray-on tan. He was wearing trendy "vintage" jeans and a designer T-shirt that showed off his newly built-up physique, and his hair was cut and ruffled into a chic choppy style. A million miles away from the spotty geek in overalls I had met less than a year ago.

'You don't look bad yourself,' he added politely.

'Yeah right, I'm a total mess. But thanks for lying.' It was true, I was scrunched from the journey, and the past couple of weeks I hadn't bothered too much about my hair and make-up. I felt about as sexy as a well-worn sports bra.

'So, what brings you to me, missy? Why so blue?'

'How long have you got?'

'All the time in the world for you, Nancy. Spill.'

I told him about what had happened, about Danny Greenslade, about Steph, about moving out, about the dreadful newspaper article. He was lovely about it, as I predicted he would be. He gave me the sympathy I needed, handed me tissues when I sobbed and made me laugh when I needed it most.

That evening we stayed up until the early hours. We drank our rum and talked and talked. We laughed about our first meeting on the airport fire escape; we talked about the island, about Joe, Coultan, Frankie and Rio. We talked about Italy, about Mildred, Barbara and her Italian Stallion. We talked about what came after, the press, the attention and the TV shows. Oh, it was really good to talk about it again, with the only person in the world who could possibly understand, who had the same feelings as me and who was the only person in the world who shared all of my guilty secrets.

The next morning passed me by completely, and I didn't rise from my pit until well after noon. Strangely, Mark had been up for hours.

'Well hello, sleepyhead,' he said gaily as I wandered out of the bedroom still in my jimjams. 'I'd offer you breakfast, but it's nearly suppertime.'

'Arf-arf,' I fake laughed at his little joke. 'Rum is evil.'

'It is when you drink one and a half bottles in one go.' He laughed.

'How come you're so annoyingly sprightly?'

'Well, I've some good news for you,' he told me, beaming like a child with a home-made Mother's Day card.

'What?' The fuzziness in my head meant I was only capable of marginal excitement.

'Guess!' He, however, was very excitable

'You've found an instant cure for rum hangovers?'

'No, sadly.'

'Oh, I don't know. George Clooney's coming for tea?'

'No, that's on Thursday.'

My brain was hurting. 'I give up.'

'I, and when I say I, I mean Malcolm, but it was my idea, have arranged for you to give an exclusive to, wait for it … *Hello!* magazine!'

'What!?'

'Yep, that's right, it's a "here's what really happened between me and Danny Greenslade" exclusive! Whaddya think, eh? Eh? Eh?'

'I can't do that!' My gast was well and truly flabbered.

'You can and you will and you are,' Mark said matter-of-factly. 'It's your chance to tell your side of the story once and for all, end of. It doesn't have to be nasty, they just want a, "what you're up to now", type of feature. They'll do a photoshoot and everything.'

I looked down at my pyjamas and bare feet. 'What!?'

Mark laughed, 'I'm sure they'll let you get dressed first.'

I sat down with my head in my hands, half laughing, half crying. 'No, no, no, no.'

'Yes, yes, yes, yes, it'll be fun.' Mark brushed the hair out of my face. 'Go on, say you'll do it. Clean slate and a bit of a make-over.'

'Thanks.'

'You know what I mean, a bit of glamming up. It'll cheer you right up. And of course, Malcolm's negotiated quite a generous fee for you.'

'I don't need the money. I've got loads of money. Ironically, since coming home, I've probably earned nearly as much money as we robbed off your dad in the first place!'

'Shhh!' Mark scanned the room out of habit. I looked too, but there was no-one there.

'Sorry,' I said anyway.

'So, are you going to do it?'

'Will you come with me?' I whined at him.

'Of course.' He smiled. 'Is that a 'yes'?'

'It's an "I'll think about it",' I said.

'Well, you'd better think quickly. It's at 10 o'clock tomorrow morning.'

'What!?'

So, I felt the fear and did it anyway … and it was brilliant fun! As the interview was only concerned about what had happened after I returned home, I could tell the truth – not quite the whole truth, but an economical version. I told the truth about mine and Danny's relationship and the fact that there had never really been one. I told the truth that I was glad that Danny and Steph had found each other and hoped they would be happy and we would remain friends. When asked if there was a man in my life at the moment, I answered truthfully that, no, there was not. I thought better of mentioning that I had been moping around in a pit of despair like a hermit for the past few months, but rather rephrased it into something about having time to find myself, enjoying the simple pleasures and contemplating what I wanted out of life.

I had my hair and make-up done by professional stylists and was dressed up in gorgeous designer outfits – I hadn't heard of most of the designers, but it felt good all the same. I was nervous about the photoshoot, but with Mark there I relaxed and even enjoyed it. After a couple of glasses of champagne, I relaxed a little too much, and we had to break several times to calm our giggling down. I usually hated having my photo taken, but knowing these professionals made a living out of making other people look fantastic and weren't in the business of publishing poor photos, it was a lot easier to let go.

I was still on a high after we "wrapped", so we finished the afternoon with a bit of retail therapy up and down Regent Street. It was brilliant fun spending our ill-gotten gains together.

With my confidence higher than it had been in ages, I suddenly had an idea.

'Mark?' I asked him as he was browsing through a row of leather jackets.

'Yes?' he asked without looking up.

'Your dad owns a huge airline and travel company, right?'

'I am very much aware of this.' He looked up at me. 'As are you.'

'Do you think he would give me a job? Writing for the in-flight magazine or something?' As I asked the question, a smile formed on my lips.

'Nancy, that's a great idea! I'm sure he'd have something you could do. Shall I call him?'

I hesitated. 'Now? Shouldn't I write to him with my CV or something?'

Mark laughed. 'Why do that when you're standing here with me? Plus, he still owes you one.'

'Well, technically I owe him about a million, but we won't mention that.'

Before I could protest anymore, Mark was phoning Max Cheriton on his mobile. 'Hi Dad, I'm here with Nancy … yes, yes good thanks … she wants to ask you something.' And with that, he passed the phone over to me.

With no time to plan my opening gambit, I ploughed straight in with my job request to which he laughed before agreeing there would definitely be a position for me at Giant, either with the magazine or writing travel posts for the Giant website. He finished by confirming that his Communications Manager would be in touch to arrange a meeting.

This was it. I felt a weight had been lifted. I had finally decided what I wanted to do and was well on my way to doing it. Yes, there may have been a bit of nepotism to get my foot in the Giant door, but morals will only get you so far. Sometimes you just have to take what you want. I'd been taught that by a wise man with beautiful blue eyes.

That evening we stepped out in our new gear and headed into town for something to eat. As it was a nice evening, we headed down to Covent Garden and sat in the courtyard of one of the Italian restaurants there.

'Thank you for today,' I said, smiling at Mark.

'No worries,' he replied, picking up his menu.

'No really, thanks for arranging that and frog-marching me in there. You were right, it was just what I needed. Thank you.' I squeezed his hand.

'You're welcome. What are friends for?' He squeezed my hand back and looked into my eyes. I wanted to cry and I think he did too, but he shook himself out of it and said, 'Actually, I've got something I have to tell you …' He put his menu back down and rubbed his eyes. *Uh-oh, this was bad.*

'What?'

He looked at me straight in the eye. 'I'm not sure how to say this.'

'Mark, just spit it out!'

'Ok, here goes …' He took a deep breath, clearly psyching himself up. Of course, I imagined the worst and implored him to tell me again. 'I spoke to Joe.' He winced in preparation for my reaction.

'What? You mean … since we left?' I swallowed hard.

'Yes, here in London.'

'What? How? When did you …? What …?'

'It was about a couple of months ago. He came over to make arrangements for Mabel. He managed to get hold of a number for me and we arranged to meet while he was here.'

I felt instantly betrayed by both of them. Joe had been in the country and contacted Mark, not me. They'd met up without me and, on top of that, Mark hadn't even told me.

'It was a five-minute chat in Hyde Park, it wasn't a night out or anything.'

'That's not the point! Why didn't you tell me? Did he ask about me at all?' Tears sprang into my eyes. All this time I had been pining for something that wasn't real. Days I had spent wallowing in self-pity when I should have had been moving on with my life, like everyone else. I felt stupid, humiliated and a little bit angry.

'Of course he did! He tried to see you. God knows how, but he found your address and waited for you to leave your flat, but you walked out with that Danny bloke and he put two and two together.'

'And got five! I wasn't seeing Danny!' I said, exasperated.

'But he wasn't to know that. Nance, you and that Danny were all over the papers. It's no wonder he assumed you were a couple, I assumed you were a couple, the entire country assumed you were a couple!'

'So, what happened when you met?'

'He decided – well, *we* both decided – that you looked happy. That you'd moved on. There was no point in rocking the boat.'

'Is that supposed to be funny?'

'No.' He bit his lip. 'I'm sorry, Nancy, we honestly thought it was for the best. There was no point in turning your world upside down again for no reason—' He paused '—but now, after what you told me last night about you and Danny, I can see that it was probably the wrong decision.'

'Probably!' I fumed.

'C'mon Nancy, cut me some slack. You know I'd never do anything to hurt you intentionally.' He touched my arm gently, which went some way to calming me down.

This was true, but it was just so frustrating. I needed time to think, to weigh things up in my mind.

'I'm sorry, I overreacted.' I squeezed his hand.

'I know, you usually do.' He smirked, trying to make me laugh, which I did.

At that point the waiter arrived with our tray of starters and laid them on the table in front of us.

'Come on, let's enjoy this lovely meal and celebrate your new job.' Mark picked up his knife and fork ready to tuck in.

'Yes, let's.' I agreed. *I'd almost forgotten about that.*

'And I promise I'll make it up to you.'

'Don't be silly, you don't have to do that.'

'Well, I think I do, and in fact, I've got an idea …'

'Oh God, what now?'

Chapter Twenty-Three

 Almost a year to the date of my kidnapping, at precisely 1:00 pm, I was standing on a small Spanish quay waiting for the ferryman. Mark's surprise was an open first-class ticket for one to Minorca. I managed to make it through the airport on my own without getting kidnapped, which made a change, and this time the journey to Spain took just over three hours. On my arrival, I got a taxi to my hotel right at the top of the island, near the small town of Cala Pueblo. After freshening up, I headed out into the warm evening and down towards the little harbour to make some enquiries about the possibility of chartering a boat to the small, little-known island of Mecinia. The evening breeze was warm and the sound of the crickets chirping, mentally transported me back to the island.

   After not having much luck in getting people to understand my arm gesturing (my Spanish was no better than my Italian), I gave up and stopped for a meal in a small open-fronted restaurant by the side of the quay. It was truly beautiful here. The sun was slowly setting as I looked out across the water in the direction of Mecinia. I was so close I could almost swim there. The waiter brought my food over and I tucked into the fresh fish, probably caught today by one of the bare-chested Spanish fishermen. The boats in the harbour were almost all well-worn fishing boats that bobbed and clinked on the gentle tide. I sat alone, enjoying my solitude. Here I didn't have to pretend; I had no apologies to make and no guilt to feel. Here there was only hope and the sense of a new adventure. There was something in the air, even if it was just the warm breeze circling around me – something was coming and it would soon be here.

The restaurant was slowly emptying as holidaymakers made their way out to bars and the only disco in this part of the island. The waiter cleared my plate and bought over half a bottle of wine. I'd had two glasses from it already so he said I could have the rest of the bottle for free, provided I stayed and talked to him for a while. It turns out his name was Felipe, and he was the owner of the restaurant. He was friendly in a non-threatening way, and as I didn't relish the idea of entering a bar alone, or going back to my hotel yet, I agreed. He pulled up a chair and another bottle of wine for himself. I asked him how he ever made a profit when he gave half his wine away and drank the rest himself. He laughed and answered in very good English.

'What is profit? A man makes enough to eat, to feed, clothe and house his children and buy his wife flowers, he has enough. What can you spend your money on that is better than this?' He waved his arm out, bottle in hand, to the view in front of us. The sun was almost touching the sea, and the sky was becoming an oil painting of reds and purples reflecting in the cool water around the silhouetted boats. I was forced to agree. I liked his way of thinking. I liked him.

'You are on your own, yes?' he asked, in a non-obtrusive, non-accusatory way.

'Yes, I am,' I answered honestly, without shame and with a hint of defiance.

'You like it here?' he asked.

I wasn't sure if he meant on this island or in his restaurant, but I liked both so answered, 'Very much so. It's beautiful here.'

'How long will you stay?'

Good question, I didn't know myself. Depending on my best and worst-case scenarios, it could be anything between three seconds and for the rest of my life. 'Erm, not sure,' I answered honestly. 'It really depends.'

'On what does this depend?' He was getting interested as the mystery English girl's plot thickened. 'Is it because of a man?'

'Kind of … well, yes, yes, it is dependent on a man.'

'A lover?' he asked, clearly intrigued and pouring himself more wine.

I poured myself some too and made a mental note that it probably wasn't the best idea to tell him the whole story. As for it being a lover, that was a tough one. How long do you have to be separated from someone before they stopped being your lover? And if you have loved no-one else since and you're still in love with them, does that mean they're still your lover or your ex-lover?

'That also depends,' I answered, creating an unintentional air of mystique.

'Ah, I see,' Felipe said, winking, and I was pretty sure that he didn't see at all but that, nevertheless, he had come to his own conclusions.

'Hey, Felipe?' I asked, changing the subject. 'Do you know how to get to the island of Mecinia?'

'Yes, of course, by boat,' he told me as if that wouldn't have crossed my mind.

'Do you know of anyone who could take me on their boat?' I ventured.

'You want to go to Mecinia?' This was obviously not a common request. 'There is not much on Mecinia.'

'I'd like to go all the same,' I answered casually, as if my whole future happiness didn't depend on it.

'In that case, it's easy,' he said. 'You come down to here tomorrow at noon and ask for Domingo. He will take you on his boat.'

'Are you sure?' I wondered if Domingo would mind Felipe offering his services to strange English women.

'It's ok, he sails to Mecinia every week, and he goes tomorrow, it's like a—' He struggled for the word '—a ferret.'

'Oh, a ferry!' I tried not to laugh. But inside I was smiling. I was grinning like the Cheshire Cat – not only for the image of ferret transporting passengers over to the neighbouring island, but because I had just received validation that Mecinia existed and it wasn't just in my imagination – and not only that, but there was an actual ferry service to it now. The last piece of my journey was in place. I had almost come full circle and all that stood in the way of my destiny now was twelve hours and a ferryman called Domingo.

After finishing the wine and saying my goodbyes and thank yous to Felipe, I strolled the short distance back to my hotel with a spring in my step. I was so full of euphoria and wine that I couldn't help swinging my handbag by my side, and once or twice even broke into a little dance.

At noon the next day, I was back at the quayside of the pretty little harbour, now almost empty of boats which had left on the early tide to begin a day's catch. My suitcase was by my feet and a smile was on my face.

The Spanish *mañana* attitude did not complement my nervous impatience, but there was no choice but to wait. I paced up and down the quayside for approximately ten minutes before I started to get a little dizzy, not to mention hot. I decided I needed to calm down before I became too sweaty and my appearance that I had spent all morning perfecting would be ruined. My choice of attire was a casual, carefree, hippy-chick ensemble. A flowing, floaty skirt with a pretty cotton top, accessorised with a chunky belt and long dangly beads. My make-up was applied very carefully for a natural flawless look, and my hair was straightened before curling it again into tousled waves with plenty of de-frizzing and smoothing lotion. How come it was such an effort to look so natural?

Attempting to postpone the inevitable make-up melt and sweaty arm-pit syndrome for as long as possible, I tried to calm myself down by sitting in the shade of Felipe's restaurant from the previous evening and ordered some bottled water. He wasn't there, and I was glad as I wasn't really in the mood for answering questions. My hands were sweating with nerves more than heat, and my stomach was churning with nervous excitement. It was like the world's ultimate second date. The best-case scenario was that nothing would have changed. I would glide in, looking fabulously serene and fragrant, see Joe who would run over to me, like Ashley and Melanie in *Gone with the Wind*, and we'd live happily ever after. This was my favourite scenario, and I didn't think it was too much to ask for.

The worst-case scenario, well, what was that? They were no longer there? They had left the island, and there was no way of finding them ever again? Oh no, I hadn't considered that possibility until now! How would my already scrambled head be able to handle that? But which was worse, that scenario, or the one where they were still there but Joe no longer loved me, or he never really did? Was there a possibility I'd just been used as a convenience? I simply couldn't bear that and decided that that scenario was too distressing even to contemplate. I pushed the image to the back of my mind and went to the toilet for the third time. I looked at myself in the mirror, like I had all those months ago at the Venice police station. *It must work out. I have no Plan B.*

At approximately 1:00 pm, a small number of people were gathered at the top of the short slip-way. There were about four or five of them, laden with cases and bags, wearing shorts and sun hats. Judging by their pasty white legs and the profuse sweating in the midday sun, I guessed they were either English or German, certainly not Spanish. About half an hour later, one man walked over to where I was sitting and spoke to the waiter who was perched at the end of the bar smoking a cigarette.

'Excuse me, I wonder if you could tell me where I might find Domingo?' he said slowly, seemingly to help the Spaniard understand more easily.

As I was after Domingo myself, I pricked up my ears to listen in to their conversation and to my surprise, the man answered, 'Yes, I am Domingo.'

'Domingo with the boat?' the British man continued.

'Yes, I am Domingo with the boat.' He shouted something to

somebody behind the restaurant counter, stubbed out his cigarette and gestured to the man to follow him. Annoyingly, he had been sitting there all the time! I grabbed my bag and case and followed the pair of them towards the slipway, clambering into the little boat waiting at the bottom. The memories of being on Joe's little boat came flooding back, and as we pulled away from the dock, the wind blew into my face and the smell of the sea filled my nostrils. It was like coming home and I closed my eyes to breathe it all in.

When I opened my eyes, I noticed a woman staring at me. She was sitting next to the man who'd asked for Domingo at the restaurant, and so I'd assumed she was his wife. As luck would have it, she was one of those women who liked to tell perfect strangers all about herself. It turns out they were from Kent and had come to Spain for a retreat to get away from their very stressful but very well-paid jobs. She told me that her PA had found this little place for her on the internet. *It was new, you know, and very exclusive.* There were only about three or four chalets, and she just had to come before the crowds came to ruin it. She was already missing her laptop and mobile phone and proper coffee. She didn't ask me any questions about myself and that suited me just fine; there was nothing about me that I wanted to tell her. After a little while, the bouncing of the little boat turned her a little green and she spent the rest of the journey with her head over the side, which also suited me fine – not that I wished her ill, but it gave me time to prepare myself for whatever lay in store across the water.

About an hour later, I finally saw it in the distance: my island. My own little utopia. I was glad my sunglasses were big and dark enough to hide the tears that sprang into my eyes. My heart pounded faster and faster as it grew bigger and bigger. As we got closer, some of the features started to take shape. I could see sand, trees, some wooden structures that I didn't recognise, but one I did, the little jetty down to the water's edge, a small boat moored at one side of it. My gateway to paradise.

I was nearly bursting with excitement as the boat slowed and gently touched the side of the jetty, my hands clenching and unclenching in anticipation at what I might find. I scanned the length of the beach for a familiar face but couldn't see anyone; I began to panic. I was the last one off the boat and Domingo took my hand to help me out. As I stood up straight, I saw a Jamaican man welcoming his new guests, picking up cases and pointing them in the right direction. As I stood on the jetty, he looked at me, smiled and turned away, but something stopped him and he turned once more to look back at me. I stood there with one hand on my hip, one brushing the hair from my face.

'Hey, Coultan,' I said, pretending to be calm but unable to stop myself breaking out into an enormous grin.

'Oh, my goodness! I don't believe it!' he boomed when the recognition hit him. He dropped all the luggage he was carrying, ran over and picked me up in the biggest of bear hugs ever, before swinging me round and round until I was dizzy. I needed that. I felt so welcome and so wanted. I wanted to cry and tried hard to compose myself.

'Come on, come on!' he ordered me, as he picked up the luggage he had dropped and strode off, following in the steps of the other holidaymakers. As he walked, he kept looking at me and shaking his head repeating, 'I don't believe it, I just don't believe it.'

'I know, I know,' was all I could say in response. I was so excited to be back I had to stop myself from skipping along.

'Shh, wait here,' he told me, and I waited outside the door to what looked to be a small reception area. It was rustic and made of wood, and I suddenly recognised it as the small hut that Rio and Coultan used to sleep in and that had sheltered us in the storm. I waited excitedly, wondering who was inside seeing to the guests. After a while I heard Coultan saying, 'C'mon woman, I have a surprise for you.'

'You been drinking again?' I heard Rio's voice accusing him from beyond the doorway.

'No, I haven't touched a drop. Just come outside, I got somethin' to show you.' He was so excitable it made me want to laugh. 'I know you'll like this surprise,' he pleaded.

I heard her give in. 'Ok, but I am very busy. We have new guests, you know? Now, what is it?'

As she came round the corner, I put out my arms and attempted my best Jamaican accent, 'Hey girlfriend, what's up?'

Rio screamed in delight and ran into my open arms. We hugged and jumped up and down. 'Oh my goodness! I don't believe it! I knew you'd come back!' she kept repeating in exactly the same way Coultan had some five minutes before. 'You are looking too good to be true, lady,' she told me as she held me at arms' length.

'You too, lady!' I said, looking at her familiar pretty face and brightly coloured clothes. I had been so fixated on Joe I hadn't realised just how much I'd missed Coultan and Rio. They were my surrogate family, and I adored them for their kindness, their humour and their love.

'So.' I took a deep breath before asking the question I had been dreaming of for months, trying to remain calm. 'Is, er, is Joe around?' Inside my head I was screaming, *please say yes, please say yes*.

'Yes, he's down by the water, over there.' She pointed out of sight. My heart leapt, but I sensed something was wrong.

'What?' I asked anxiously, 'What's wrong?'

Rio looked at Coultan, and I inwardly pleaded with her to tell me. I was finding it hard to breathe.

'There's somethin' I think you should know before you go down there,' she said softly.

'What? What? Tell me?' I implored, about to explode.

'He, he's not on his own.' I could tell by the way she spoke she wasn't referring to Frankie.

'Who?'

'It's a girl.'

Shit shit shit shit! I was not expecting that. Why wasn't I expecting that? I instinctively put my hand up to my face and noticed that it was shaking.

'Oh.' I didn't know what to say. What could I do? March down there, announcing that I was the love of his life and he must dump her immediately? But what if I wasn't the love of his life? Just because I'd built it up to colossal proportions in my head, it didn't mean it was true. Perhaps to him, I'd been a holiday romance, or even worse, a mere convenience; someone to help him get their plan off the ground. Maybe after his conversation with Mark, assuming that I'd moved on with Danny Greenslade, he'd done the same? And why wouldn't he? Another woman hadn't been in any of my possible scenarios – but why not? Who wouldn't fall for the good-looking barman-come-hotel owner with the handsome face and the sexy smile? I had. Why hadn't I so much as considered that someone else who came along would do too? Had I really been that stupid?

Chapter Twenty-Four

What should I do now? There wouldn't be another "ferret" boat for a week, and I did so want to spend time on the island with Rio and Coultan, and of course Frankie. The question was, could I be just friends with Joe? Could I watch him with his new long-legged, blonde girlfriend without bursting into tears, or even worse, lamping her one. I didn't know. Rio spoke and brought me out of my thoughts.

'I think you should at least go and say hello,' she said kindly. 'I'm sure he'll be pleased to see you.'

'You think so?' I asked timidly. 'Perhaps I'll have a drink first.' I knew I was wimping out.

Coultan drew a hip flask out of his pocket and handed it to me. I took a swig of his crazy rum, the familiar burning sensation running from the top of my throat to the pit of my stomach.

'Off ya go then.'

I had run out of excuses, so I cleared my throat. 'Ok,' I croaked, pulling down my sunglasses, smoothing my hair and straightening my clothes. I turned in the direction Rio had indicated and began walking. *What should I say?* I still didn't know. I turned back to Rio and Coultan, who proceeded to shoo me away like a chicken in a farmyard. At that moment I was saved as Frankie came bounding over. He spotted me and stopped in his tracks.

'Hey! Nancy!' he shouted, looking over at Rio and Coultan to check if they'd noticed me.

'Frankie, Frankie! Come here for a minute,' Rio shouted.

He looked at me, confused. 'I'll come and say hello in a minute,' I told him, kissing him on the cheek. 'I just have to do something first.'

'Ok,' he said, still clearly confused but with an enormous grin on his face nonetheless. He went over to where Rio and Coultan were standing, and I continued walking, each step taking me closer and closer to my ultimate fantasy and my worst nightmare.

I had almost reached the tree – the tree that I'd once sat under with a burning face and burning feet, from where I'd walked down to the water's edge to cool down before Joe unceremoniously dragged me out by my armpits. At the tree, I stopped short. *There he was*. His back was turned towards me, his hair was a little longer, but I would have recognised him anywhere. He was wearing long shorts and nothing else, his body as tanned and muscular as the last time I'd seen him. For a second, I stopped breathing. He was looking at something down at the water's edge, but from my position I couldn't make it out. All I cared about was the fact that it didn't look like his girlfriend was with him. I was momentarily relieved, but I knew she had to be here somewhere. Any minute now she would come strutting back out of the trees, bringing him a cold beer, or performing some other girlfriend duty. I looked behind me, but there was no-one there. Facing forwards again, I realised I was so near to what I wanted and yet so far from getting it. This was my time – I had to do something now before that boyfriend-stealing goddess came back. I just wanted him to be alone when he saw me. I needed to catch his genuine reaction to my presence, good or bad; it had to be spontaneous, natural and true.

I had the sensation that my heart must have almost been visible, beating hard from the inside of my rib cage; so loud and so strong. I tried to compose myself by taking a deep breath and striding, as purposefully as is possible in flip-flops, down the beach towards the figure I knew so well and that I had touched so often in my mind.

I reached the halfway point, and he still hadn't looked around. I was clammy and shaking with uncontrollable nerves. What was I to do, if he didn't turn round? Tap him on the shoulder with a "Hi, do you remember me?" But then it happened. He must have heard me walking or my deep breathing, and he turned slowly to face me. I stopped in my tracks.

'Hey, Joe,' was all that I could manage without my voice cracking up. He ducked his head a little, squinting to make sure his eyes weren't deceiving him. *God, he was gorgeous.*

'Nancy? Nancy, is that you?' I couldn't tell if it was excitement in his voice or complete panic.

'It's me,' I answered almost curtseying for want of something else to do, and I immediately felt very silly.

He began to walk slowly towards me, gesturing for me to meet him halfway. I walked, thankful that the unevenness of the sand masked my shaky legs. When I was almost close enough to touch him, he reached out and grabbed me, pulling me close to him.

'You're here, you're here. I can't believe you came back!' he said into my hair.

This is more like it, I thought. This would have been my perfect scenario number one … if I hadn't been so continually aware that his girlfriend might come back at any second to spoil it all. I was so happy and so sad all at the same time. I was back where I wanted to be, with my Joe … but he wasn't my Joe anymore.

'Oh shit!' he exclaimed, as he jumped back and turned away from me. Well, I'd had my minute alone with him, before he remembered about his girlfriend. I couldn't ask for more than that. I wiped my eyes and he took my hand. 'Hey Nancy, come here. I want you to meet someone.'

Great, here we go. Now I'd have to be all polite to the woman who had broken my heart.

'Nancy, this is Mecinia,' he announced. I was confused, and watched Joe as he bent down to scoop up a baby girl of about six months who had been sitting in the sand, her white nappy stark against her dark skin. I must have still looked confused as Joe explained that Rio had found out she was pregnant shortly after I had left the island. Mecinia was such a gorgeous baby, with both Rio's beauty and Coultan's smile in her little face, and she happily grabbed for Joe's hair.

'I was gonna cut it but she likes it like that,' he said, laughing.

'So … she's your new girlfriend?' I said as the realisation of Rio's little joke hit me.

Now it was his turn to be confused. 'Well, that depends …' he said, grinning at me in the way I had pictured in my memories and in my dreams. *No way was this happening.*

Everything I had been dreaming of was here within my grasp, and after the past year, I suddenly just thought *sod it*; I deserved it. Joe put his free arm around my shoulder, and as I breathed in the familiar smell of his suntanned skin, I couldn't stop the tears from rolling, this time with pure happiness.

'C'mon, let's go get a drink in the bar.' He held me close and guided me back up the beach. 'Hey, have you met Mabel yet?'

'Mabel's here already?' I asked in surprise.

'Yep, thanks to you.' He kissed my forehead. 'She'll probably be in the bar.' He laughed. 'She usually is.'

We walked up the beach towards a newly built wooden structure. The front and sides were open to the summer breeze, the roof matted with leaves and branches. The tables were rustic as were the benches, although brightly coloured cushions covered them to add comfort for the poor backsides of those weary of sunbathing. Above the doorway to the bar was a sign, carved neatly and meticulously out of a plank of wood. *NANCY'S BAR*, it read. I smiled. It seemed I had never really left after all.

Later, as the sun began its daily descent over my corner of paradise, I looked around the bar. Rio had finished clearing the plates from her guests and was sitting across the table from me, little Mecinia asleep and content on her knee. The English couple from the boat were in the corner of the bar and, like the other guests, were well fed and relaxed, staring out to the horizon as I had so many times before them. Coultan was the perfect host, making sure everyone's glasses were kept topped up with his home-brewed rum. I knew it would be an experience the island's guests today would never forget. Frankie and Mabel were duet-ing The Beatles' 'Here Comes the Sun' at the karaoke, and Joe was right where I wanted him to be – by my side, until the sun set on both of our lives.

THE END

Acknowlegements

This first novel has been a real labour of love, having been dragged out of the cupboard (and subsequently put back in again) periodically over the last 20 years. Finally, with much help from many self-publishing websites, several writing podcasts and one global pandemic, I eventually managed to get it finished.

I would like to thank all those who have read *Getting Away* through the many stages of its life and who offered such helpful feedback. A special thank you to my fabulous friends Sarah B and Clair P who have put up with my many, *many* procrastinations and provided enough heartfelt encouragement for me to finally get it out into the world.

My love and gratitude also goes to my family for always being there and of course my ever-patient husband, Derek, who loyally supports me in all my ideas and dreams. Oh and for making my lovely website.

Thanks to Lusana Taylor for her fantastic editing skills which helped make Getting Away to be as good as it can possibly be. And also to Clarissa Kezen at ckbookcoverdesigns.com for her skilful work with my fabulous book cover. I just hope my would-be readers love it as much as I do.

If you enjoyed this book, please leave a review wherever you bought it. Thank you, lovely reader.

Getting Away

About the Author

Having grown up in Nottinghamshire, Amelia Short moved to the South West to study English and now lives by the sea on the East Coast of Devon with her husband.

An Interior Designer by trade she is always looking to find the beautiful and the colourful in everyday life. She loves to travel and explore new places, gathering story inspiration along the way.

After years of writing stories and poetry, *Getting Away* is her first novel to be published.

To find out more about Amelia visit her website at www.ameliashort.co.uk or connect with her on Facebook at **ameliashortauthor** or Instagram at **ameliashort_writer**

Printed in Great Britain
by Amazon

74176017R00144